Friends of the People

FRIENDS OF THE PEOPLE

UNEASY RADICALS
IN THE AGE OF THE CHARTISTS

Owen R Ashton and Paul A Pickering

THE MERLIN PRESS

First published 2002 by The Merlin Press Ltd.
PO Box 30705
London WC2E 8QD
www.merlinpress.co.uk

ISBN: 0850365198

British Library Cataloguing in Publication Data
is available from the British Library

Printed in Great Britain by J.W. Arrowsmith, Bristol

CONTENTS

Acknowledgements   vi

Introduction   1

Chapter 1: The 'People's Advocate':
Peter Murray Mcdouall (1814-1854)   7

Chapter 2: An 'Earnest Radical':
The Reverend Henry Solly (1813-1903)   29

Chapter 3: The Aristocrat Of Chartism:
William Stephen Villiers Sankey (1793-1860)   55

Chapter 4: The 'Remarkable Work' of
The Reverend Benjamin Parsons (1797-1855)   81

Chapter 5: 'The Chaplain Of The Manchester Chartists':
The Reverend James Scholefield (1790-1855)   101

Chapter 6: 'A Newspaper Genius':
Richard Bagnall Reed (1831-1908)   127

Conclusion: Friends Of The People   149

Bibliographical Note   164

Index   165

ACKNOWLEDGEMENTS

For all but a few weeks, this book has been written while we have been in different time zones on opposite sides of the world. With the aid of technology that many Chartists would probably not have approved of, and with fewer difficulties than might be imagined, it is offered as a work of joint scholarship.

We are grateful for the assistance of staff at the following institutions: the British Library, St Pancras; the British Newspaper Library, Colindale; Cheltenham Public Library; Chifley Library, the Australian National University; the University of Durham Library; Gloucester City Library; Jersey Library; Manchester Central Library; National Library of Australia, Canberra; Newcastle-upon-Tyne City Library; Staffordshire University Library (The Dorothy Thompson Special Collection); State Library of Victoria; Tyne and Wear Archives; The Working Class Movement Library (Salford); Yeovil Library.

Thanks are also due to the Australian Research Council; the staff of the Humanities Research Centre at The Australian National University; the School of Humanities and Social Sciences, Staffordshire University; the Newcastle Chronicle; and the Registrar's Office at Newcastle-upon-Tyne City Council. Paul Pickering's research is funded by the Australian Research Council.

We would also like to place on record our appreciation to the following individuals: Glenn Airey; Glen Barclay; Martin Brown; Greg Claeys; Chris Clowes; Tom and Lily French; Bob Fyson; David Gatley; Vic Gatrell, David Goodway; Brian Harrison; Ron Heisler; Joan Hugman; Joanna Innes; Nev. Kirk; Iain McCalman; Alun Munslow; Ann Parry; Andrew Prescott; Debbie Roberts; Alan Ruston; Barry Smith; Miles Taylor; Dorothy Thompson; Caroline Turner; Philip Walmsley; and Anthony Zurbrugg and Adrian Howe at Merlin Press.

We offer special thanks to Stephen Roberts and Alex Tyrrell for reading our manuscript and for making valuable suggestions.

Last and by no means least, we would like to acknowledge the unfailing support of our respective families: Angela, Faye and Ian Ashton; and Daniel, Jessica, Timothy and Suzanne Pickering (Sue also helped by finding many mistakes and lapses of clarity in the first draft of the book).

This book is affectionately dedicated to our families.

The cover illustrations are (first row) Peter McDouall, Henry Solly, William Sankey, and (second row) Benjamin Parsons, James Scholefield and Richard Reed. The image of James Scholefield is reproduced here by kind permission of Manchester Archives and Local Studies at Manchester Central Library.

INTRODUCTION

Riding on the top of an omnibus towards my brother's house, I got into conversation with a gentleman beside me … A little time before I got down I gave him my address in exchange for his own; but when he saw my name, he said 'What! William Lovett, the Chartist?' 'Yes,' I replied, 'the same individual'. 'Why,' said he, scrutinising me very earnestly, '*you don't look like one …*'[1] (Original Emphasis)

As a respectable artisan, the author of the People's Charter was understandably concerned by his encounter with an anonymous Metropolitan commuter, but he could have hardly expected otherwise. According to Benjamin Parsons, a Chartist who is the subject of one of the chapters in this book, this was a time when the hostile portrayal of Chartists was endemic. 'Who has heard of Chartism or the People's Charter without feeling queer?', Parsons admitted in 1847, 'Pikes, blunderbusses, brickbats, and lucifer matches almost instantly seem to bristle and flash through the country'.[2] Even in the colony of New South Wales at the far end of the British world, a Chartist émigré complained that a hostile press depicted Chartists 'with dark colours and … hideous features'.[3] Implicit in the stock image of the menacing Chartist that prevailed from Land's End to Sydney's Rocks, were assumptions about gender and class: the typical Chartist was invariably a horny-handed son of toil. Lovett did not look like a Chartist, not because he was unarmed, but because he did not look like an ordinary labourer. Unlike the associations with violence, however, the identification of the cause with the characteristics of a social class was not only welcomed, it was actively encouraged by some Chartists themselves. In particular, the celebration of the attributes of everyday working-class life was undertaken by the most important leader of the movement, Feargus O'Connor, who famously addressed his weekly epistles in the *Northern Star*, to the 'fustian jackets, unshorn chins and blistered hands'.

O'Connor did not look like a Chartist either, although in one of the most important gestures of the 1840s, he donned a suit of fustian for his release from York Castle in 1841.[4] The ubiquitous O'Connor was one of a handful of 'gentlemen leaders' who continued to play a significant role in popular politics in the nineteenth century and beyond,[5] but his symbolic gesture pointed to a profound shift that was taking place below the level of the national leadership. Other signs of this were many. For example, whereas a majority of delegates to the inaugural meeting of the Chartist General Convention of the Industrious Classes in February 1839 were not working men, the first president and secretary of the National Charter Association (NCA), formed the following year, were respectively a factory operative and a power-loom weaver before their election. Presumably, they looked like Chartists.

The careers of the 'gentleman leaders', from Henry Hunt to Joseph Cowen, are well-known, but, as Asa Briggs noted in an end of the twentieth-century survey of Chartism, there is still 'ample scope for continuing study and for reflection' on the composition of the movement.[6] This book arises from our belief in the need for a better understanding of those who remained loyal to the Chartists, even though a commuter on a London bus would never have guessed by looking at them. Students of politics have long understood the role of outsiders: from Lenin who ascribed an historic mission to a 'vanguard' driven by déclassé intellectuals and professional revolutionaries, to Max Weber who identified the importance of what he called the 'pariah intellectuals'.[7] The emergence of a fiercely independent working class radicalism that reached its apogee in the 1840s, should not obscure the fact that Chartism enjoyed the support of many individuals who did not have 'blistered hands'. Hence we have written this book about three ministers of religion, a doctor, a leisured gentleman, and a newspaper magnate. Some of our subjects had been born into the ranks of the aristocracy or the rapidly expanding middle class, while others had risen from a humble background to occupy a place in the professions. Invariably they are an odd fit when measured against the hardening social realities of early Victorian Britain: they were 'friends of the people', because they were not, or were no longer, of the people.[8] They did not look like Chartists.

Our approach is biographical, rather than thematic. There are a number of reasons for this. First, the study of whole careers highlights some of the continuities of nineteenth century radicalism that can be easily overlooked by the treatment of Chartism in isolation. Similarly biography provides a better opportunity to explore the relationship between Chartism and the plethora of other reform movements that operated at the same time. Chartist lives were often rich, diverse and unexpected. Our case studies take us on an extraordinary journey through time and place: from Grattan's parliament to gun-running for Garibaldi; from the massacre of Peterloo to Masonic lodges; from rural Ireland to far north Queensland. Secondly, recent developments in political theory suggest that to understand political action we must explore, first and foremost, the multi-layered micropolitics of everyday life. Inevitably, an examination of what William E. Connolly has called the 'visceral register' must begin with the study of the individual.[9] Each of the chapters is written to stand alone, but we have not left it at that: the book concludes with an extended comparative essay. Despite the small number of cases, the aim of this chapter is, in part, prosopographic. By comparing and contrasting the sociological and ideological profiles of the six cases we attempt to define some of the features of an 'identikit' friend of the people. Without wishing our subjects to bear too much strain, this chapter also seeks to use their experiences – individual and collective – to reflect on aspects of the broader movement, and to offer some tentative new conclusions about popular politics in the age of the Chartists.

On what basis have our subjects been selected? When G.D.H. Cole compiled his 'Chartist portraits' he opted for 'leading Chartists' and 'men whose fortunes were, at one point or another, so closely linked with Chartism as to be inseparable from its story'.[10] As Brian Harrison later noted, this approach led Cole to include four men who were not actually Chartists and another who turned his back on the movement shortly after its commencement.[11] The first and most important criterion that our case studies had to meet was that they were Chartists. Unlike many other 'friends of the people', who held working-class radicals at arm's length or who shunned the movement after 1839, the men studied in this book called themselves Chartists. In terms of E.P. Thompson's well known statement that the 'middle class Radical and idealist intellectual were forced to take sides between the two nations',[12] these men made their choice, at a time when it was difficult and dangerous to do so. By sticking with the Chartists they imperilled reputation, social standing, income and, in some cases, liberty. They were men who took risks. In this sense, they belonged to the 'uneasy class' (a term originally coined by Edward Gibbon Wakefield) which is recognised to have been a fertile breeding ground for a wide range of radical opinions.[13]

One consequence of the strict application of our first criterion is that we have not selected a subject from what might otherwise seem like an obvious source: the Members of Parliament who voted for the People's Charter when it came before the House of Commons. Apart from O'Connor and Thomas Slingsby Duncombe, none of this diverse group joined the principal Chartist organisation, the NCA, and, more importantly, none would have welcomed the epithet 'Chartist' after their name.[14] In one respect, however, we have followed Cole – by selecting subjects about whom there is sufficient biographical material.[15] For this reason we have not included an example of the most obvious contrast to the stereotypical Chartist of the 1840s: a woman. Eileen Yeo has shown how much can be achieved in her study of Mary Lovett, but significant gaps in information remain.[16] Unfortunately there was no female Chartist who was prolific enough with the pen or vociferous enough on the platform to sustain a chapter length study.

In only one case have we sought to recover an unknown career. William Sankey has been virtually ignored by all previous historians of the movement, despite the fact that he brought to it an almost unique set of ideas and associations. For Peter McDouall (probably the best known of our subjects), James Scholefield, Benjamin Parsons and Richard Reed, we have sought to build on existing work; and, in the case of Henry Solly, we have endeavoured to save him from his own distorted account of his Chartist career. Finally, the six case studies have been chosen because they offer important insights into the struggle in different regions: from the Scottish Lowlands and the North East, to Lancashire, London and the South West of England. Thus the book is also intended as a contribution to the study of the regional history of early and mid Victorian Britain. Needless to say we might have chosen others to study.

Although each of our subjects was associated for some or all of their career with the mainstream of the movement that revolved around the leadership of Feargus O'Connor, all of them (with the exception of McDouall) were also involved with the more conciliatory initiatives within the movement, and with middle-class reform campaigns separate from it, including the Complete Suffrage Union, the Anti-Corn Law League and the Parliamentary and Financial Reform Association. On the one hand, this may simply help to reinforce a point made in a recent book about the League, that middle-class reform politics in this era was more radical than has been acknowledged,[17] but, at the same time, it also helps us to understand the ease with which the nascent Liberal Party later captured support from many former Chartists. The mid-Victorian consensus was built on the relationships that these men, and others like them, sustained during the difficult 1840s. Although our subjects participated in public life at a time when politics was no longer an exclusive preserve of the independently wealthy, they were not anachronisms. On the contrary, they demonstrated that individuals of goodwill could work together across the divide of social class and, in this way, they helped to preserve a pattern that persists in popular politics to this day. More immediately, by helping to make sure that Victorian Liberalism was a radical creed replete with good causes, they helped to ensure that, in the words of George Julian Harney, 'Chartist principles did not die with the organisation'.[18]

Notes

[1] W. Lovett, *Life and Struggles of William Lovett In his Pursuit of Bread, Knowledge & Freedom*, 1876 repr. London, 1967, p. 201.

[2] B. Parsons, *Tracts for the Fustian Jackets and Frock Smocks*, no. 2-3, [1847], p. 13.

[3] *People's Advocate*, 3 February 1849.

[4] For the significance of fustian see P. A. Pickering, 'Class Without Words: Symbolic Communication in the Chartist Movement', *Past and Present*, no. 112, August 1986, pp. 144-162.

[5] See J. Belchem & J. Epstein, 'The Nineteenth Century Gentleman Leader Revisited', *Social History*, vol. 22, no. 2, May 1997, pp. 174-193.

[6] A. Briggs, *Chartism*, Stroud, 1998, pp. 93, 107

[7] See V.I. Lenin, *What is to Be Done*, 1902, repr. Moscow, 1973, chapters 4-5; Weber cited in I. J. Prothero, *Radical Artisans in England and France 1830-1870*, Cambridge, 1997, p. 2. See also D. Thompson, *The Chartists*, London, 1984, pp. 152-172; T.J. Nossiter, *Influence, Opinion and Ideas in Reformed England. Case Studies from the North East 1832-74*, Hassocks, 1975.

[8] Dorothy Thompson has shown that by 1842 'the people' had become synonymous with the working classes. See D. Thompson, 'Who were "the People" in 1842?', in M. Chase & I. Dyck (eds), *Living and Learning: essays in honour of J.F.C. Harrison*, Aldershot, 1996, pp. 118-132.

[9] We are grateful to Professor W.E. Connolly, Johns Hopkins University, for bringing this concept to our attention. See W.E. Connolly, *Why I Am Not a Secularist*, Minneapolis, 1999, pp. 24, 146-8

and *passim*.

[10] See G.D.H. Cole, *Chartist Portraits*, London, 1941, p. 23.

[11] B. Harrison, 'Chartism, Liberalism and the life of Robert Lowery', *English Historical Review*, vol. LXXXII, July 1967, p. 505.

[12] E.P. Thompson, *The Making of the English Working Class*, Harmondsworth, 1980, p. 902.

[13] See E.G. Wakefield, *England and America*, 1834, repr. New York, 1967, pp. 60-74; R.S. Neale, 'Class and Class Consciousness in Early Nineteenth Century England: Three Classes or Five', *Victorian Studies*, vol. XII, no. 1, September 1968, pp. 5-32. By using the term here we do not wish to imply that we accept Neale's cumbersome model.

[14] For a prosopographical analysis of forty-five of the parliamentary supporters of Chartism see D. Nicholls, 'Friends of the People: Parliamentary supporters of popular radicalism 1832-1849', *Labour History Review*, no. 2, Summer 1997, pp. 127-146. The career of Duncombe is long overdue for a major re-assessment.

[15] Cole, *Chartist Portraits*, p. 24.

[16] See E. Yeo, 'Will the Real Mary Lovett Please Stand Up? Chartism, Gender and Autobiography', in Chase & Dyck (eds), *Living and Learning*, pp. 163-181

[17] See P.A. Pickering & A. Tyrrell, *The People's Bread: A History of the Anti-Corn Law League*, London, 2000.

[18] This quotation is from the *Northern Tribune*, vol.1, no. 2, January -May 1854.

CHAPTER 1

THE 'PEOPLE'S ADVOCATE'[1]:
PETER MURRAY McDOUALL (1814-1853)

'I have claims upon the Chartist body, and upon the working men, of more than a common character', wrote Peter Murray McDouall, from a dank prison cell in Kirkdale Gaol in July 1849. McDouall was understandably embittered by a second long term of imprisonment, and he was clearly tormented by reports that his wife and children were suffering when he was less than half way through his period of incarceration. Perhaps with his medical insight he feared the death of one of his young children – a fear that came to pass the following year, a few weeks before his release. Since becoming the 'people's advocate', McDouall continued:[2]

> I have suffered imprisonment twice – exile once – and endured the privations of a wandering, houseless lecturer, during a period of ten years. I have sacrificed time that might have been more profitably employed – health, that ought to have reaped a better reward – and talent, that might have secured a far higher and lasting remuneration.

McDouall's outburst was suffused with both anger and self-recrimination: he went on to admit that he had 'spared neither property, person, nor family. I have been unjust to myself, negligent to my children, and forgetful of my private duties, that I might concentrate all upon the people'. Claims of self-sacrifice were a familiar trope to Chartist audiences, but McDouall had a point. During a public career that lasted about fifteen years he was never far from the headlines. Apart from his numerous arrests, three years in prison and two years in self-imposed exile in France, in 1841 McDouall topped the poll in the inaugural election for the executive of the National Charter Association (NCA) – a feat he repeated in 1842 – and he was triumphantly re-elected in the midst of the crisis of 1848.[3] McDouall's standing alone is sufficient reason to write about him, but, as a man who exchanged the relatively comfortable life of a medical practitioner for the uncertainty of the 'trade of agitation', he is also a good case study of those members of the 'uneasy class' who served the Chartist movement in significant numbers.[4] Moreover, an examination of how and why McDouall came to be politicised sheds important light on the social polarisation of early Victorian Britain. Unlike other case studies in this book, McDouall never claimed that he was a working man; on the contrary he clung to the notion that he was a 'professional' member of the middle classes even when a decline in his material circumstances made it difficult to do so:[5] it was, it seems, only as a 'people's advocate' that he could proselytise on behalf of those whose cause he had embraced.

Peter McDouall was born in 1814 in Newton-Stewart, a market town on the river Cree about 80 miles from Glasgow in the south-west of Scotland. During the years that he was growing up among its 2000 or so inhabitants, Newton-Stewart was undergoing an abortive attempt at industrialisation. The failure of speculative ventures in cotton spinning and coarse carpet manufacture dashed expectations of rapid expansion; and, McDouall later commented, occurred at the same time as a sharp decline in the condition of the local hand loom weavers.[6] A Scottish gazetteer noted that Newton-Stewart was a centre for two Presbyterian secessionist groups - the Relief and the Cameronians. Growing up in an area with a strong tradition of religious dissent may well have been the catalyst that, as in so many other cases, led on to radical causes.[7] Addressing Chartist crowds McDouall was an astringent critic of the 'rotten and slimy slough of Churchism', but not of 'true religion': 'he honoured and revered Christianity and the Bible'. He shared a sense of public duty with many religious radicals: 'It is the duty of a good man', he wrote, 'to leave the world better than he found it'. This predisposition to public life may have also owed something to a family radical tradition - he was, he told an audience in Edinburgh, the grandson of a man who fought alongside Washington.[8]

McDouall's father, Andrew, was a poet, known locally as 'Will Wander, the poet of the Cree'. He published a collection entitled *Will Wander of Benarrow's Trip to America and Other Poems*;[9] what else he did for a living is not clear, but it was sufficient for the family to accumulate some property and provide McDouall with a comfortable and secure childhood. The funds for the boy's education, however, came from a trust established for that purpose by his uncle, Peter McDouall, the Baillie of Newton-Stewart.[10] Thanks to his benefactor the young McDouall embarked on a medical education, studying for five years with Mr McMillan, a surgeon in Newton-Stewart, before completing his training in Glasgow and Edinburgh.[11] We know what was involved from the experience of another Scot, Samuel Smiles, who did a medical apprenticeship at this time. Smiles learned to mix potions, to bleed and to bandage, and he assisted in 'attending the poorer class of patients'. A couple of years into his apprenticeship Smiles began sitting in on classes at Edinburgh University and after six years he applied for his diploma. Following an oral examination of 'about an hour' he commenced his career as a doctor. McDouall passed a similar examination conducted by the Royal Edinburgh College of Surgeons in the mid-1830s before relocating to Lancashire.[12]

McDouall lived briefly in Burnley, managing a medical practice there, before moving, in 1835, to Ramsbottom, on the outskirts of Bury, where he established a successful practice among the residents of a cluster of small factory towns in the Irwell valley. In the three decades before McDouall's arrival, Ramsbottom had been transformed from a typical eighteenth century village comprising a handful of cottages into a booming industrial township with about two thousand inhabitants. The architects of this transformation were members of the nascent Lancashire industrial elite: the Grants and the Ashtons.[13] The spectacular rise of the Grants attracted the attention of Samuel Smiles, who re-told their story in *Self Help*. They arrived in Ramsbottom in 1783 penniless and began work at a small dyeing establishment, but went on to build a cotton spinning and dyeing empire in the Irwell valley. William Grant's rise was also marked by the acquisition of political and social power commensurate with his wealth; he became a magistrate and deputy-lieutenant of the county.[14] Early in the nineteenth century the Ashtons established a large cotton mill at Ramsbottom (they also owned extensive factories at Middleton and Hyde). Engels found Thomas Ashton to be a typical 'Liberal manufacturer' who gave guided tours of his 'superb, admirably arranged building'; 'he calls your attention to the lofty, airy rooms, the fine machinery, here and there a healthy-looking operative'. But, Engels continued, all was not as it appeared: 'the people hate the manufacturer, this they do not point out to you, because he is present'; the factory school trained 'children to subordination' and employees who read 'Chartist or Socialist papers and books' were dismissed.[15] Despite Ashton's best efforts the air at Ramsbottom was thick with radicalism. The town had sent a contingent to Peterloo and in 1826 there had been a pitched battle at Ashton's Mill over the introduction of power looms (William Grant had read the Riot Act). Engels pointed out that the Ashtons were given further reason to hate radicals five years later in 1831 when Samuel's son was shot and killed in Hyde during an industrial dispute.[16]

McDouall's experience as a practising doctor in this setting was crucial to his politicisation and resulted in him becoming a vehement opponent of the factory system. At a time when the statistical inquiry was coming of age as a tool of social investigation, McDouall undertook a detailed survey of his adopted home, visiting over 300 cottages occupied by factory labourers and their families. What he found shocked and appalled him; the conditions were 'miserable in the extreme'. The cottages were severely over-crowded and sparsely furnished; weekly wages were low – 'five shillings on an average' – leading to hunger and debt; infant mortality was high – 'of 10,000 children, not half of that number survive five years'; and illiteracy was widespread. The conclusion was inescapable: 'rags, starvation and death were the fate of these unfortunate people'.[17] McDouall first publicised his research in a presentation to a meeting of the British Association at Newcastle-upon-Tyne in August 1838 which later appeared in the *Journal of the Statistical Society*. Finding that the British Association was more interested in a paper that concluded that employees of Thomas Ashton enjoyed the best pay and conditions in England, McDouall extended his investigations to Hyde.[18]

Here he discovered, much as Engels did a few years later, that all was not as it seemed. The occupants of one house received 17s each week from Ashton's Mill, but from this sum 'they paid Mr. Thomas Ashton 5s. 5d. for coals, rent and water, not forgetting 2d. for the [factory] Sunday School, leaving a sum of 11s. 7d. for nine persons to live on during the week'. There were many similar instances of people receiving 'nominal payments subject to deductions by the masters'.[19] As McDouall testified before a Parliamentary Select Committee on the payment of wages in 1842, the district where he practised was rife with this oppressive 'truck system' whereby employees were paid in kind or compelled to patronise shops and rent houses owned by their employer, often at exorbitant prices. Smiles was wrong when he stated that the Grant brothers were 'honoured and respected by all who knew them'; McDouall accused them of engaging in truck. The working people, 'Consider themselves robbed in a variety of ways', he told the Committee; they were 'afraid' to bring action under existing legislation as 'a great majority of the magistrates are factory masters' – an unmistakable reference to William Grant.[20]

McDouall's critique of the system did not end here. As a doctor he was in a privileged position to comment on the impact of factory labour on the health of the population: 'we find repeated diseases of the structure amongst the adults; diseased lungs, diseased livers, and diseased stomachs'. In addition accidents were common, particularly involving children. Factories were, he concluded, 'hospitals of disease' where 'death presented itself under a hundred different forms'.[21] For McDouall the victims of the factory system were not only those confined to the 'hospitals of disease', but also those whose labour had been de-valued by the machine. He had witnessed the distress of the hand loom weavers in his home town and in the Irwell valley and in both places he saw a 'once noble race ... in rags and want'.[22] 'Oh! for the days of the rattling loom', he wrote in a poem (published in 1849) that imaginatively explored the weaver's perspec-tive[23]

> In the days of my father I lived by the loom,
> My song with my shuttle kept pace,
> I knew not starvation nor poverty's gloom,
> Strong was my arm and ruddy my face.

In 1850 he went further by noting that '[n]othing can compensate society for the loss of its producers. Instinct tells us to preserve life – Reason points out to us the equal necessity of preserving labour'.[24] For McDouall the principal solution to these problems was political: 'I believe the only law which the people believe would be effectual, is a law which the people should have a voice in making'.[25] Although it is too simplistic to reduce Chartism to a 'knife and fork' question involving the revolt of displaced outworkers, economic issues were crucial for

Peter McDouall. The 'manifold evils of the factory system' formed the basis of his first major address to the Chartist National Convention of 1839, and, subsequently, 'White Slavery' was the most common subject matter of his many lectures, articles and poems as an active Chartist. Political reform was not about abstract philosophical concepts, it was about practical solutions; as he bluntly told a group of Parliamentarians in 1842, he believed that 'if the people in the manufacturing districts had had their social miseries remedied by the law in former times, they would never have sought for political remedies now'.[26]

McDouall's opposition to the factory system earned him powerful enemies. He came to appreciate the vulnerability of the 'White Slaves' first hand when he found that his patients were being instructed not to attend him by their employers and that he was prevented from attending cases at local factories. At his first trial in August 1839 he drew attention to the fact that the principal Crown witness against him was Thomas Ashton's brother-in-law.[27] Opposition to the factory system was thus at the core of McDouall's political radicalism in more ways than one.

The immediate cause of McDouall's involvement in Chartism was his friendship with Dr Matthew Fletcher, a surgeon in nearby Bury. Although McDouall had made a name for himself in a debating society in Castle Douglas, not far from his home town, he was very nervous when, in October 1838, Fletcher introduced him at a public meeting. A fellow Chartist, R.G. Gammage, recorded that those who heard McDouall that day 'held little hope of his success in that department'. Yet in time McDouall became a skilled orator.[28] His rise through the Chartist ranks was rapid. The arrest of the enigmatic Tory-radical preacher, J.R. Stephens, in December 1838, created a vacancy at the Chartists' first General Convention that was due to commence its proceedings in London in the new year. Stephens recommended McDouall to his Ashton constituents, who duly elected the 'little doctor' in January 1839. At the Convention McDouall quickly earned a reputation for extremist views on the right of the people to bear arms, and he urged the delegates to adopt a plan of 'ulterior measures', including a national strike. 'He did not come to the Convention merely to present a petition', he declared, 'if they were not to recommend ulterior measures he had better go home'. 'If such views caused alarm', he continued, it should be understood that they had 'sprung from the feelings of a benevolent heart'.[29] There is evidence to suggest that McDouall was also involved in clandestine arrangements for an armed uprising in the spring of 1839. According to a military veteran and Anti-Corn Law League stalwart, Alexander Somerville, McDouall was part of a secret insurrectionary committee and saw himself as a potential commander-in-chief of Chartist forces.[30] In May he was implicated in the purchase of muskets and bayonets in Birmingham, where the Convention had reconvened. During the Bull-Ring riots that gripped Birmingham in mid-July 1839, however, McDouall had urged rioters to throw down their weapons.[31]

As early as April 1839 McDouall had come to the attention of the Home Office as 'one of the most violent of the Chartists' and in June 1839 he was arrested.[32] At his trial in August McDouall spoke for over four hours justifying his earlier calls to arms on the basis of Britain's 'ancient constitution', and detailing the condition of the manufacturing districts 'to which he attributed the agitation commenced by [the working classes] for the increase of their political power'. According to William Aitken, an Ashton-under-Lyne Chartist, who sat in the crowded courtroom gallery, McDouall defended himself 'with a firmness and an eloquence which even his enemies could not but admire. There was no shrinking before that high tribunal from the principles he had advocated …' In a public house the following day, another Chartist, Thomas Dunning, found the special constables 'ordering in jugs of ale and drinking the health of Dr McDouall whose speech had converted them to Chartism'. The speech did not, however, have the desired effect on the jury who convicted McDouall of sedition without even bothering to retire, and he was sentenced to 12 months imprisonment at Chester Castle.[33]

McDouall's life in prison was notable for an acrimonious dispute with his former mentor and fellow inmate, J.R. Stephens, and a love affair with a turnkey's daughter whom he married upon his release.[34] Gammage remembered that McDouall was of 'an ardent fiery temperament' and his feud with Stephens, which involved allegations of mis-appropriation of funds and sexual impropriety,[35] was the first of many spectacular clashes that marked McDouall's public career. In prison he also followed in his father's footsteps by giving free reign to his muse. Unlike his letters, pamphlets and the thousands of reports of his speeches, McDouall's poetry draws attention to his Scottishness which was also evident in a Lowland accent when he spoke. Although there is evidence of anger and regret, the poetry is characterised by a steely sense of defiance and hope, without any of the self-recrimination and doubt evident in 1849:[36]

> Now winter is banished, his dark clouds are vanish'd,
> And sweet Spring has come with her treasures so rare;
> The young flowers are springing – the wee birds are singing,
> And soothing the beast that is laden wi' care.
>
> But lov'd ones are weeping – their long vigils keeping –
> The dark prison cell is the place of their doom:
> The sun has nae shining to sooth their repining –
> To gild or to gladden their dwelling of gloom …
>
> But! Look not so proudly, and laugh not so loudly,
> Nor dream that the struggle of freedom is o'er;
> Your prisons may martyr the chiefs O'our Charter,
> But the bright spark it kindled shall burn as before.

When he emerged from prison in August 1840 it was into the 'trade of agitation'. This existence was not, however, a comfortable one. McDouall 'sacrificed a lucrative profession' (the words are Gammage's) for the cause, and, without payment during his time at the Chartist Convention, used up 'a good round sum in the Bury Bank'.[37] In 1848 he detailed his losses during this period: when he first became a Chartist in 1837, he claimed that he had savings of £338-11s; in 1838 he was forced to sell property in Newton Stewart (a dwelling house, barn and stable) for £409 to boost the cash on hand. By the time he entered prison in 1839 McDouall claimed that all he had left in the bank was £27-3-7d.[38] After his release, like many other Chartists who took tentative steps into the world of professional politics (often following a brush with the law), McDouall lived by a combination of lecturing, journalism, and pamphleteering including editing his own Chartist newspapers: one between April and October 1841 and a second, less well known journal, in 1850.[39]

McDouall also supplemented his income with the proceeds of a concoction called 'McDouall's Florida Medicine' which he first marketed to Chartist audiences in 1842 for 1s-1d a box.[40] Previous historians, including one of the present authors, have implied that these pills were nothing more than a tenuous link to his former profession, but, in fact, their manufacture and the philosophy that lay behind it are worthy of further exploration. In more than one respect McDouall was part of the burgeoning challenge to orthodoxy that characterised the medical culture of his day. On the one hand he became a pill manufacturer in what was surely becoming the age of pills. F.B. Smith has shown that from humble beginnings in the 1820s one pill merchant (James Morrison) was selling approximately 1.1 million boxes of patent medicine a year by 1834.[41] As a faithful mirror of working-class culture the leading Chartist newspaper, the *Northern Star*, never appeared without advertisements for patent medicines, including the famous 'Chartist Pills', which were guaranteed to 'avert much of the illness usually affecting the working classes' and had as their principal agent, Joshua Hobson, the publisher of the newspaper.[42]

The fact that McDouall's pills were manufactured from an ingredient imported from United States of America (hence the name), however, makes them fashionable in another respect: they formed part of the rage for the folk beliefs of the American frontier that swept Britain during these years.[43] The principal advocate of American-style alternative medicine in England was Dr A.I. Coffin. Coffin arrived in England in the mid-1840s to promote the therapeutic virtues of 'internal heat' which was promoted by a concoction of capsicum, cayenne pepper and lobelia or 'Indian tobacco'. As Smith has shown, Coffin built an extensive following across the north of England and numbered among his patients the leading defender of the Chartists in the House of Commons, Thomas Slingsby Duncombe.[44] Whether McDouall had any contact with Coffin or his followers is unclear, and, in fact, he claimed that the recipe for 'McDouall's

Florida Medicine' had been gleaned from 'travellers, and from my own relatives who have mixed with the Indians'.[45]

Either way the pills underscored McDouall's support for reform across a very broad front that extended well beyond the realm of parliamentary politics. 'Society', he proclaimed in a medical tract published in the early 1840s (and hitherto unused by historians), 'rests upon an artificial foundation'.[46] 'To eradicate physical suffering', he continued, 'would require two grand remedies'. As noted, by the time he got to Ramsbottom it had become clear to him that the first recourse 'should be through the law'. Prisons, mad-houses, hospitals, poor houses, he argued, all bore witness to the 'ruin' of man's 'god-like reason and the wreck of nature's bodily strength, health and vigour'. The list of causes was familiar to any witness to industrialism: long hours of labour, insufficient food, scanty dress, and 'comfortless homes' were antithetical to the 'mental elevation and the physical well-being of the people'. Here was a Chartist's simple faith in the power of politics to rectify social problems.[47]

Secondly, however, McDouall argued that physical suffering could be assuaged by the 'administration of rational medical remedies, found in nature, and applied according to her never-erring laws'.[48] As noted, McDouall offered his Florida Pills as a natural remedy practised by the Amer-indians, but this natural therapy was only one in a six-point regimen that he recommended to working people. His other 'laws' sound like little more than home-spun aphorisms to the modern ear: strict temperance in eating and drinking; regular meals; never proceed to work 'without breakfast, warm milk or coffee'; 'rather wear a bad hat than a bad pair of shoes'; and, at dinner, 'eat first and most, and drink last and least'.[49] In its own day, however, McDouall's regimen (even including the pills) would have done little harm to those able to follow it, and it was radical in what it rejected. It is important to remember that in this respect McDouall was among legions of professional, semi-professional and amateur physicians who spurned the often alcohol-based products favoured in conventional medical practice and looked instead to hydropathy, homeopathy, phrenology, vegetarianism, and all manner of 'natural' pills and potions.[50]

The market for McDouall's pills and pamphlets was one that he built up while plying the principal trade that he followed for the remainder of his public life: lecturer. Beginning within days of his release from Chester Castle on 13 August 1840, McDouall was fêted at a succession of 'liberation' parades and soirées. It was a punishing programme. In the five weeks between his release and 21 September, when he arrived in Glasgow, he had addressed 27 meetings throughout Lancashire, Yorkshire and into Scotland. Although his health had begun to fail he continued to meet his commitments: Edinburgh (24th), Dalkeith (25th), Bathgate (28th), Airdrie (29th), Hamilton (30th), Strathaven (1st), Newmills (2nd), Cumnock (5th), Kilmarnock (6th), Saltcoats (7th), Paisley (8th), Johnston (9th), Kilbarchan (10th), Eagelsham (12th), Kirkintilloch (14th) and

Campsie (15th).[51] And on it went. With understandable exaggeration he claimed in July 1841 that since his release he had spoken to nearly 5,000,000 Britons from the Isle of Wight to Aberdeen.[52]

On the platform McDouall cut an impressive figure. Gammage wrote:[53]

> M'Douall was rather short, but possessed a straight and well-erected frame; in personal appearance he was decidedly handsome; his general features were extremely prepossessing; his mouth was small but well formed, void of any unpleasant compression of the lips, his face rather inclined to the oval; his eyes were full, and in moments of excitement sparkling and fiery; his brow was moderately high, very full and broad, and his eyebrows dark and finely pencilled; his hair was light, approaching to sandy (although a government description once stated it to be black), was parted in the centre and hung in long graceful curls behind his ears, and his whole appearance was highly interesting.

McDouall supplemented his natural good looks by wearing black cloths and a long cape which gave him, in the words of another Chartist, 'the appearance of a hero of melodrama'.[54] The tone of his message had not changed, but the emphasis had. 'The first great error was the physical force idea', he told the Manchester Chartists; 'if you want to defeat your oppressors then...ORGANISE, ORGANISE'.[55] His preoccupation with the organisational requirements of the movement was reflected in his editorial contributions to his *Chartist and Republican Journal*. In February1841 he outlined a comprehensive plan to amend the NCA structure which had been adopted the previous July. He envisaged an organisation that combined the virtues of centralisation – a national executive and national delegates' conferences – with intimacy, in the form of small trade-based Chartist Associations in which 'Every man will know his neighbour'. It is questionable whether McDouall's model would have been any more successful than the NCA in evading the legal obstacles that confronted a national organisation, and his call for the trades to form political associations was a process that was already well under way.[56]

Although McDouall's plan was not adopted, his standing was not diminished. Later in 1841 he put it to the test in two important electoral contests. In June he topped the poll in the election for the National Executive of the NCA, gaining 3795 votes.[57] A month later he stood before the electors of Northampton as Chartist candidate in the General Election. His campaign was based on the demands for political reform contained in the People's Charter as well as opposition to the New Poor Law and the Rural Police. He also approved of the 'unfettering of commerce in every respect' – a reference to the repeal of the Corn Laws – provided that the people were given the protection of universal suffrage. He won, he claimed, 'the largest show of hands ever given to any ... candidate'; but at the poll he received 170 votes (compared to 990 and 970 for the two Whigs and 896 for the Tory). McDouall took credit for reducing the Whig vote by 120 based on the result of the previous election – 'they have got a rub they will not forget for some time' – but he probably succeeded in ensuring the defeat of the Tory.[58] Not that he cared for either of the major parties. Although he sought to damage the Whigs in Northampton, in August 1842 he used his fists on the Tories in a wild brawl at Nottingham in the course of providing unsolicited help to the by-election campaign of the Quaker radical philanthropist and corn magnate, Joseph Sturge.[59]

McDouall's activities in 1840-2 proved to be an *entr'acte* between brushes with the law. His role on the NCA executive put him at the centre of the massive wave of strikes that swept through Lancashire, Cheshire and the Potteries in August 1842. As the industrial action entered its second week McDouall arrived in Manchester to represent the London Chartists at a routine national conference.[60] The Chartist deliberations took place in Scholefield's Chapel (see chapter 5), a stone's throw from the headquarters of the striking trades who had resolved not to return to work until the Charter was enacted. McDouall penned an address from the NCA executive 'to the people' that unambiguously supported the adoption of a political objective for the strike:[61]

> … we have solemnly sworn, and one and all declared, that the golden opportunity now within our grasp shall not pass away fruitless, that the chance of centuries, afforded to us by a wise and all-seeing God, shall not be lost; but that we do now universally resolve never to resume labour until labour's grievances are destroyed, and protection secured for ourselves, our suffering wives, and helpless children, by the enactment of the People's Charter.

On the question of whether violence would be needed to resolve the issue, however, the language of the placard was considerably more ambiguous:

> ENGLISHMEN! the blood of your brothers reddens the streets of Preston and Blackburn, and the murderers thirst for more. Be firm, be courageous, be men. Peace, Law and Order have prevailed on our side – let them be revered until your brethren in Scotland, Wales, and Ireland, are informed of your resolution; and when a universal holiday prevails, which will be the case in eight days, then of what use will bayonets be against public opinion?

McDouall, it would seem, felt that he had little choice in taking this stand. 'The question of having or not having a strike was already decided, because the strike had taken place', he later wrote, 'the question of making or not making that strike political was also decided, because the trades had resolved, almost unanimously, to cease labour for the charter alone'. The only question unresolved was 'whether chartism should or should not retain its ascendancy in its natural territory'.[62] His decision to offer leadership to the struggle was costly. The authorities seized on the placard as the pretext for issuing the first of several warrants and

McDouall was lucky to evade capture. Gammage recounts several anecdotes of McDouall's daring life as fugitive, before he successfully escaped to France in September 1842.[63] He was not the only Chartist who took the option of exile in 1842; his friend, William Aitken, fled to the United States.

While he was avoiding the police, McDouall was attacked by the editor of the *Northern Star*, William Hill, over the expenses incurred by the NCA Executive. On top of this, his absence made him a convenient scapegoat for the actions of the Chartist leadership during the strikes.[64] From his self-imposed exile he penned intermittent justifications of his fiscal and political conduct; he was soon also actively engaged in French politics, contributing articles to Etienne Cabet's communist journal, *Le Populaire*.[65] McDouall had probably met Cabet in London in 1839 at the end of the Dijon lawyer's long exile in Britain.[66] In Paris their relationship seems to have blossomed. McDouall set about translating ('at the especial request of the author') Cabet's ponderous utopian novel, *Voyage en Icarie*, the first twopenny instalment of which was ready for publication in May 1845.[67] No copy of McDouall's translation (that appeared under the title 'The Adventures of Lord William Carisdale in Icarie') is extant, but its completion is a testimony to his education. It is easy to understand what attracted him; mythical Icarie was a democratically-controlled state where families enjoyed happy lives free from want and full of healthful and rational pursuits and minimal labour (even the factories are clean, brightly painted and well lighted). There was an Icarian Committee formed in England in the mid-1840s that included in its ranks John Goodwyn Barmby, a man with extensive Chartist and radical connections. 'Our intention is to prove, experimentally', claimed the Committee in a public address, 'that individual property is *the* cause [of social] evil; and, by establishing a Communist State, to prove not only the possibility of its existence, but its superiority in all respects over any other form of government'.[68] Whether McDouall had any connections with the English Icarians is unclear, but they certainly upheld objectives that he approved of:[69]

> We will gather your orphans from your [poor law] unions, your outcast children from your gutters, and instead of becoming acquainted with misery and vice in the streets and the prison, they shall be the Brethren of our Children, and shame your miscalled society by their virtues, developed according to our doctrine of Fraternity, and by our system of Education.

Little other information about McDouall's activities in France has come to light, although he further displayed his education in occasional public letters.[70] It is also clear from these letters that McDouall suffered considerable hardship on the Continent (as did his family who had been left behind in a newly rented house in London) in spite of receiving assistance from collections taken at several Chartist localities and £50 from Feargus O'Connor.[71] By the end of 1844 it was clear that most of McDouall's fellow conspirators, although convicted, were not going to be called for sentence, and he judged it safe to return. He stepped off the boat into controversy. McDouall's first action was an attempt to reorganise Chartism in Scotland together with a plan to commence a Chartist newspaper based in Glasgow. When it became clear that he envisaged a Scottish organisation separate from the NCA he found himself in direct conflict with O'Connor. He also quarrelled with a former close friend and colleague on the NCA executive, James Leach, over the administration of a fund that had been collected during his exile for the ostensible purpose of assisting McDouall to establish a medical practice in Manchester. Not content to settle one score at a time, McDouall also renewed his public dispute with William Hill, and levelled allegations of spying at two of his long-standing Manchester comrades, James Wheeler and Abel Heywood.[72]

Early in 1847 McDouall took steps to set up a medical practice at Oldham, but as soon as the formation of the Chartist Land Company sparked a demand for lecturers, he answered the call, and, despite his earlier conflict with O'Connor, established himself as a prominent promoter of the Land Plan.[73] Much to his great satisfaction, he came into conflict with the authorities in the Potteries. After the police tried to break up his meeting in Newcastle-under-Lyme, he confronted the local magistrates; and in Burslem he was 'escorted by a posse of policemen out of the town'.[74] McDouall's enthusiasm for rural resettlement was a corollary of his passionate opposition to the present factory system. The Land Plan offered the victims of 'White Slavery' nothing less than 'social redemption'; it was, McDouall argued, 'not only practically, but scientifically correct', a point he illustrated with experiments in agricultural chemistry during his lectures.[75]

McDouall spent the early months of 1848 on a lecture tour in Scotland, 'although, God knows', he wrote, 'I should be at my profession. I have sacrificed much valuable time and feel keenly the frequent and long separation from my family'.[76] His return to prominence was capped in the spring of 1848 with his re-election to the executive of the NCA.[77] In the aftermath of 10 April, the day the Chartists sought to present their last petition to Parliament, and the subsequent proscription of Chartist meetings, McDouall again became embroiled in conspiracy, chairing a secret insurrectionary committee in London.[78] It was a speech at Ashton-under-Lyne, however, that led to his arrest in the middle of the night of 16 July. At his trial for sedition and illegal assembly in August 1848 he was defended by the well known radical lawyer, W.P. Roberts, but the result was no different than in 1839; McDouall was convicted and sentenced to two years imprisonment at Kirkdale. 'It is not for myself that I care about', he told Roberts, 'but what are the children to do?'[79]

At Kirkdale McDouall was subjected to the worst of a prison system designed for 'grinding men good'.[80] Conditions there were poor. A fellow Chartist inmate, John West, described the cells:[81]

[they] are lofty with arched roofs, and a small aperture to admit air over the door, and an iron-girded window in front. There is no glass in this window, but wooden slides inside which close to. In the morning the bed clothing is quite wet, the blankets about our shoulders presenting the appearance of a field after driving rain or a heavy fall of dew.

Another Chartist inmate, George White, reported that McDouall was 'suffering sorely': 'He was in solitary confinement and not *allowed* to see, or speak to, any one'. In a public appeal McDouall's wife, Mary-Ann, complained that her husband's health was failing as a result of 'twenty three hours' *close confinement* out of twenty-four'.[82] Despite regular assistance from Chartist victim funds, Mary-Ann McDouall and their young children also suffered severe hardship during his imprisonment. As noted at the outset, their anguish was greatly intensified by the death of their oldest daughter a few weeks before McDouall's release in June 1850.[83]

McDouall emerged from prison claiming that he was going to 'retire from the talking arena' and confine himself to 'the pen and lancet' and he subsequently commenced a medical practice at Ashton-under-Lyne aided by his long time friend and fellow Chartist, William Aitken.[84] But McDouall had not retired from politics. As an old Chartist later wrote, 'agitation had unfitted him for a regular life'. Within weeks of his release he addressed a large Chartist meeting at Blackstone Edge on the Pennine moors telling the crowd 'he had been imprisoned for two years in a small cell, yet he treated the authors of it with the most sovereign contempt'.[85] By July 1850 McDouall had embarked on another eponymous democratic newspaper, but this proved to be a short-lived enterprise.

Only one edition (number two) of *McDouall's Manchester Journal* has survived but, together with extensive extracts from the first number published in the *Northern Star*, there is sufficient material to provide an insight into his mature views. The leading article in the first edition (reprinted in full in the *Star*) begins by pondering, with a 'philosophical mind', 'THE GREAT SECRET OF NATIONAL WEALTH'.[86] The answer, as McDouall recognised, was no revelation - 'labour is the source of wealth' -but he then proceeded to probe the far more interesting questions of 'What is meant by labour' and 'What is useful labour?' Firstly, McDouall rejects 'all consideration of personal profit, and the separate interest of either employer or employed' as bench marks, making 'the public good the standard, the national benefit, the sole test of ability'. In determining public utility, however, McDouall eschews any distinction between mental and physical labour:[87]

a little reflection must convince any reasonable man that there is not any real difference between the man who labours for the good of society with his head, and him who works for the same end with his hands.

This is the closest he ever came to blurring the dividing line between himself as a 'professional' and the workers he treated and campaigned for:

> The worldly distinction consists in the names of salary and wage, as the result of their respective industry. The two are identical in interest. Both are necessary in the present state of society, and therefore should exercise and enjoy equal rights, and proportionate benefits.

But McDouall was no leveller, as he demonstrated when he continued this discussion in the second edition of the *Journal* under the heading 'Capital'. Here he showed clearly that he had not embraced communism during his association with Cabet. 'Some go so far as to say, that all profit is theft', McDouall noted, 'Not so; whilst society allows a field to be let and hired. He who takes it, and tills it, deserves profit for his outlay'.[88] What concerned him was the 'rapid accumulation of capital' 'to enrich the few'. 'Such a capitalist', he felt, 'is a curse to society, because, to secure a present advantage, he robs society of a future gain'. Not surprisingly, given his faith in the power of politics, McDouall's solution to this problem was regulation – 'Such an employment of capital should be restrained by law' – in order to produce a balanced economy: 'Good profit, and good wages, mean equal justice'.[89]

The second article (an Address to the Trades) bemoans the economic consequences of machinery – overproduction – and rejects the prevailing response: wage reduction. In the course of this discussion, McDouall covers familiar ground:

> It is a very moderate statement to say, that half a million handloom weavers' families were thrown out of regular employment; no social provision existing in anticipation of such a calamity, and no suffrage power having been prepared to meet it, because the steadiness of our previous progress forbade the mere supposition.

For him politics and economics remained inextricably linked with dire consequences: 'To destroy labour, and to provide no other means of self-support, than poor rates, is an act of [social] suicide'.[90]

Under the rubric 'Family Medical Advice' McDouall next extolled the virtues of fresh air and clean water. Gone is the inevitability of defeat in the face of the factory and the city. In fact McDouall introduces a plea for 'self-help' into the struggle to survive modern urban industrialism:

> Open your windows, chimneys, and doors; throw the bed cloths, every morning, on chairs or hang them on skreens [sic] or lines; let the breath of heaven sweep away all impurities and sweeten your homes, give the toilworn man blessed, healthful, and pleasant rest, after his labour.

Even fever, he continued, would retreat before 'whitewash, Soap and a scrub-bing brush'. Again, practical experience informed McDouall's prescription. 'When I used to attend the fever patients, in the plague districts of Edinburgh', he recalled, 'I could easily trace the dreadful mortality to overcrowded rooms, want of ventilation, and the absence of water'.[91] But self-help could only achieve so much, the intervention of government was still necessary: 'All narrow lanes and streets should be swept away … and open spaces should be multiplied, as they are the lungs of town and cities. All cemeteries, burial grounds, and offen-sive manufactories, should be removed from the habitations of men'.[92]

The remainder of the newspaper comprised a lecture on the chemistry of agriculture – undoubtedly a left over from his days as a Land Plan advocate – a fictionalised account of the conditions of a Parisian workman, a string of home-spun remedies for removing stains, and advertisements for McDouall's latest poems. The *Journal* concluded with the a promise to provide 'MEDICAL ADVICE' for a fee of two shillings and sixpence, a final attempt to combine politics and pills: 'the requisite prescriptions can be given, either privately, or in a printed form in the *Journal*.[93] The *Northern Star* 'heartily' recommended *McDouall's Manchester Journal* to its readers, hoping that it would enjoy more success than his previous journalistic endeavour,[94] but it was not to be.

In 1852 McDouall again stood for the NCA Executive but on this occasion he was not elected, attracting a paltry fifty-one votes. It was possibly this defeat, together with the parlous nature of the Chartist movement in decline, that con-vinced him to emigrate to Australia, an intention which he publicly announced in June 1852.[95] By this time tales of fabulous wealth from the goldfields that had opened up in New South Wales and Victoria had become a regular feature in the British press, which led the editor of the *Star* to insist that 'no workman need starve at home while comfort and independence await him in Australia'. 'The future Australian republic', continued the editor, 'will be a refuge and a home for those of our workers in the cause of the people, whose souls shall yearn for liberty, should they ever be … compelled to abandon in despair the people of the British Islands'.[96] He might have had McDouall in mind. As late as November 1852 McDouall was still actively engaged in Chartist debates on his old stomp-ing ground of Manchester, but shortly thereafter the McDoualls left for the antipodes. According to later testimony of Mary-Ann McDouall, her husband died shortly after they arrived. He was forty years old.[97] His widow and five children (aged between two and twelve) later returned to England where they lived as parish paupers in Liverpool before a subscription among old Chartist comrades of the 'little Doctor' helped them establish a stationery business at Nottingham.[98]

McDouall's opposition to the 'White Slavery' of the factory system is crucial to understanding his motivation for becoming 'the people's advocate': 'The scenes I have witnessed in Edinburgh, Glasgow, Burnley, and many places in

Lancashire', he wrote in 1848, 'convinced me that some remedy was required for the grave and serious evils I discovered whilst in pursuit of my professional duties'.[99] His medical practice provided him with tangible evidence of its horrors, but his condemnation of the system was also tinctured with moral outrage. 'The factory system is rooted upon the worst passions of the human heart, avarice and ambition', he wrote, a revelation that gave him cause to fear for the future of Britain: 'for one moment contemplate and believe and dread that this race of pale-faced slaves is to be the spring of another generation of people, the mind of the patriot sinks with fear, that of the philanthropist with horror, and that of the man with loudly expressed indignation'.[100]

For an alternative McDouall urged 'English radicals' to 'Read your history'.[101] Although the 'manifold evils of the factory system' were a relatively recent curse – 'as late as 1793, the hand-loom weaver could earn enough by the labour of his hands' – the outline of his hopes for a better future was to be found in the past. Like many Chartists, McDouall invoked a supposed golden age of Saxon democracy during the reign of Alfred the Great as the basis of the case for radical reform. From his prison cell in 1849, he penned an ode to Queen Victoria which made this point forcefully:[102]

> The people claim the ancient suffrage right,
> Chief corner stone of this nation's might …

F.B. Smith records W.J. Linton's disapproval of McDouall's ode, implying that it can be considered along with a 'Loyal Address' adopted by the Chartist Convention, as evidence of monarchism, but this is too simplistic.[103] Although there can be little doubt about McDouall's republican instincts,[104] by urging Victoria to act to restore the 'ancient suffrage right' his poem reflects the ambiguity felt by many Chartists who were prepared to receive their rights by royal intervention:[105]

> … resurrection from the ancient dead,
> Will beam a halo round thy royal head.

Perhaps it was his discomfort at praying to one monarch to restore the rights granted by another that led McDouall to delve deeper into the past to 'the very beginning of our history' where he discovered Britain's 'primitive Parliament', the Kyfr-y-then. Long before the 'Norman Yoke' had enslaved the democratic Saxon institutions of Alfred (the point at which most radical theories of a past golden age commenced[106]), McDouall found 'a savage hand' that had 'First rudely fashioned' the 'ancient suffrage right'.[107] The Kyfr-y-then, McDouall argued, was the apex of a truly republican democracy based on a communal property ownership. This system had been suppressed by the Saxons in the middle of the fifth century and from there it was all down hill: 'We are now in 1841, contending against, and endeavouring to remove evils originating in the year 449'.[108] Delving into the mystical past was a common feature of a wider European romantic revolt against modernity.[109]

One reason why Peter McDouall has failed to find a biographer is that he was, in the words of Mark Hovell, 'one of the least attractive as well as the most violent of the Chartist champions'.[110] He could be petulant and self-opinionated, and it is indisputable that he advocated arming and dabbled with insurrection. His belief, however, that physical force would ultimately be necessary to change Britain's political structure was based on an assessment of the unlikelihood that the occupants of the benches of the House of Commons could be persuaded to simply vote themselves out of existence. It was 'absolute folly', he maintained, to expect that 'anything' would be 'done for the people, either by the present parliament or any other parliament, until they got universal suffrage'.[111] Hovell further displayed his dislike of McDouall by suggesting that he operated out of 'self interest' – an accusation that was often levelled at nineteenth century popular leaders, and not always by their opponents. For example, in 1839 the Attorney General had alleged that McDouall's object was to fill 'his own pockets at the expense of the poor', and a fellow Chartist, William Hill, brought similar charges against him in 1842 by questioning the NCA expenses.[112] As one who clung tenaciously to his status as a member of the middle classes, this accusation cut him to the quick. On this score he deserves to be defended. There is no reason to doubt his claim in 1849 that he spent 'upwards of £1,000 in hard cash' in the early years of Chartism, and, although he subsequently lived off the movement, he strenuously denied that he had profited from either 'pills, pamphlets or politics'.[113] If he was guilty of anything, he admitted in an appeal to the 'Middle Classes' published in 1848, it was 'a pardonable ambition to imitate great philanthropists and reformers'. In this cause McDouall exchanged the relatively comfortable existence of a doctor for a life of uncertainty and hardship in the 'trade of agitation' at a time when the modern concept of professional politics had not won acceptance. In this regard he was a pioneer.

Notes

[1] *Northern Star*, 4 August 1849.

[2] Ibid. See also *Democratic Review*, March 1850.

[3] *Northern Star*, 5 June 1841; 25 June 1842; 20 May 1848; 1 July 1848. G.D.H. Cole admitted that he 'seriously' considered McDouall for *Chartist Portraits*, and in 1975 David Jones suggested that the 'little doctor', Peter Murray McDouall, 'deserves a biography', but despite his prominence McDouall has not attracted much attention from historians; he has not even received an entry in one of the ten volumes of the *Dictionary of Labour Biography* published to date. See G.D.H. *Chartist Portraits*, London, 1941, p. 25; D. Jones, *Chartism and the Chartists*, London, 1975, p. 23. The only exceptions are the brief portraits in C. Godfrey, *Chartist Lives: An Anatomy of a Working Class Movement*, New York, 1987, pp. 517-519, and E. & R. Frow, *Chartism in Manchester 1838-*

1858, Manchester, 1980, p. 24; short articles by H. Weisser, 'Dr Peter Murray McDouall' in J.O. Baylen & N.J. Gossman (eds), *Biographical Dictionary of Modern British Radicals*, Sussex, 1984, vol. 2, pp. 323-326; T. Park, 'The Mysterious Doctor McDouall', *Ramsbottom Heritage Society News Magazine*, no. 7, Summer 1993, pp. 9-11; and a more detailed piece in a relatively obscure political journal by R. Challinor, 'P.M. McDouall and Physical Force Chartism', *International Socialism*, vol. 2, no. 12, 1981, pp. 53-84. See also P.A. Pickering and S. Roberts, 'Pills, Pamphlets and Politics: the career of Peter Murray McDouall (1814-1854)', *Manchester Region History Review*, vol. XI, 1997, pp. 34-43. The present chapter draws on that article.

[4] E. Royle has suggested that only about half the delegates to the first Chartist Convention were 'working men', *Chartism*, London, 1980, p. 23.

[5] P.M. McDouall, *The Charter, What it Means! The Chartists, What they Want. Explained in an Address to the Middle Classes of Great Britain*, London, 1848, p. 2.

[6] *The Topographical, Statistical and Historical Gazetteer of Scotland*, vol. 2, 1848, pp. 443-4 (we are grateful to Alex Tyrrell for this reference); *Northern Star*, 24 August 1839; *Manchester and Salford Advertiser*, 24 August 1839.

[7] *The Topographical, Statistical and Historical Gazetteer of Scotland*, p. 443. See also S. Roberts, 'Joseph Barker and the Radical Cause, 1848-1851', *Publications of the Thoresby Society*, Second Series, 1 (1990), pp. 59-73.

[8] *Northern Star*, 3 October 1840; 10 July 1847; *British Statesman*, 26 November 1842; L.C. Wright, *Scottish Chartism*, Edinburgh, 1953, p. 122.

[9] For notice of the death of Andrew McDouall see *Northern Star*, 8 January 1842. His volume of poetry can be found in Dumfries Public Library; there is no date of publication.

[10] McDouall, *Address to the Middle Classes*, p. 2.

[11] Ibid.

[12] T. Mackay (ed.), *The Autobiography of Samuel Smiles LLD*, London, 1905, pp. 28-9, 34, 45-6. Weisser, 'Dr McDouall', p. 323, suggests that he took his examination in 1836 before moving to Lancashire, although McDouall consistently stated that he moved to Ramsbottom in 1835.

[13] B.T. Barton, *History of the Borough of Bury and Neighbourhood in the County of Lancaster*, 1874 repr. Manchester, 1973, pp. 208-12; *Victoria History of the Counties of England* [Lancashire, 8 volumes], vol. 5, (1911), p. 144.

[14] S. Smiles, *Self-Help*, 1859, repr., London, 1968, pp. 253-4; W. E.A. Axon, *Annals of Manchester*, Manchester, 1886, p. 216; J. Mortimer, *Industrial Lancashire: Some Manufacturing Towns and their Surroundings*, Manchester, 1897, pp. 20-1. Dickens is reputed to have based the Cheeryble brothers of *Nicholas Nickleby* on William and Daniel Grant.

[15] F. Engels, *The Condition of the Working Class in England*, 1845, repr. Moscow, 1977, pp. 197-8n.

[16] Barton, *History of Bury*, pp. 210-12; Engels, *Condition of the Working Class*, p. 227; *Voice of the People*, 8 January 1831; 15 January 1831.

[17] *Northern Star*, 23 March, 1839; 24 August 1839; *McDouall's Chartist and Republican Journal*, 5 June 1841; *Manchester and Salford Advertiser*, 24 August 1839.

[18] P.M. McDouall, 'Statistics of the Parish of Ramsbottom, near Bury, in Lancashire', *Journal of the Statistical Society*, vol. 1, January 1839, pp. 537-39; W. Felkin, 'An Account of the Situation of a Portion of the Labouring Classes in the Township of Hyde, Cheshire', *Journal of the Statistical Society*, vol. 1, November 1838, pp. 416-20. Both papers had been read to the same meeting in August 1838. In 1842 William Cooke-Taylor wrote that Felkin's paper 'excited much attention at the time; it was copied into nearly all the newspapers of Great Britain and America', *A Tour of the Manufacturing Districts of Lancashire*, 1842, repr. London, 1968, p. 184.

[19] *Northern Star*, 23 March 1839; 24 August 1839; *McDouall's Chartist and Republican Journal*, 22 May 1841.

[20] PP. *Select Committee on the Payment of Wages*, 1842, (471), vol. IX, pp. 96-105; Smiles, *Self Help*, p. 253.

[21] *Northern Star*, 22 August 1840; *McDouall's Chartist and Republican Journal*, 24 April 1841; 10

July 1841.

[22] *Northern Star*, 23 March 1839; 24 August 1839; *Chartist Circular*, 19 December 1840; *McDouall's Chartist and Republican Journal*, 10 April 1841; 17 April 1841.

[23] *Northern Star*, 27 October 1849. See W.E. Adams, *Memoirs of a Social Atom*, 1903, repr. New York, 1967, pp. 212-13, and *Northern Star* 5 May 1849 for other poems by McDouall.

[24] *McDouall's Manchester Journal*, 20 July 1850.

[25] PP. *Select Committee on Payment of Wages*, p. 107. See also *Northern Star*, 22 August 1839.

[26] PP. *Select Committee of Payment of Wages*, p. 107.

[27] *Ibid*, p. 106; *Northern Star*, 22 August 1839; 4 August 1849.

[28] R.G. Gammage, *History of the Chartist Movement*, 1854, repr. New York, 1977, p. 67; *Charter*, 7 April 1839.

[29] *Charter*, 17 February 1839; 24 February 1839 (we are grateful to Stephen Roberts for these references); *Manchester and Salford Advertiser*, 2 February 1839; 16 February 1839; 27 April 1839; W. Lovett, *The Life and Struggles of William Lovett*, 1876 repr. London, 1976, p. 169; B. Harrison & P. Hollis (eds), *Robert Lowery: Radical and Chartist*, London, 1979, p. 143.

[30] Cited in A. Plummer, *Bronterre: A Political Biography of Bronterre O'Brien 1804-1864*, London, 1971, p. 108.

[31] M. Hovell, *The Chartist Movement*, Manchester, 1918, p. 145; Lovett, *Life and Struggles*, p. 180; C. Behagg, *Politics and Production in the Early Nineteenth Century*, London, 1990, pp. 211, 214.

[32] HO 40/53 fol. 371, Wemyss to Napier, 20 April 1839. For the story of McDouall's arrest see R.G. Hall & S. Roberts, eds. *William Aitken: The Writings of a Nineteenth Century Working Man*, Tameside, 1996, pp. 34-8.

[33] *Manchester and Salford Advertiser*, 24 August 1839; *Northern Star*, 24 August 1839; Hall & Roberts, *William Aitken*, p. 39; 'Reminiscences of Thomas Dunning' repr. in D. Vincent (ed.), *Testaments of Radicalism*, London, 1977, pp. 137, 140.

[34] See *People's Paper*, 9 August 1856; C. Godfrey, 'The Chartist Prisoners, 1839-41', *International Review of Social History*, vol. XXIV, no. 1979, pt. 2, pp. 216-17.

[35] *Manchester and Salford Advertiser*, 22 June 1839; 29 June 1839; 5 October 1839; *Northern Star*, 22 August 1840; T.M. Kemnitz & F. Jacques, 'J.R. Stephens and the Chartist Movement', *International Review of Social History*, vol. XIX, 1974, pt. 2, p. 224. McDouall alleged that Stephens had attempted to commit 'a most indecent assault upon a young lady'; Stephens and his supporters retaliated claiming that McDouall had diverted part of the Stephens Defence fund for his own legal expenses.

[36] Repr. in *Newcastle Weekly Chronicle*, 8 March 1884. McDouall's accent was noted in the description of him on a wanted poster published in 1842. See Pickering & Roberts, 'Pills, Pamphlets and Politics', p. 38.

[37] Gammage, *History*, p. 67; Hall & Roberts, *William Aitken*, p. 30. Dorothy Thompson has pointed out that so-called 'interested agitators' often earned less than in the trade they had foregone, *The Chartists*, London, 1984, p. 163.

[38] McDouall, *Address to the Middle Classes*, p. 3.

[39] We are grateful to David Goodway for bringing this journal to our attention.

[40] For advertisements of McDouall's pamphlets and pills see *inter alia Northern Star*, 19 September 1840; 5 March 1842; 23 April 1842; 14 December 1844; 2 September 1848; 5 May 1849, *Place Collection*, set, 56, vol. 16 (c.1842), p. 298. For a discussion of this issue see P.A. Pickering, 'Chartism and the "Trade of Agitation" in Early Victorian Britain', *History*, vol. 76, no. 247, June 1991, pp. 221-237.

[41] F.B. Smith, *The People's Health 1830-1910*, Aldershot, 1993, p. 343.

[42] *Northern Star*, 26 January 1839; 5 December 1840; 24 December 1841; 5 March 1842; 12 March 1842; 16 April 1842. See also *Poor Man's Guardian*, 24 November 1832.

[43] Smith, *The People's Health*, p.339.

[44] Ibid, pp. 339-42.

[45] P.M. McDouall, *The People's Medical Tract*, (London, n.d.), p. 9. This rare pamphlet is in the

Place Collection, set 56, vol. 16 (c.1842), p. 299f.

46 Ibid, p. 3.

47 Ibid, pp. 3-4.

48 Ibid, p. 4.

49 Ibid, p. 9.

50 This point has been helped by a discussion with Alex Tyrrell.

51 *Northern Star*, 22 August 1840; 5 September 1840; 12 September 1840; 19 September 1840; 3 October 1840; 17 October 1840; 24 October 1840; D. Thompson, *The Early Chartists*, London, 1971, pp. 139-74.

52 *McDouall's Chartist and Republican Journal*, 17 July 1841. McDouall ended the Scottish tour after he quarrelled with John Collins. George White recalled: 'When in Scotland I have been ready to vomit at the paltry jealousies between Collins and McDouall'. Cited in S. Roberts, *Radical Politicians and Poets in Early Victorian Britain*, Lampeter, 1993, p. 7. *English Chartist Circular*, no. 30, p. 117, gives details of McDouall's lecture tour for the spring of 1841; Derby Local Studies Library holds handwritten police reports of two lectures given by McDouall in September 1841.

53 Gammage, *History*, p. 67; HO 45/249c fols. 325, 333.

54 Adams, *Memoirs*, p. 212.

55 *Northern Star*, 22 August 1840; 5 September 1840.

56 *Northern Star*, 13 February 1841; *McDouall's Chartist and Republican Journal*, 17 April 1841; 24 April 1841. See also E. Yeo, 'Some Practices and Problems of Chartist Democracy', in J. Epstein & D. Thompson (eds), *The Chartist Experience*, London, 1982, pp. 345-80; P.A. Pickering, *Chartism and the Chartists in Manchester and Salford*, Basingstoke, 1995, pp. 66-8.

57 *Northern Star*, 5 June 1841.

58 *McDouall's Chartist and Republican Journal*, 17 July 1841; *Northern Star*, 3 July 1841; M. Hovell, *The Chartist Movement*, p. 239. John Foster suggests that McDouall failed to attract even a majority of the artisan vote. See *Class Struggle and the Industrial Revolution*, London, 1974, p. 104.

59 T. Cooper, *The Life of Thomas Cooper*, 1872, repr. Leicester, 1971, pp. 156-61. See also *McDouall's Chartist and Republican Journal*, 12 June 1841.

60 McDouall was on bail having been arrested in the last week of July in Deptford. His treatment by the police was raised in Parliament by Thomas Duncombe. See *Hansard* [House of Commons], LXV, 1 August 1842, cols 898-922.

61 HO 45/249c fol. 218, enclosure, August 1842.

62 P.M. McDouall, *Letters to the Manchester Chartists*, Manchester, 1842, p. 9.

63 Gammage, *History*, pp. 228-9; *British Statesman*, 1 October 1842.

64 *Northern Star*, 26 November 1842; 3 December 1842; 17 December 1842; 24 December 1842; 7 January 1843; 4 February 1843; *British Statesman*, 19 November 1842; *Poor Man's Guardian*, 5 August 1843. See also D. Jones, *The Last Rising*, Oxford, 1986, p. 202.

65 *British Statesman*, 1 October 1842; 22 October 1842; 26 November 1842; 3 December 1842; 17 December 1842; *Northern Star*, 20 August 1842; *English Chartist Circular*, no. 89, pp. 147-8; R. Challinor, 'McDouall', p. 83n.

66 A Member of the Chamber of Deputies, Cabet had fled to England in 1834 after criticising the government.

67 *Movement: Anti-Persecution Gazette and Register of Progress*, 2 April 1845; R. Challinor, 'McDouall', p. 72. See also C.J. Johnson, *Utopian Communism in France: Cabet and the Icarians 1839-1851*, Ithica, 1974, pp. 48-61. Aitken spent part of his self-imposed exile on the Mormon community at Nauvoo in Illinios which was later taken over by the Icarians. Another Chartist who was interested in Cabet was G.J. Harney who used a translation by the London radical publisher, Henry Hetherington. See R.G. & R.M. Black (eds), *The Harney Papers*, Assen, 1969, p. 241.

68 *Community of Icarie: Address of Icarien Committee*, London, 1847, p. 3. See also W.H. Armytage, *Heavens Below: Utopian Experiments in England 1560-1960*, London, 1961, pp. 205-7.

69 *Address of Icarien Committee*, p. 4.

70 See, for example, his essay, 'The Sedition of Tiberius and Caius Gracchus', *Poor Man's Guardian*,

22 July 1843.

71 *British Statesman*, 1 October 1842; 8 October 1842; 22 October 1842; 26 November 1842; 17 December 1842; *Northern Star*, 17 February 1844; 25 January 1845; *English Chartist Circular*, no. 129, p. 305, for John Cleave on McDouall's reluctance to flee to France and the need to support him and his family.

72 *Northern Star*, 25 January 1845; 8 February 1845; 15 February 1845; *Poor Man's Guardian*, 5 August 1843; R.G. Gammage, *History*, pp. 258-9; A. Wilson, *The Chartist Movement in Scotland*, Manchester, 1970, pp. 209-11.

73 *Northern Star*, 2 January 1847. For his appointment as an official lecturer on behalf of the Company and reports of his tours see *Northern Star*, 10 July 1847; 28 August 1847; 25 September 1847; 6 November 1847.

74 *Northern Star*, 31 July 1847; 14 August 1847; 4 September 1847.

75 'Rules of the National Land Company', *PP. First Report from the Select Committee on the National Land Company*, 1847-8, vol. XIII, App. 1, p. 50; *Northern Star*, 11 September 1847.

76 *Northern Star*, 12 February 1848; 19 February 1848. In March McDouall stood, at short notice, as a Chartist candidate at a by-election for Carlisle. After a victory at the nomination he came last in the poll securing 55 votes. See *Northern Star*, 18 March 1848; *The Times*, 7 March 1848; 16 March 1848.

77 *Northern Star*, 20 May 1848; 1 July 1848.

78 D. Goodway, *London Chartism 1838-1848*, Cambridge, 1982, pp. 86-9, 228; J.C. Belchem, 'The Spy-System in 1848: Chartists and Informers - An Australian Connection', *Labour History*, no. 39, November 1980, p. 25.

79 *Northern Star*, 22 July 1848; 29 July 1848; 2 September 1848; R. Challinor, *A Radical Lawyer in Victorian England*, London, 1990, pp. 162-3.

80 See M.E. DeLacey, 'Grinding Men Good? Lancashire's Prisons at Mid-Century', in V. Bailey (ed.), *Policing and Punishment in Nineteenth Century Britain*, London, 1987, pp. 182-216.

81 *Northern Star*, 17 March 1849.

82 George White to Mark Norman, 1849, in Black (eds), *The Harney Papers*, p. 90; *Northern Star*, 5 May 1849.

83 *Northern Star*, 5 May 1849; 4 August 1849; 25 August 1849; 8 September 1849; 17 November 1849; 5 February 1850; 23 March 1850; 8 June 1850.

84 *Red Republican*, 3 August 1850; *Northern Star*, 29 June 1850; W.E. Adams, *Memoirs*, p. 212; *Newcastle Weekly Chronicle*, 8 March 1884.

85 W.E. Adams, *Memoirs*, p. 212; *Northern Star*, 20 July 1850.

86 *Northern Star*, 13 July 1850.

87 Ibid.

88 *McDouall's Manchester Journal*, 20 July 1850.

89 Ibid.

90 Ibid.

91 Ibid.

92 Ibid. McDouall ended this article on a positive note by suggesting that '[w]e are fast overcoming these nuisances'.

93 Ibid.

94 *Northern Star*, 13 July 1850.

95 *Star of Freedom*, 19 June 1852; *People's Paper*, 21 August 1852.

96 *Star*, 10 April 1852; *Star of Freedom*, 19 June, 1852; 26 June 1852; 31 July 1852. See also P.A. Pickering, 'The Finger of God: Gold's Impact on New South Wales', in I.D. McCalman, A. Cook & A. Reeves (eds), *Gold: Forgotten Histories and Lost Objects of Australia*, Cambridge, 2001, pp. 37-51.

97 *People's Paper*, 6 November 1852; *Newcastle Weekly Chronicle*, 8 March 1884. There is no record of McDouall's arrival in Australia in the Colonial Secretary's *Reports of Vessels Arrived*, 1853, (Victorian State Library, Mf. AO LOC., 4/5243, 4/5244). The story that he drowned in the

shipwreck of the *President* off the Australian coast is apocryphal. During this period the *President* was permanently anchored in Hobson's Bay, Melbourne, where it served as a prison hulk. See M.A. Syme, *Shipping Arrivals and Departures: Victorian Ports*, vol. 2, 1846-1855, Melbourne, 1987, p. 698; J. Loney, *Australian Shipwrecks*, vol. 2, 1851-1871, Sydney, 1980. McDouall's death is not recorded in any of the official notices of the Australian colonies. In his reminiscences Robert Gammage raises and rejects the notion that McDouall did not in fact emigrate, but died in poverty near Manchester. See W.H. Maehl (ed.), *Robert Gammage: Reminiscences of a Chartist*, Manchester, 1983, pp. 23-4.

[98] W.E. Adams, *Memoirs*, p. 212; *People's Paper*, 9 August 1856; *Newcastle Weekly Chronicle*, 8 March 1884; C. Godfrey, *Chartist Lives*, p. 519; R. Challinor, 'McDouall', p. 81.

[99] McDouall, *Address to the Middle Classes*, p. 3.

[100] *McDouall's Chartist and Republican Journal*, 3 April 1841; 26 June 1841.

[101] *Operative*, 17 March 1839.

[102] *Dr P.M. McDouall's (State Prisoner) Poetical Petition to Queen Victoria, on Behalf of the Oppressed Working Classes of Great Britain and Ireland and in Demand of their Political Rights and Liberties*, Liverpool, 1849, p. 3.

[103] F.B. Smith, *Radical Artisan: William James Linton*, Manchester, 1973, p. 34.

[104] See *McDouall's Chartist and Republican Journal*, 3 April 1841; 24 April 1841.

[105] *P.M. McDouall's (State Prisoner) Poetical Petition to Queen Victoria*, p. 3. For a fuller discussion of this issue see P.A. Pickering, '"Hearts of the Millions": Chartism and Popular Monarchism in the 1840s', *History*, forthcoming.

[106] See C. Hill, 'The Norman Yoke', *Puritanism and Revolution*, London, 1968, pp. 58-125.

[107] *P.M. McDouall's (State Prisoner) Poetical Petition to Queen Victoria*, p 3; *McDouall's Chartist and Republican Journal*, 10 April 1841; 8 May 1841.

[108] *McDouall's Chartist and Republican Journal*, 8 May 1841; 15 May 1841.

[109] See, for example, J. Hutchinson, *The Dynamics of Cultural Nationalism: the Gaelic Revival and the Creation of the Irish Nation State*, London, 1987.

[110] Hovell, *The Chartist Movement*, p. 263.

[111] *Manchester and Salford Advertiser*, 27 April 1839.

[112] Hovell, *The Chartist Movement*, p. 263; *The Trial of Dr McDouall*, cited in J. West, *A History of the Chartist Movement*, London, 1920, p. 128.

[113] *British Statesman*, 3 December 1842; *Northern Star*, 4 August 1849.

CHAPTER 2

AN 'EARNEST RADICAL'[1]:
THE REVEREND HENRY SOLLY (1813-1903)

Few men in our own age and generation have striven more zealously for the promotion of the welfare of their fellow-men than Mr Solly, who has, to our knowledge, and for many years past 'spurned delights and lived laborious days' in order that he might aid the working classes in their efforts to emerge from the dark realms of ignorance, to which a hateful system of legislation had relegated them, and place themselves in the full light of the sun of knowledge. In this direction he has been largely successful ...
Foreman Engineer, c.1881[2]

Henry Solly's life was crowded with efforts to improve the condition of the working class and to promote fellowship between the social classes. Inspired by a Unitarian's faith in 'rational religion', which he believed had to be applied to all aspects of life, Solly became, in the view of one historian, the 'Omnibus Radical'.[3] Although he still awaits his biographer, we now have studies that recognise his contributions to the abolition of slavery, the working men's club movement, the promotion of charity organisations, and the concept of the garden city.[4] Appropriately, too, before the end of the twentieth century he was given an entry in a standard work of biographical reference.[5] The aspect of Solly's multi-faceted career which has been least celebrated, however, was his involvement in Chartism. Solly was a figure of secondary importance in the Chartist move-ment, but, he achieved national prominence in 1841-2. Firstly, he captured the public eye as the author of a radical Christian pamphlet interrogatively entitled *What Says Christianity to the Present Distress?* and, secondly, he gained national notoriety as a result of his role as a delegate to the Anti-Corn Law League's Convocation of Ministers and to the Complete Suffrage conferences organised by the Birmingham corn magnate and radical philanthropist, Joseph Sturge. By the close of the latter, as Robert Gammage noted in his *History of the Chartist Movement*, Solly had earned much respect for his courageous stand in support of Chartist rather than Suffrage resolutions.[6]

Ironically, Solly has done much by his own hand to obfuscate his Chartist ca-reer. In his absorbing autobiography *These Eighty Years* (1893), as well as in the semi-fictional *James Woodford, Chartist and Carpenter* (1891), the characters of

which were modelled on his comrades among the Yeovil Chartists, Solly depicted a movement soiled by Feargus O'Connor's 'imperious' style of leadership.[7]
Influenced, as he was, by the success of Victorian Liberalism, Solly cast the real
hero of Chartism as William Lovett, a rational man dedicated to the pursuit of
class conciliation with the radical middle class through education and temperance.[8] Whether or not Solly wilfully contrived a historical distortion, the record
speaks for itself. As will be shown from hitherto neglected sources, Solly was as
much at home with the mainstream O'Connorites as he was with the so-called
'moral force' Chartists. In effect, he worked with Chartists of all persuasions
during a succession of pastorates in Yeovil (1840-1842), Tavistock (1842-1844),
Shepton Mallet (1844-1847), and Cheltenham Spa (1847-1851). The aims of
this chapter are thus twofold: to save Solly from himself by establishing an ac-
curate record of his role as a 'great conciliator' in Chartism,[9] and to illustrate
how the genesis of the principal achievement of his later career, the formation
of the Working Men's Club and Institute Union in 1862, was to be found in the
Chartist-based prototypes that he developed in the West Country before 1848.

Henry Solly was born on 17 November 1813 in the City of London, the
youngest in a solidly middle class family of ten children. His father, Isaac, was
a successful merchant and business man who had married Mary Harrison, the
daughter of a London solicitor; their wealth and social standing was such that
they kept servants and farmed about sixty acres at Leyton in north London.
The family was originally Presbyterian, and they had established links with
Unitarianism. It showed, for example, in the construction by Solly's grandfather
of a meeting house for worship in 1730; in their love of books and of the arts; in
a commitment to respectability through temperance; and, in the private sphere,
in the humane treatment of their retinue of domestic servants and agricultural
employees.[10]

As a child Solly attended a number of Unitarian educational institutions
including the well-known school run by Dr John Morell at Hove, Brighton.[11]
At Morell's he imbibed those values for which the Unitarians were still held
in opprobrium by members of other religious faiths. These included a liberal,
rational outlook based on the denial of the concept of original sin as the key to
man's true nature, and a commitment to 'an open, ever-developing religion,
with no subscription to articles of faith'.[12] Arguably, the greatest strength of the
Unitarians' influence lay, according to Ruth Watts, in an educational philosophy which deemed that 'knowledge is power': thus 'rational' religion and 'rational' education preached from the pulpit and disseminated in the classroom,
regardless of gender, would change society.[13] Unitarianism, therefore, was a
Christian denomination linked to a belief in human improvement and progress.
Following the 1813 Act of Unitarian Toleration, the wide range of thought allowed to Unitarians became very appealing both to a significant minority of the
rising middle-class industrialists championing municipal reform and free trade,

and to the new working class involved in defending press freedom and campaigning for political reform.[14]

With a liberal education and the financial support and encouragement of his parents behind him, Solly entered the new University of London in 1829. Here he continued to do well in classical and mathematical studies; he also excelled in the art of public speaking which he honed in a debating club called the Academic Society. The oratorical skills gained at University were to be of essential service to him in adult life: in the Unitarian pulpit, on the political platform, in the mutual improvement club and in the lecture hall. Having completed his degree, however, Solly was dismayed that his father insisted he begin a business career in a shipbroker's counting house belonging to a relative in Leadenhall Street, London. 'Book-keeping' and 'quill-driving' were never Solly's forte.[15] Despite several attempts, the work and world of the commercial clerk seemed 'to crush the very life out of me' he recalled at the beginning of his autobiography.[16] Illness and depression accompanied him when he tried other business-orientated work, first in a science laboratory and then at a number of London banks. By his own estimation his sanity was saved only by falling in love, writing a play, and by attending night classes and meetings of debating societies.[17] Ironically, it was a crisis in capitalism, the economic system that he instinctively disliked, which first provided Solly with the opportunity to escape. In 1837, his father faced financial ruin in the commercial crash of that year. His social conscience stirred by the distress and poverty he witnessed first hand in London, Solly approached a family friend, the Rev. Robert Aspland, about the spiritual rewards of becoming a Unitarian minister. Suitably encouraged by Aspland, in 1840 Solly was briefly engaged as a man of the cloth in the General Baptist Academy at Worship Street Chapel, London under the supervision of another friend, the Rev. Benjamin Mardon.[18] On certain theological and doctrinal questions – for example, the rejection of the divinity of Christ – the General Baptists were drawn towards Unitarianism. However, by this time Solly had also become influenced by the preaching and writings of two of the most advanced Unitarian thinkers of the day: William Johnson Fox from the South Chapel, London, who had become an active supporter of Chartism and one of the Anti-Corn Law League's star performers;[19] and William Ellery Channing, the ablest defender of Unitarianism in America.[20] Inspired by Channing's belief in the innate goodness of humanity and that strand in Unitarianism now professing vociferously for social reform,[21] the idealistic Solly boldly put himself forward for the vacant Unitarian ministry in Yeovil. Given a three months trial on a fixed salary of £65, Solly remained in this West Country town until the end of November 1842 when he was forced to leave by a hostile section of the congregation.[22] The explanation for Solly's expulsion was his adoption of a social gospel mission that preached Chartism as a panacea for contemporary society's poverty and economic ills that proved completely unacceptable, despite his attempts aimed at class conciliation.

Neither his age – he was only twenty-seven – nor his open-mindedness were adequate preparation for the turbulent times Solly experienced in Yeovil. Whilst the town was not a modern industrial centre like Manchester or Bradford, it did have its fair share of political, social and economic problems by the time Solly arrived. A traditional market town with a population of only 2,774 inhabitants in 1831, it had failed a year earlier to secure a Parliamentary seat under the Reform Act.[23] Although the trappings of rural deference remained intact, there was an element of defiance present: the workers were experiencing much upheaval as a result of a depression in two of the town's industries, glove-making and leather dressing.[24] Faced with stiff competition from the north of England in the machine age, the prospect of more unemployment, and high food prices resulting from a bad harvest in the district, two hundred gloving operatives had formed their first trade union in January 1834.[25] Significantly, this action had followed rapidly on the visit in 1833 by 'Orator' Henry Hunt during which he addressed the men on the radical political issues of the day.[26] By 1838, the harsh realities of the withering glove trade, combined with the glaring inequalities that existed between the masters and the men, had led the impoverished glove-makers and other small-town craftsmen into enthusiastic support for Chartism.[27]

Although Solly's most loyal friends were ultimately to be the working men and their wives, when he first arrived in Yeovil he was met with hostility from at least one of the glove makers. The confrontation was, not surprisingly, generated by social class. After all, Solly was middle class and not free from the insensitivity and prejudice that went with it. As he later recalled: 'for the first twenty-five years of my life I looked on the working classes as a sort of inferior race, like many employers of labour'.[28] Moreover, the first mass protests by the Chartists, whom he had witnessed presenting their Petition to Parliament in 1839, had interested him little.[29] In Yeovil's streets Solly was confronted for the first time with the realities of social distress when he enquired of a glove-worker about the state of trade in the town. Solly was taken aback by the reply to his well-intentioned question and, in particular, by the way in which the glove-cutter immediately linked it to his gentlemanly dress code. In a situation where 'genteel' poverty met 'real' poverty, the concern shown by Solly unwittingly compounded the worker's sense of grievance. 'I asked (the glove-cutter) if the staple manufacture of the town was tolerably flourishing', Solly recalled,[30]

'No', he answered gloomily, 'and you don't seem to be doing much to help it'. Then I became guiltily conscious that I was wearing cotton gloves, and was too poor to buy kid!

Undeterred, Solly began his life's mission by deliberately involving himself in discussion and debate with the distressed working-class members of his Unitarian congregation, some of whom were now leading lights in the recently formed National Charter Association (NCA) in Yeovil. Slowly he moved from the position of the politically and socially naïve 'outsider', to one in which he was regarded, by virtue of his status, education and conviction, as a 'gentlemanly radical leader'.[31] Indeed, it was an image that he self-consciously cultivated and a concept that was to become a cornerstone of his future plans for class conciliation.

Unitarians were better known for advocating social reform than for engaging in theological controversy. In Solly's case this meant applying Christ's teachings in profoundly radical ways in order to address the special needs of the poor and defenceless members of his congregation, rather than to applaud the material success of its wealthy members. He found in Chartism an important vehicle for achieving the abolition of 'class legislation' against working men and women. In his later account, Solly gave special attention to the influence of two Yeovil Chartists both on his own thinking and on local Chartist policy: John Bainbridge, a journeyman upholsterer originally from Yorkshire, and John Stevens, a local man who earned his living as a house-decorator.[32] It was they who taught him to apply his religious convictions to an egalitarian mission – to help 'the will of God to be *done on earth*, as it is done in Heaven'; both men became life-long role models – born 'gentlemen' in their class[33] – who represented all that was admirable in working-class life. Bainbridge in particular was put on a pedestal by Solly because he subsequently worked for William Lovett's 'moral force' National Association in the 1840s. He became the key 'mascot',[34] an exemplar of Solly's vision of a Unitarian-inspired working-class 'gentleman' involved in club-work and promoting fellowship between the classes.[35]

In the highly charged atmosphere of 1840, however, employers in Yeovil were 'notoriously cruel and selfish' (Solly's words[36]) and class conciliation seemed a long way off. Local Chartist policy at this time was shaped by a group of about forty members operating from their rooms in Brunswick Street.[37] Encouraged by a visit from Robert Gammage, who was on tour in the West Country during 1840,[38] the local Chartist association appeared to be in a flourishing state from the summer of that year until May 1841. During these months Chartist tracts were widely distributed; funds were raised every week for the wives and families of incarcerated Chartist leaders; the Queen was memorialised to pardon John Frost, Zephaniah Williams and William Jones; and a petition requesting the liberation of Feargus O'Connor from York Castle prison was collected for presentation by Thomas Wakley MP. Among the names of local leaders reported in the *Northern Star* in connection with all this activity, those of John Edmunds, William Hewlett, Emanuel Hooper and George Wheadon – all glovers – as well as George White and 'Mr Woodward' (both artisans and prominent Unitarians) figure as prominently as those of Bainbridge and Stevens.[39]

Although Solly never formally joined the NCA, the full cut and thrust of his Chartist apprenticeship now began. Much to the annoyance of the more respectable elements in his congregation, he attended an important public meeting arranged for 6 October 1840 to hear a welcome address from George Bartlett, who had just been released from Ilchester prison.[40] A West Country leader from Bath, Bartlett had been serving a nine-month prison sentence for sedition.[41] Reports indicated that it was a highly charged evening meeting with over two hundred present. Bartlett made a powerful speech which was all the more moving because, despite having been visibly weakened by his prison experiences, his spirit remained as strong as ever. From the platform Bartlett told the crowd that:

> Chartism is not considered by me to be a bread and cheese question; nor do I advocate it merely because it would, if established, better the condition of the people. I advocate Chartism principally because it is founded on truth and justice .... What we demand is even-handed justice.

Despite the presence of Solly, Bartlett then proceeded to 'ridicule the middle classes':

> They obtained their privileges by our assistance, and though they have, to a great extent, failed in their object; yet, because we are contending for the rights of all, and against injustice of every description, they shake in our faces the halter and the keys of the dungeon .... They thought that we were to be put down by persecution, but they have been deceived.

Before concluding early through exhaustion, Bartlett showed how, since history was on their side, the 'popular agitation' in which they were presently engaged would bring the Charter.[42] Significantly, Solly's recollection of the meeting in his autobiography is both slight and distorted. In Solly's view, Bartlett appeared 'to have suffered too much to have enough spirit left in him to speak at all effectively'.[43] Predictably, Bainbridge was made the hero of the moment: from the chair he gave 'an excellent address'.[44] By contrast, the report in the *Northern Star* records how Bainbridge apologetically confessed to the assembled Chartists that he was 'inexperienced in public speaking'.[45] Unfortunately, no evidence has been unearthed to indicate whether Solly subsequently attended a liberation dinner organised by the Yeovil NCA. What is clear is the fact that Bartlett was a well-known supporter of O'Connor.[46] Other lecturers of a similar persuasion, such as Ruffey Ridley, also visited Yeovil. Solly, however, appears to have remembered only meeting those like Charles Clarke, who followed the initiatives of Lovett, Henry Vincent and Arthur O'Neill, the founder of the Christian Chartist Church in Birmingham. From the spring of 1841, these leaders were advocating strategies designed to attract radical middle-class support to the cause of universal suffrage. For many O'Connorites compromise was a euphemism for surrender.

Solly's Unitarian background predisposed him favourably to Lovett's scheme for the provision of education and rational recreation. Accordingly, Solly wrote to him but did not receive a reply until six months later in October 1841,[47] by which time there was open hostility at national level between Lovett and O'Connor over the direction Chartist strategy should take. In the mean time the local Chartists considered Lovett's initiative at a crucial meeting held on 3 May 1841. After a lengthy discussion, the following resolution, proposed by Bainbridge and seconded by Hewlett, was carried:[48]

> That this meeting is of the opinion that a good system of education is highly neces-sary in this country, and we highly approve of the plan laid down by Messrs Lovett and Collins; but for the purpose of carrying the Charter, we are of the opinion that the present National Charter Association is calculated to effect it more speedily, and therefore we shall still continue to give it our warmest support.

Not surprisingly, Solly mentions none of this in the autobiography, even though it was to remain the local Chartists' twin objective over the next two years. In his influential essay on Chartism in Somerset and Wiltshire, R. B. Pugh sug-gests that from May 1841 the Yeovil Chartists harboured 'a sneaking fondness for Lovett'.[49] This may be correct, but evidence gleaned from the *Northern Star* points to another conclusion: despite financial difficulties the Chartist Association in Yeovil remained overwhelmingly committed to agitating for 'nothing short of the People's Charter' and regularly reaffirmed its loyalty to the National Executive of the NCA that was supported by O'Connor.[50]

As luck would have it, a change in personal circumstances – for the better as it proved to be – prevented Solly from taking part in the discussion. On 22 April – eleven days before the Chartists' meeting – Solly had married Rebecca Shaen, the daughter of a leading Unitarian with land and influence in Crix, Essex, where they spent part of the next three weeks because they 'could not afford a proper honeymoon'.[51] Typical of members of that faith (male and female), Rebecca Shaen had received a sound liberal education that prepared her for the teaching profession in adult life.[52] Like Solly, too, she possessed an inquiring mind and a strong social conscience. As a result she came to share some of the burdens connected with the realisation of her husband's social gospel in Yeovil. For example, she supplemented his 'meagre salary' through occasionally teaching pupils at their vicarage home; she also showed an active interest in Chartism by accompanying him to hear itinerant lecturers, and in accepting invitations to attend the NCA's soirées and balls.[53] Doubtless, her involvement exacerbated Solly's already strained relations with the more conservative and wealthy mem-bers of his congregation, who objected strongly to the way he was politicising the ministry.

Soon after he returned from his honeymoon, Solly was thrust into national prominence. Early in August 1841 John Bainbridge, conscious of mounting distress in the town, wrote opportunistically to the *Northern Star*.[54] A confer-ence of clergymen of all denominations was being organised by the Anti-Corn

Law League in Manchester to consider both the cause of the current distress and how to alleviate it. Hopeful about the influence clergymen might usefully exert over the growing crisis, Bainbridge urged readers of the *Star* to 'send honest and talented men to represent them at this important meeting'. Significantly, the *Northern Star* did not dissent; indeed, it also included the address of George Thompson, one of the organisers, to whom further representation could be made. Here was an opportunity, it seemed, for all Christian Chartist ministers and Rational Religionists to follow Bainbridge's call and actively participate. All the evidence suggests that by this time Solly had become not only a convinced Chartist, but also a tried and tested friend of the working class. Earlier doubts which he had expressed in his letter to Lovett about the necessity of universal suffrage,[55] were finally removed in a series of debates with the full Chartist committee,[56] that took place shortly before he left for the 'National Convocation' in Manchester.

The decision to elect Solly as their representative emerged out of these debates. To the approval and satisfaction of all shades of opinion in the local NCA,[57] and with additional financial support from Bridport radicals to cover his expenses, Solly agreed to attend to oppose the Corn Laws, but also to speak vigorously for the People's Charter.[58] The stage-managed affairs of the Manchester Convocation, however, were undoubtedly an eye-opener for Solly, as was the experience of witnessing, at first hand, the depth of distress prevailing in the cotton capital of the world. Solly arrived 'with high hopes of putting the case for reform', but the League had other ideas. He was perhaps fortunate to avoid the brawl at the entrance that prevented many like-minded ministers – the Christian Chartist preachers and Rational Religionists – from being part of the assembly of 645 delegates,[59] but once inside his dogged persistence got him further than others (including the Chaplain of the Manchester Chartists, James Scholefield, see chapter 5). On the afternoon of the final day of the Convocation, admittedly when the members were tired and half of them already absent, Solly spoke passionately about the three point mandate that had been mutually agreed upon with the Yeovil Chartists: on the need for practical measures to alleviate distress; the requirement of education for all; and for 'the removal of unjust authority usurped by the higher classes over the lower'.[60] There was little response, but Solly felt that at least 'he had kept faith with my friends at Yeovil and Bridport'.[61]

Solly returned to Yeovil emboldened by his conference performance. Soon he would call public attention to the Chartist cause by taking the highly provocative action of interfering in a celebration of the monarchy. At a great public meeting in early February to celebrate the birth of Queen Victoria's first child, a son and successor to the throne, Bainbridge moved and Solly seconded a resolution that asked the Queen to consider:[62]

that poverty, misery and human degradation prevails to an alarming extent in every part of this our favoured land, and which if not speedily removed will, in all probability, lead to results the most fearful to contemplate.

The context for this remarkable outburst in the winter of 1841-2 was a classic convergence of hunger and politics. Class hostility between masters and men had reached crisis proportions.[63] Both Bainbridge and Stevens had been sacked shortly after a lecture in the town by Charles Clarke of Bath.[64] The local authorities – 'the squirearchy and the priesthood' – had redoubled their efforts 'to put Chartism down'.[65] There is no doubt that Solly and Bainbridge caused a great sensation: the authorities felt publicly embarrassed. The failure to show proper respect for the Queen marked the beginning of the end of Solly's fragile relationship with the more wealthy Unitarians in his congregation who paid his stipend.[66] In due course the ruling family of bankers withdrew their annual subscription of £20 towards his salary, a move designed to put pressure on him to leave. For a time Bainbridge fared better. Although ostracised both inside and outside the Unitarian chapel, he managed to find work as a self-employed grocer for the rest of 1842 and was defiantly active in Chartist branch life.[67] Stevens, however, appears to have been successfully hounded out of town almost at once. He left for Trowbridge where he was again active in the NCA until 1847, at which time, with the help of a loan from Solly and his wife, he emigrated to Philadelphia, USA.[68]

Solly's standing in the Chartist ranks now made him an obvious choice as a delegate to Sturge's Complete Suffrage Union conference scheduled for the beginning of April in Birmingham. Earlier in the year, Sturge, whom Solly had already met, along with the Rev. Edward Miall, editor of the *Nonconformist*, launched a new initiative with the expressed aim of achieving reconciliation between the middle and working classes on the basis of a programme of advanced radical reform.[69] The Sturge proposals certainly appealed to a section of the Yeovil Chartists, including Bainbridge, Woodward and Solly, who were devout Unitarians. They were, like Sturge, just as interested in curbing the power of the Anglican Church as in schemes for working class education and temperance.[70] Once again, however, Solly's memory is selective. In his autobiography Solly records unequivocal enthusiasm for Sturge's scheme for class conciliation on the eve of the Birmingham conference.[71] Yet the report in the *Northern Star* of the meeting at which he was elected as conference delegate outlined a non-sectarian approach:[72]

> … we return our sincere thanks to Feargus O'Connor, Esq., and other leading Chartists, for their increasing exertions for the rights of the working classes of this empire: that we will not unite with any party having for their object any thing short of the Six Points of the Charter, which we consider the only effective remedy for the prevailing distress; but that where that measure is made the primary object, we

will cordially join with all classes of our country men in ameliorating the condition
of our fellow creature.

Solly's formal contribution to the first Complete Suffrage Conference was modest, but not unimportant. Although he was overshadowed by the idiosyncratic
radical Anglican preacher and Complete Suffragist, the Rev. Thomas Spencer,
Perpetual Curate of Hinton Charterhouse near Bath,[73] who moved an important resolution for the adoption of universal suffrage on the opening day, Solly,
together with Lovett and others, rose to second it. Moreover, Solly again teamed
up with Lovett to second the latter's resolution calling for another conference
to work out in detail both the name and joint programme for radical political reforms. Finally, perhaps in recognition of his role as a conciliator, he was
asked to move the resolution in which the Complete Suffrage party conceded to
Annual Parliaments in their programme for future action.[74] On his return, Solly
reported with some confidence to the local Association that he thought that the
'Charter would soon be obtained'.[75]

Solly now also employed his pen in support of Sturge's agenda. In the summer
of 1842 he published (again with financial sponsorship from Bridport friends)
a pamphlet entitled *What Says Christianity to the Present Distress?* At a time
of severe economic distress and social tension it was not the only pamphlet
that was critical of the ineffective role of the clergy in mediating class conflict.
Solly's colleague at the Complete Suffrage Conference in April, the Rev. Thomas
Spencer, for example, had also produced *The People's Rights and How to Get
Them.* However, the sharply contrasting reception afforded to these two pro-
Sturge pamphlets in the mainstream Chartist press is worthy of note. While the
Northern Star's reviewer slated Spencer's plan as 'well intentioned but naïve',
the *English Chartist Circular* hailed Solly's as 'an admirable work'.[76] Drawing
on first hand experiences of the gulf that existed between the classes in Yeovil
and his observations of the widespread poverty around Manchester in August
1841, Solly argued forcibly that the cause of the people was a Christian cause.[77]
Ministers like himself had a God-given duty to lead their congregations in supporting the two campaigns which would remove class legislation and poverty
and improve their earthly existence: the Chartist movement and the Anti-Corn
Law League. A particularly open-minded Unitarian, Solly could appreciate the
arguments articulated by the defenders of both causes; he now cast himself in
the role of mediator; his task was to persuade others that the two causes were
compatible and should be allied.[78]

To this general end Solly applied himself vigorously in two ways. Firstly,
he went on a missionary tour of the West Country as an official delegate
of the Provisional Council of the Complete Suffrage Union that was set up
at Birmingham. Its function was to persuade and prepare the public for a
December meeting, which would then consummate the union of Chartists and

non-Chartists, including many Anti-Corn Law Leaguers.[79] His lectures in towns such as Tiverton and Bridgwater and cities like Bristol were well received; he also used his platform appearances to publicise the arguments for class conciliation that he had set out in his pamphlet.[80]

At the same time, Solly and others launched a 'Democratic Improvement Society' in Yeovil. His lofty aim was to create an alcohol-free environment that would promote social harmony; members, he hoped, would come to appreciate that the existing system offered the best and, in fact, the 'only guarantee that the interest of capital and labour would be well and equitably served'.[81] It was an objective that he shared with others, including William Sankey (see chapter 3). Although Solly received friendly overtures about cooperation, the Yeovil society remained separate from William Lovett's National Association that had been launched in the autumn of 1841.[82] More importantly, the Yeovil Mutual Improvement Society was the prototype of the national scheme that Solly launched in 1862 as the Working Men's Club and Institute Union.[83] For a time the Yeovil Society worked well: meetings – conducted in a converted hayloft – were well attended; lectures were organised; and concerts, readings and recitations undertaken. Bainbridge appears to have been a key figure in the early days, particularly when Solly was on tour. Like Stevens before him, however, Bainbridge was finally forced to leave Yeovil at the end of 1842, when, jobless, he went to London to work for Lovett's National Association.[84]

Notwithstanding his involvement in the Improvement Society, Solly continued to play an active political role in the affairs of the local NCA. Early in August 1842, for example, he hosted a visit by the London Chartist leader, Ruffey Ridley, who lectured in the town as part of a tour of Chartist strongholds in the West Country. Typically, Solly made no reference to the well attended lecture in his memoirs. At a time when the movement was rent by bitter recriminations about the role some leaders had played in the Plug Plot strikes, Ridley's lengthy report of his meeting with Solly provides telling evidence of the latter's characteristic fair mindedness towards his fellow men. Apparently Solly had voiced some misgivings about O'Connor's leadership at their private meeting, but Ridley was able to report publicly that following a 'long discussion on the prospects of our movement' Solly acknowledged that Ridley 'had disabused his mind regarding the "chief stave" of our movement'.[85]

Within a month of this meeting, Solly's Chartist career finally led to his dismissal from his Ministry. It was not unexpected. The leaders of his congregation, who already believed that he had been disrespectful to the Queen and deplored him for allowing himself to be made a Chartist spokesman on a national stage, now came to regard his Chartist-inspired Improvement Society as nothing less than 'a very hot-bed of mischief'. Solly was told to leave immediately.[86] 'The grief and dismay of the members of our little society when they heard that my wife and I would have to leave the town', recalled Solly, 'was very genuine'.[87] Solly's departure greatly weakened the group, which became just a boot and shoe savings club; alas, the treasurer then added to their gloom by decamping with the funds.[88] The Yeovil NCA survived, however. Early in 1843 it regrouped, continuing its loyal support for O'Connor, and becoming particularly enthusiastic about the Land Plan.[89]

From the parochial and conflict-torn town of Yeovil, Solly moved to the 'freer air'[90] of the larger borough town of Tavistock (population approximately 6,000) in Devon. The Unitarian congregation at its Abbey Chapel, which consisted almost equally of middle and working class members, were favourably impressed and hired him to fill their vacant pulpit in November 1842 on a slightly higher salary of £70.[91] In the market town of Tavistock, Solly was left alone to continue his Chartist associations, but he found that the local NCA members – shoemakers, tailors, carpenters and basket-makers – were sceptical of the aims of the Complete Suffrage Union.[92] At a meeting held just before Christmas 1842, Solly tried unsuccessfully to persuade the local NCA to adopt him as their delegate for the Complete Suffrage conference arranged for 27 December in Birmingham. Disappointed and disheartened, Solly blamed O'Connorites in the Tavistock Association for his rejection, although the Northern Star furnishes no evidence to support this allegation.[93] Late in the day, he was chosen to attend as the delegate for the Scottish burgh of Stirling.

As is well known, at the December Complete Suffrage gathering in Birmingham, disagreement broke out between delegates who believed that it would be better to base the Complete Suffrage Union around a new name – the Bill of Rights – and those determined to retain the People's Charter as the basis of their campaign. Typically, Solly worked at attaining harmony. For example, he endorsed a series of resolutions that sympathised with the victims of government oppression and he helped to organise the collection of funds for their families.[94] When the crucial decision had to be made over the name for the organisation, however, Solly agonised long and hard before deciding to support Lovett's motion, gleefully backed by O'Connor, to retain the name of the Charter. Sturge thereupon led a secession of the majority of the middle class Complete Suffrage delegates to a local temperance hall to prepare the Bill of Rights. Solly remained with the predominately working class Chartists, earning himself accolades for his 'unbending firmness'. Alex Tyrrell has argued that personality and religious conviction were more important than class in understanding the split, and he has made the point that some high profile working men, such as Henry Vincent and Arthur O'Neill, followed Sturge out of the hall.[95] By remaining behind with the 'rationalist' Lovett, Solly represents an exception to this thesis.

Before leaving Birmingham Solly tried again to find a compromise by interesting Sturge and his colleagues in a scheme for the creation of Democratic Improvement Societies along the lines of the one he had successfully, if briefly, founded in Yeovil. Acutely aware now of the general failure of middle class social reforming efforts to appeal effectively to large numbers of working men, Solly argued that the educational benefits which would flow from such organisations would lead to 'the enfranchisement and elevation of the working classes'.[96] Although the plan received ample publicity over three consecutive weeks in the *English Chartist Circular* at the end of 1842 and the beginning of 1843,[97] it failed to convince.

Solly returned to Tavistock 'much depressed' by the failure of the conference.[98] Despite the set-back, he continued to work passionately to try to break down the mistrust and prejudice that existed between the classes. By now a proud father, he took the pledge and became active in encouraging working men to join the local temperance club. He began, too, his long association with the Peace Movement at a time when it was being radicalised under the influence of Sturge and others. Solly was a controversial recruit, lending his weight to Sturge's efforts. As he recalled in his autobiography, he had earlier become a devotee of the extreme 'Non-resistance' ideas of the American anti-slavery campaigner, William Lloyd Garrison, and, with Sturge's blessing, he used his first appearance at a Peace Conference in 1843 to try to foist these ideas on the moderate delegates.[99] Solly also continued to lecture on the need for class conciliation and rational recreation in a variety of venues, from the local Mechanics' Institute to the Sunday School of his Unitarian Chapel.[100] Although he had not joined Struge in walking out of the December Conference, Solly remained an ardent supporter of the Complete Suffrage Union. Early in 1843 he even tried to persuade Sturge to stand for Tavistock at a by-election. Although Sturge declined, he encouraged Henry Vincent to contest the borough. The 'Demosthenes of English Democracy' proved to be an able substitute giving a string of speeches that Solly remembered as a potent combination of 'pathos and humour, facts, figures, and fierce invective with extraordinary power'.[101] Despite a lingering concern that their Unitarian beliefs would alienate potential voters, both Solly and his wife campaigned vigorously on behalf of Vincent who, although he lost, secured a respectable sixty-nine votes.[102] Solly attributed the defeat to the pressure exerted by the Duke of Bedford, who rounded up his tenant farmers to vote against the former Chartist.[103] Solly's ongoing support for the Complete Suffrage Union, however, should not obscure the fact that he still approved of the aims of mainstream Chartism. In the *Northern Star* of 18 March 1843, for example, Solly is listed as having donated 5 shillings for the Defence Fund of 'Feargus O'Connor and 58 others' who were facing trial for their part in the Plug Plot disturbances the previous August. Significantly, in a list covering two columns of the paper, Solly's donation represented the largest sum of money provided by any one individual.[104]

Solly and his young family left Tavistock in the latter part of 1844 to take up the position of pastor at the Unitarian chapel in the Somerset town of Shepton Mallet. His salary in this post, which he held for three years, was considerably higher at £125.[105] Like Yeovil, the town had suffered a decline of its manufacturing base, in this case its woollen industry. Solly again took up the grievances of the working people but, as in Yeovil, he met with opposition, particularly in the form of pulpit attacks from the local Methodists and Congregationalists.[106] Solly found that, although these Nonconformists would cooperate with him on the temperance cause, in other spheres of activity they would have nothing to do with him.[107] Thus he worked single-handedly to found a local Institute for holding lectures and discussion groups, and successfully improved working conditions for shop-workers, a neglected economic group, by securing from their employers the early closing of local shops. At his Unitarian chapel he was also particularly concerned with promoting both greater unity and stronger regional links between the poorer congregations in the West Country. To this end he helped form the Western Unitarian Christian Union by preaching a rallying call at their annual meeting in Dorchester in June 1845: it was subsequently published under the title of *The Midnight Cry*.[108] Apart from contacts with the Rev. Joseph Barker, the Unitarian Chartist minister and printer-publisher in Wortley, Leeds,[109] Solly does not appear to have been involved in any way with the Chartist movement whilst in Shepton Mallet.

His reputation well-established, Solly was invited in the autumn of 1847 to take the pastorate at the newly built Unitarian chapel in Bayshill, Cheltenham Spa, on the modest salary of £100. Despite the steep cut in salary, Solly confessed in his autobiography that by comparison with his previous ministries Cheltenham offered a 'much wider sphere of action' and 'a more intellectual society'.[110] This was certainly true. Over the next four years Solly experienced some of the pride and prejudice which flowed from those who directed or controlled power and authority in the Spa. A pocket Whig borough in the political control of the liberally-inclined Berkeley family, Cheltenham was an exciting mix of traditional market town, tourist centre for the wealthy and evangelical stronghold of the Anglican Church. Its population, which had grown to approximately 34,000 by the time Solly arrived in 1847, was composed of many professional people – clergymen, architects, solicitors, journalists, surgeons, accountants and bankers. They provided a range of service industries for the wealthy residents and visitors. Equally vital to the town's functions were its large numbers of skilled workers – printers, shoe-makers, bricklayers, decorators and tailors – and numerous small shopkeepers, traditionally labelled lower middle class, such as grocers, bakers, brewers and butchers.[111]

Like Bath, Cheltenham was a stronghold of radicalism and Chartism. The members were drawn not only from the ranks of the skilled workers, but also from fringe professionals who had flocked to the Spa in large numbers. All who joined the Chartist movement had become resentful of their exclusion from full political and social participation in the affairs of the town after it had been granted a parliamentary seat in 1832. Undeterred by the discord between the national leaders, the Cheltenham Chartists had built up a reputation for un-swerving loyalty to the NCA and a passion for self-improvement through educa-tion and temperance. Such activities were anathema to the evangelical Francis Close, the incumbent of the Parish Church of St. Mary's in Cheltenham, who sought to improve the cultural and religious tone of the town with Christian and Tory principles, and to diminish the influence of the Berkeleys. So supreme and inquisitorial was his empire that opponents nicknamed the Spa 'the Close Borough' and his thirty-year clerical reign the 'Close Season'.[112]

The decade after 1838 was therefore characterised by an intense and often bitter class struggle between a lively artisan culture, which encompassed all the active Chartist tendencies as well as the Owenite socialists, and the evangeli-cal cleric, the Rev. Francis Close, who, backed by his middle- and upper-class congregations, proselytised vigorously, striving to recruit working men and women to the established Church and opposing Catholicism, Nonconformity, Radicalism, Owenism and temperance with equal vigour. Even after the de-mise of Chartism, Close continued to oppose teetotalism until 1860 precisely because he perceived it to have 'dangerous' radical connections and unaccept-able theological implications. Solly's efforts to promote class cooperation were unwittingly aided by Close's confrontational style. Uniquely in the Spa, during the 1840s and 1850s Close's authoritarianism had the effect of bringing many Nonconformists, Unitarians and Chartists into cross-class alliances over such issues as freedom of speech, opposition to church rates, education, temperance, the vote and foreign affairs.

Apart from fundamental theological differences, there were several specific reasons why the Unitarians in particular incurred the wrath of Close. Firstly, amongst its Bayshill congregation (even before Solly arrived) were a number of energetic shopkeepers and artisans, who were Chartists and temperance ad-vocates, but also respected figures of influence in the local government of the Spa. William Hollis, gunsmith, and John Goding, grocer and local historian, were two such prominent Unitarians and Chartists. They also worked alongside mainstream Chartists such as W. E. Adams, Edwin Wilkes and J. P. Glenister, in promoting educational and temperance work at their People's Institute in Regent Street. At the same time they had managed to get themselves elected not only to the Parish Vestry, where they opposed Close over his exacting of church rates, but also to the board of the Poor Law Guardians, where they were equally hostile to his views.

Secondly, the Unitarian congregation included some of those fringe profes-sionals who supplied political radicalism in the nineteenth century with much of its fierce energy. The most influential member was probably Samuel Charles Harper, editor of the *Cheltenham Free Press*, the main voice of the Spa's radical middle class and a man who was also sympathetic to the cause of the Chartists. Solly does not mention Harper by name, but paid a glowing tribute to his role:

'we were fortunate in having the courageous and manly support given by the Editor of the *Cheltenham Free Press*, who allowed me to answer, in his columns, an attack made upon us by Mr Close'.[113]

Finally, there was the arrival of Solly himself, an event that was celebrated by a tea party in the Chapel in early September 1847.[114] Almost immediately he began to work on an ambitious plan of educational fellowship between the classes. Within a year his efforts resulted in the establishment of the progressive Cheltenham Working Men's Institute under Unitarian patronage. Even before the Institute was launched Solly was battling against the prevailing evangelical temper in other ways. On the first Sunday succeeding the French Revolution of 1848, for example, there was a meeting of minds between Solly and the radical elements hitherto described. They gathered together after morning service to agree on an address to be conveyed to the revolutionaries in France proclaiming sympathy with their aims.[115] Solly also started to give talks to the Chartists on educational and temperance subjects. For this involvement he won great affection and respect, not least from their leader, W.E. Adams, who remembered him as the 'venerable friend of my youth'.[116]

The Cheltenham Working Men's Institute was formally established at the beginning of December 1848.[117] Helped by a range of people, from a leading local Nonconformist minister, Rev. Morton Brown, and the president of Cheltenham Temperance Society and successful seed merchant, C. Hale Jessop, to Edwin Wilkes, a prominent Spa Chartist, Solly enrolled almost one hundred members. The plan was an important advance on what had been set up in Yeovil in that it began to combine education with an element of rational amusement.[118] Backed by adequate financial resources from his own chapel and from those groups who sympathised with his cause, Solly opened three reading rooms in the centre of the Spa, formed separate classes in each of them for debate and discussion, and established a general lending library.[119] Over the next three years Solly built up a successful Institute where education, temperance principles, rational amusement and ideas on promoting social harmony between the classes were all inextricably linked and actively encouraged. In 1849, for example, Solly supported the highly symbolic move to make William Hollis, a Chartist, president of the Institute.[120] Speakers at the Institute ranged from local Chartists such as John Goding on 'The Evils of Capital Punishment',[121] to a national leader Thomas Cooper, who lectured on 'The Prospects of Coming Changes at Home and Abroad'.[122] Other local Chartists, such as J. P. Glenister and Edwin Wilkes, were prominent either as chairmen or in providing concluding remarks and votes of thanks.[123] Among the radical middle class figures who came to lecture were William Tweedie, a leading voice in the National Temperance League,[124] George Dawson, the spell-binding orator and popular campaigner for civil and religious liberties,[125] and the Rev. Ben Parsons -- the subject of another chapter in this book – who left his audience in no doubt that his 'hobby was the advancement of the working classes, the most honourable members of society'.[126] At the close of his address, Parsons paid tribute to the healthy state of the Institute.

The Institute's progress was impressive, especially when measured against a similar scheme for working men sponsored by Close at this time. The *Education Census* of 1851 reveals that Solly's Working Men's Institute had 651 members (one female member only), paying 6d per month, 200 volumes in its library, and held weekly lectures and debates on 'Any Subject but Religion'. By comparison, Close's Church of England Reading Association is listed as having only 154 members (five of whom were women) paying one guinea per annum, 300 volumes in its library, and holding debates which were restricted to 'Religion and Science Subjects'.[127] Given this marked disparity in membership, it is not difficult to appreciate why Solly remarked in his autobiography that his Institute met with both 'bitter *odium theologicum*' and general obstructionism on the part of Close and his conservative supporters.[128]

Solly's role in the Cheltenham Working Men's Institute offered him the opportunity to develop some of the ideas which he later applied to the development of the nation-wide Working Men's Club and Institute Union. The most important of these was the Unitarian-inspired campaign to posit a new concept of a 'gentleman'.[129] A key element in the progressive education Solly had received was the need to challenge the 'barbaric' codes of honour of the aristocracy. They were to be replaced by those that emanated from a new type of gentleman, who was honest, educated, upright and caring.[130] Solly honed this message in a series of lectures at the Institute under provocative tiles such as 'What is a Gentleman?'[131] In these lectures, which he was still delivering across the country in the 1880s, Solly argued that wealth and position were not the only criterion for being a gentleman. Education, courtesy, honour, ethical conduct and truthfulness were, regardless of social class, elements essential to the 'constitution of a thorough gentleman' in the modern age. From his experiences with the Chartists, Solly felt the need for 'gentlemen' role models with these qualities to be nurtured in the working class itself.[132] Hence the overwhelming emphasis placed by Solly on the pervasive activities of working men like John Bainbridge who, until his death in 1867, rendered invaluable service both to Lovett's educational schemes, in Sunday School work at Little Portland Street Chapel and for the Club and Institute Union in London.[133]

What is equally important about this initiative is the fact that Solly did not talk down to working-class audiences. Genuine participation was the order of the day; his lectures were routinely thrown open for discussion after he had finished, often with impressive results. For example, when one member of an audience asked 'Whether Lawyers, Doctors, or Parsons are the most useful to Society?', it provoked a robust exchange that resulted in important refinements to their definition of a 'gentleman' within the middle class. Another discussion on the

'Development of Religious Life' did much to illuminate 'what a true Christian Church should be'.[134]

Beyond the Cheltenham Working Men's Institute, Solly also enjoyed considerable social standing and political respect amongst a range of dissenting groups in the Spa. He was the guest speaker, for example, at the Christmas Teetotal Festival of the Cheltenham Temperance Society, which was attended by over 500 enthusiasts at the Town Hall in late December 1847.[135] Solly's support for teetotalism did not preclude him from adding his voice to that of Sydney Dobell, a local wine-merchant, minor English poet and a spokesman for Cheltenham's literati,[136] in support of persecuted nationalities in Europe, a position also heavily underlined by his membership of the nationally influential Peoples' International League.[137] Organised under the aegis of Mazzini, this organisation had been established in England in April 1847 to support self-government and nationality in Europe, and brought together a number of influential middle-class radicals, such as James Stansfeld and P. A. Taylor, and Chartists such as Thomas Cooper and W. J. Linton. Finally, by 1849, when partnership between the classes became a little easier,[138] he was working with radical middle-class peace campaigners such as Samuel Bowly of Gloucester, the O'Connorite Chartist in Cheltenham, J. P. Glenister, and the influential Rev. Morton Brown, in mobilising petitions that were sent to Richard Cobden in the House of Commons. They collected signatures from the Spa's sympathetic 'uneasy' class of small traders and fringe professionals, and its solidly working class, in favour of arbitration instead of war.[139]

At the end of 1851 Solly was forced to resign his Bayshill pastorate. The reason for this decision was personal rather than, as previously, linked either to ecclesiastical bigotry or political persecution. Early in 1851 the family received a sad blow when their eldest daughter, aged seven, fell victim to scarlet fever and died. The child had accompanied Solly's wife on one of her visits to the Cheltenham slums where she was actively engaged in helping the very poor.[140] The tragic consequence coupled with their doctor's concern for the health of the remaining children, led the family to move to London, where Solly became pastor at the Carter Lane Unitarian Church in 1852.[141]

Before leaving the Spa, Solly was given a warm send-off with tea parties held in his honour both in the Bayshill Chapel and, appropriately, at the Cheltenham Working Men's Institute.[142] Unfortunately, the optimism expressed by Solly at these farewell gatherings about the future prospects of the Institute was not borne out by subsequent events. Within a year it appears that, in Solly's own words, the Institute 'fell into bad hands and closed ingloriously'.[143] Unfortunately, no evidence has been unearthed to explain its demise, though ever watchful and very bitter enemies, especially in the person of Francis Close, surrounded the Unitarians in Cheltenham.[144] Solly's successor however, the Rev. John Dendy, did allow those who remained in the Institute, which included Chartists like W.

E. Adams, to use the vestry rooms of the Unitarian Chapel for meetings of a new educational club, the Cheltenham General Literary Union.[145]

After leaving Cheltenham, Solly does not appear to have become involved again in the Chartist movement, although in the course of his work as a social reformer he maintained contact with former Chartists such as G. J. Holyoake, Thomas Cooper, Henry Vincent and J.B. Leno.[146] Instead, under the influence of Christian Socialism, and in particular through an association with one of its leading figures, F.D. Maurice, Solly turned increasingly to social questions such as charity provision and better working-class housing.[147] Again, as with his involvement with the Club and Institute work of the 1860s, Solly was fundamentally concerned with the condition of the working class and improving the fragile relationships that existed between the classes.[148]

Although he remained an active Unitarian, in 1862 Solly's career as a Minister came to an end, and the following year he took up a post as the first paid secretary of the Working Men's Club and Institute Union in London, a position he held intermittently over the next twenty years. He also earned a living from his writings. Because of these and his important contributions to a range of progressive causes from the Charity Organisation Society (1868) to the Society for the Promotion of Industrial Villages (1884), Solly helped to shape working-class life and culture and remained a prominent public figure throughout the rest of the nineteenth century. Recognition of his contribution to Chartism and, within it, to healing the breach between the classes is long overdue.[149] Solly remained loyal to Chartist demands, though he came to regret their tactics. He firmly believed that the grievances which had brought the movement to life were genuine and serious, and he deplored the failure of the churches to act with a social conscience and ameliorate their position. Solly was also, as Ridley recognised, sufficiently open-minded to be able to see the other man's point of view. As an enthusiast for repeal of the Corn Laws and the Charter he sought to persuade both sides of his sincerity. Solly learned from his insensitive encounter with an impoverished glover in Yeovil. As the historian, Betty Fladeland, has concluded in relation to his activities in opposition to slavery, 'Solly tried hardest and succeeded best at learning to know and respect working people on their own terms'.[150] From this sense of the special needs of working people, Solly developed mutual improvement societies to promote good fellowship, rational recreation and class conciliation. Ironically in Cheltenham, because of the impact of Close's evangelical straightjacket, cooperation between the Chartists and the radical middle class was not quite as difficult as it was elsewhere. Facilitated by Solly's good hand, reconciliation in the Spa during 1848-9 offered a glimpse of the mid-century configuration of class relationships and cultural forms that tentatively began to emerge in towns and cities more typical of the industrial age.[151]

Another historian, Alan Ruston, has pointed out that it is important 'not to take Solly at his own evaluation'.[152] As we have seen, this is particularly true with respect to his involvement in Chartism. In the 1880s Solly invented myths about the nature of the movement to suit his present needs, but his motive was benevolence rather than remorse or hubris. Canvassing for donations for his cash-strapped Club and Institute movement, Solly was trying to impress would-be patrons, like Lord Lyttelton and Earl Ducie, with the capacity of working men – natural 'gentlemen' – to benefit from the Clubs as they had in the past. Old Chartists like John Bainbridge, John Stevens and, of course, William Lovett, were thus shining examples of the potential for working-class respectability.[153] Conveniently therefore Solly ignored the fact that he had worked constructively with Chartists of all shades of political opinion. Many of those whom he left out were just as keen as Bainbridge and Stephens on self-improvement through education and temperance, but they had committed the cardinal sin of supporting Feargus O'Connor. Solly's selective memory later in life is a testimony to the lingering fear of independent working-class radicalism that had blossomed under the leadership of Chartism's 'Lion of Freedom'. Solly's less than frank attitude to what constituted the best in Chartism, however, should not obscure the fact that he was a genuine, well-intentioned and decent man – an 'earnest radical' and a true apostle of class cooperation – who was trying to ameliorate the disturbed condition of England in the 1840s.

Notes

[1] The description is from W. E. Adams' column in the *Newcastle Weekly Chronicle*, 26 March 1898.

[2] H. Solly, *These Eighty Years or The Story of an Unfinished Life*, London, 1893, vol. 1, particularly p. 11 on the reception of Solly's *James Woodford, Carpenter and Chartist*, London, 1881, 2 vols.

[3] A. Ruston, 'The Omnibus Radical: Rev. Henry Solly (1813-1903)', *Transactions of the Unitarian Historical Society*, vol. 19, pt. 2, 1988, pp. 78-91.

[4] See, for example, R.N. Price, 'The Working Men's Club Movement and Victorian Social Reform Ideology', *Victorian Studies*, vol. 15, pt. 2, Dec. 1971, pp. 117-147; K. Woodroofe, 'The Irascible Reverend Henry Solly and His Contribution to Working Men's Clubs, Charity Organisations, and "Industrial Villages" in Victorian England', *Social Services Review*, 1975, vol.49, pt. 1, pp. 15-32; P. Bailey, *Leisure and Class in Victorian England: Rational Recreation and the Contest for Control 1830-1885*, London, 1978, pp. 106-123; B. Fladeland, *Abolitionists and Working Class Problems in the Age of Industrialisation*, Baton Rouge, 1984, pp. 111-131. Political scientists, too, have paid tribute to Solly's contribution to the formation of citizenship in the nineteenth century. See D. Lloyd & P. Thomas, *Culture and the State*, London, 1998, pp. 126-143.

[5] C. S. Nicholls (ed.), *The Dictionary of National Biography: Missing Persons*, Oxford, 1993, entry on Solly by Alan Ruston, pp. 622-623.

[6] R. G. Gammage, *History of the Chartist Movement 1837-1854*, 1894, repr., New York, 1969, p. 244.

[7] Solly, *James Woodford*, vol. 1, p. 147 where O'Connor is described as 'the imperious demagogue'. For the significance of *James Woodford* in Solly's career see Price, 'The Working Men's Club Movement', pp. 108-109 and Fladeland, *Abolitionists and Working Class Problems*, pp. 125-127.

[8] Solly, *James Woodford*, vol. 1, Introductory letter to J. R. Seeley, from Solly. See p. x & xii regarding Lovett's attributes.

[9] We have borrowed this concept from L.J. Satre, *Thomas Burt, Miners' MP 1837-1922 The Great*

Conciliator, London, 1999. Solly had a great respect for Burt. See Mf. *Solly Papers*, British Library of Political and Economic Sciences, Reel 2, Item 2, letter from Thomas Burt to Solly, 8 Jan. 1890, folio nos. 86-87

[10] Solly, *These Eighty Years*, vol. 1, pp. 18-37.

[11] R. Watts, *Gender, Power and the Unitarians in England 1760-1860*, London, 1998, p. 45.

[12] Ibid, pp. 3-4.

[13] Ibid, pp. 7-9, see also generally.

[14] The Act of Toleration of 1813 abolished the legal penalties for non-belief in the Trinity. Unitarians were henceforth free to practise their faith and disseminate their views. For Unitarianism and municipal reform see, for example, J. Seed, 'Unitarianism, political economy and the antinomies of liberal culture in Manchester, 1830-1850', *Social History*, vol. 7, No. 1, Jan. 1982, pp. 1-25; and J. Seed, 'Theologies of Power: Unitarianism and the Social Relations of Religious Discourse, 1800-50', in R. J. Morris (ed.), *Class, Power and Social Structure in Nineteenth Century Towns*, Leicester, 1986. For the Anti- Corn Law League and Unitarianism, see P. A. Pickering and A. Tyrrell, *The People's Bread: A History of the Anti-Corn Law League*, London, 2000, pp. 102-105,131 & 223. For the Unitarians and Chartism, see H. U. Faulkner, *Chartism and the Churches*, 1916, repr., London, 1970, pp. 17-19, 27-28, & 105-107.

[15] Solly, *James Woodford*, vol. 1, p. 190.

[16] Solly, *These Eighty Years*, vol. 1, p. 166.

[17] Ibid, pp. 187-190, & 243-248.

[18] Ruston, 'The Omnibus Radical', pp. 79-80.

[19] Faulkner, *Chartism and the Churches*, p. 19.

[20] Watts, *Gender, Power and the Unitarians*, pp. 100-101.

[21] Woodroofe, 'The Irascible Reverend Henry Solly', p. 18.

[22] Solly, *These Eighty Years*, vol. 1, p. 399.

[23] L. C. Hayward, *From Portreeve to Mayor: the growth of Yeovil 1750-1854*, Castle Cary, 1987, p. 41.

[24] Ibid, p. 47.

[25] Ibid.

[26] See J. Belchem, *'Orator Hunt'*: *Henry Hunt and English Working Class Radicalism*, Oxford, 1985.

[27] Hayward, *From Portreeve to Mayor*, p. 49. See also R. B. Pugh, ' Chartism in Somerset and Wiltshire', in A. Briggs (ed.), *Chartist Studies*, London, 1959, chap. 6.

[28] Solly, *These Eighty Years*, vol. 1, p. 43.

[29] Ibid, p. 345.

[30] Ibid, p. 355.

[31] See J. Belchem & J. Epstein,'The Nineteenth Century Gentleman Leader Revisited', *Social History*, vol. 22, no.2, May, 1997, pp. 174-193, particularly pp. 176-179.

[32] Solly, *These Eighty Years*, vol. 1, pp. 334-347.

[33] Ibid, p. 335.

[34] Bailey, *Leisure and Class*, p. 109.

[35] See Watts, *Gender, Power and the Unitarians*, pp. 99-100 & pp. 141-143. The philosophy of the 'true gentleman', who was to be the standard bearer of a new moral code, was also popularised at this time by another Unitarian, Samuel Smiles. See, for example, A. Briggs, *Victorian People*, London, 1954, pp.124-147, particularly, pp. 142-143. We are grateful to Alex Tyrrell for this bringing this point of comparison to our attention.

[36] Solly, *These Eighty Years*, vol. 1, p. 368.

[37] See *Northern Star*, 26 September, 1840; 21 October 1843. The estimate of the numbers is based on nominations to the NCA, Balance Sheets of the Executive, and Returns of Votes for the candidates for the 1842 Convention.

[38] W.H. Maehl (ed.), *Robert Gammage: Reminiscences of a Chartist*, Manchester, 1983, p. 48.

[39] See *Northern Star*, 26 September, 10 October, 31 October 1840; 30 January, 6 March & 10 April

1841. This was not the George White of Ireland who became a prominent Chartist leader in Leeds, Birmingham and Bradford. See S. Roberts, *Radical Politicians and Poets in Early Victorian Britain. The Voices of Six Chartist Leaders*, Lampeter, 1993, pp. 11-38.

[40] *Northern Star*, 10 October 1840.

[41] Pugh, 'Chartism in Somerset and Wiltshire', pp. 191-192 & 195.

[42] *Northern Star*, 10 October 1840.

[43] Solly, *These Eighty Years*, vol. 1, p. 349.

[44] Ibid.

[45] *Northern Star*, 10 October 1840.

[46] Pugh, 'Chartism in Somerset and Wiltshire', p. 207. G. M. Bartlett died in September 1842, but Solly, who was still in Yeovil, made no reference to his passing; he was widely mourned in the West Country. The dinner was also in celebration of the release of Charles Bolwell, a Bath Chartist.

[47] Solly, *James Woodford*, vol. 2, Appendix A, p. 321, 'An Original Letter by the Late William Lovett', 10 October 1841. Lovett attributed the delay to administrative matters connected with the formation of his National Association.

[48] *Northern Star*, 8 May 1841.

[49] Pugh, 'Chartism in Somerset and Wiltshire', p. 205.

[50] *Northern Star*, 29 May 1841; 19 June 1841; 8 January 1842.

[51] Solly, *These Eighty Years*, vol. 1, pp. 365-366.

[52] See Watts, *Gender, Power and the Unitarians*, pp. 77-96.

[53] Ibid, pp. 384-385; Solly, *These Eighty Years*, vol. 1, pp. 366-367; S*olly Papers*, Reel 2, Item 1, 22 March 1842, lady's and gentleman's ticket, accompanied by a written invitation from Messrs Woodward and White to Mr and Mrs Solly, folio nos. H1-H3.

[54] *Northern Star*, 7 August 1841.

[55] Solly, *James Woodford*, vol. 2, Appendix A, pp. 321-326.

[56] *Northern Star*, 21 August 1841.

[57] Ibid, 14 August, 21 August 1841.

[58] Solly, *These Eighty Years*, vol. 1, p. 370.

[59] Pickering & Tyrrell, *The People's Bread*, pp. 95-97.

[60] *Northern Star*, 14 August1841.

[61] Solly, *These Eighty Years*, vol. 1, p. 372; *Northern Star*, 21 August 1841, contemptuously referred to the 'Clerical Anti- Corn Law Conference at Manchester' as a 'palaver'.

[62] *Northern Star*, 5 February 1842.

[63] Ibid, 22 January 1842.

[64] Ibid, 11 December 1841. Interestingly, in *These Eighty Years*, vol. 1, pp. 384-385, Solly has this meeting taking place in 1842, conveniently after the first Complete Suffrage initiative had raised expectations of closer association with men of good will amongst the radical middle class.

[65] *Northern Star*, 22 January 1842.

[66] Fladeland, *Abolitionists and Working Class Problems*, p. 123.

[67] Solly, *These Eighty Years*, vol. 1, p. 394.

[68] Ibid, p. 395.

[69] See F. C. Mather (ed.), *Chartism and Society. An Anthology of Documents*, London, 1980, p. 221, & pp. 221-225.

[70] Ibid, p. 221.

[71] Solly, *These Eighty Years*, vol. 1, pp. 375-376.

[72] *Northern Star*, 26 March 1842.

[73] See Faulkner, *Chartism and the Churches*, pp. 22-23, 28 & 31-33. See also Pickering & Tyrrell, *The People's Bread*, pp. 89-90.

[74] The conference proceedings are covered in detail in the *Northern Star*, 9 April 1842, 14 January 1843. See also Solly, *These Eighty Years*, vol. 1, p. 379 & 380-381. Solly also spoke at a public meeting in Birmingham Town Hall, along with Lovett, Vincent, O'Brien and Sturge, after the conference ended.

[75] Solly, *These Eighty Years*, vol. 1, p. 383.

[76] *Northern Star*, 2 July 1843; *English Chartist Circular*, vol. 2, no. 102, p. 200. As Dorothy Thompson has stressed, the *English Chartist Circular* remained within the mainstream of Chartism and was pro Feargus O'Connor, see *The Chartists*, London, 1984, p. 261.

[77] H. Solly, *What Says Christianity to the Present Distress?*, 1842, repr. New York, 1986, pp. 72-75 & 85-86.

[78] Fladeland, *Abolitionists and Working Class Problems*, p. 124.

[79] Ibid.

[80] Solly, *These Eighty Years*, vol. 1, p. 110.

[81] Bailey, *Leisure and Class in Victorian England*, p. 110.

[82] Solly, *James Woodford*, vol. 2, Appendix A, pp. 321-326.

[83] Ibid, vol. 2, p. 69.

[84] Solly, *These Eighty Years*, vol. 1, pp. 395-396.

[85] *Northern Star*, 16 September 1842.

[86] Solly, *These Eighty Years*, vol. 1, p. 398.

[87] Ibid, p. 399.

[88] Ibid, p. 400.

[89] *Northern Star*, 14 January, 21 October 1843.

[90] Woodroofe, 'The Irascible Reverend Henry Solly', p. 19.

[91] Solly, *These Eighty Years*, vol. 1, pp. 400-402.

[92] See *Northern Star*, 26 March, 30 July 1842; 28 January 1843.

[93] Ibid, 24 December 1847.

[94] See Ibid, 31 December 1842; 7 January 1843.

[95] See A. Tyrrell, 'Personality in Politics: The National Complete Suffrage Union and Pressure Group Politics in Early Victorian Britain', *Journal of Religious History*, vol. XII, 1983, pp. 382-400.

[96] Solly, *These Eighty Years*, vol. 1, p. 409.

[97] *English Chartist Circular*, vol. 2, nos.102 -4 [c. December 1842– January1843].

[98] Solly, *These Eighty Years*, vol. 1, p. 409.

[99] Ibid., vol. 1, p. 329; A. Tyrrell, *Joseph Sturge and the Moral Radical Party in Early Victorian Britain*, London, 1987, chapters 11 & 13; M. Ceadel, *The Origins of War Prevention: The British Peace Movement and International Relations, 1730-1854*, Oxford, 1996, pp. 316, 317-18, 340. As Ceadel notes, Solly later abandoned Garrisonism.

[100] Solly, *These Eighty Years*, vol. 1, pp. 420-423, 432-434.

[101] Ibid, vol. 1, p. 416.

[102] Solly, *These Eighty Years*, vol. 1, p. 417. See J. Vincent & M. Stenton (eds.), *McCalmont's Parliamentary Poll Book. British Election Results 1832-1918*, 8th ed., Brighton, 1971, p. 290: Trelawney (Liberal)113 votes; Vincent (Chartist) 69 votes. See also B. Harrison 'Henry Vincent', in J. Saville & J. Bellamy (eds), *Dictionary of Labour Biography*, London, 1972, vol. 1, p. 329. The *Northern Star* had no reports on Vincent's campaign.

[103] Ibid. Vincent attributed his defeat to prejudice stemming from his former imprisonment. See *Plymouth, Devonport and Stonehouse Herald*, 23 March 1843. We are grateful to Brian Harrison for this reference.

[104] *Northern Star*, 13 March 1843.

[105] Solly, *These Eighty Years*, vol. 1, p. 430.

[106] Ibid, vol. 2, p. 10.

[107] B. Harrison, *Drink and the Victorians*, London, 1971, p. 167.

[108] *Solly Papers*, Reel 2, Item 2, H. Solly, *The Midnight Cry. A Sermon preached before the Somerset and Dorset Association at their Annual Meeting, Dorchester, June 1845*, London, 1846, folio nos. 156-169.

[109] Solly, *These Eighty Years*, vol. 2, p. 15.

[110] Ibid, p. 25.

[111] A. J. Mayer, 'The Lower Middle Class as Historical Problem', *Journal of Modern History*, vol. 47, no. 3, September 1975, pp. 409-436, particularly 426-427.

[112] For Radicalism and Chartism in Cheltenham Spa, see O.R. Ashton, 'Radicalism and Chartism in Gloucestershire, 1832-1847', Ph.D. University of Birmingham, 1980; and O.R. Ashton, 'Clerical Control and Radical Responses in Cheltenham Spa 1838-1848', *Midland History*, vol. viii, 1983, pp. 121-147. See also A. Courtenay, 'Cheltenham Spa and the Berkeleys, 1832-1848: Pocket Borough and Patron?', *Midland History*, vol. xvii, 1992, pp. 93-108. For an opposing view of Close's contribution, see A. F. Munden, 'Radicalism versus Evangelicalism in Victorian Cheltenham', *Southern History*, vol. 5, 1983, pp. 115-121. Although there was a contested election in Cheltenham in 1848, which was a protracted affair owing to corruption, Solly does not appear to have got involved.

[113] Solly, *These Eighty Years*, vol. 2, p. 35.

[114] *Cheltenham Free Press*, 11 September 1847.

[115] Solly, *These Eighty Years*, vol. 2, pp. 40-41. It was a contrite Solly who recalled this action later in his autobiography.

[116] W. E. Adams, *Memoirs of a Social Atom*, 1903, repr., New York, 1968, p. 115.

[117] Solly, *These Eighty Years*, vol. 2, p. 50. This action occurred at almost the same time as the Rev. F. W. Robertson's scheme, which Solly was aware of, was taking shape in Brighton.

[118] H. Solly, *Working Men's Social Clubs and Educational Institutes*, 1867, repr. London, 1980, pp. 22-23.

[119] *Cheltenham Free Press*, 9 December 1848.

[120] Ibid, 12 May, 1849.

[121] Ibid.

[122] *Northern Star*, 5 October 1850; Solly, *These Eighty Years*, vol. 2, pp. 72-73. Cooper lectured on several occasions at the Institute.

[123] *Solly Papers*, Reel 1, Item 4a, vol. ii, Section 2: Education. Cheltenham Working Men's Institute, Report of a lecture by Rev. Henry Solly, ' The Peasant War in Germany'. This was Solly's first lecture, which was chaired by Edwin Wilkes, and the vote of thanks seconded by J. P. Glenister, both Chartists, Folio no. B18.

[124] Solly, *These Eighty Years*, vol. 2, p. 73.

[125] Ibid, p. 44.

[126] *Cheltenham Free Press*, 12 May 1849.

[127] *The Education Census*, London, 1851, Division vi, West Midlands Counties, Gloucestershire, p. 234.

[128] Solly, *These Eighty Years*, vol. 2, pp. 50-51.

[129] Watts, *Gender, Power and the Unitarians*, p. 99.

[130] Ibid, pp. 119 & 141-142.

[131] *Solly Papers*, Reel 1, Item 1, vol. ii, Section 2: Education. 'Prospectus of Lectures delivered at Athenaeums and Mechanics' Institutes by Henry Solly of Cheltenham', c.1850, Folio nos. B1-B2. Solly also developed this theme in other lectures including 'The Peasant War in Germany in the Sixteenth Century: or Labour and Leadership' and 'A Voice from the Middle Ages, or a Glance at the Enthusiasm of By-gone Days'.

[132] Fladeland, *Abolitionists and Working Class Problems*, p. 126.

[133] Solly, *These Eighty Years*, vol. 2, p. 221.

[134] Ibid, vol. 2, p. 51.

[135] *Cheltenham Free Press*, 1 January 1848. See also 26 February 1848 when Solly lectured again on Temperance to members of the Cheltenham Literary and Philosophical Society.

[136] For Dobell, see J. Goding, *Norman's History of Cheltenham*, Cheltenham, 1863, p. 478; Contem Ignotus, *The Golden Decade of a Favoured Town*, London, 1884, pp. 154-193; V. Cunningham (ed.), *The Victorians. An Anthology of Poetry and Poetics*, Oxford, 2000, pp. 574-577.

[137] M. Finn, *After Chartism, Class and Nation in English Radical Politics,1848-1874*, Cambridge, 1993, pp. 71-72.

[138] E. Royle, *Victorian Infidels*, Manchester, 1974, p. 146.

[139] *Cheltenham Free Press*, 3 February 1849.

[140] Solly, *These Eighty Years*, vol. 2, p. 72.

[141] Ibid, vol. 2, p. 81.

[142] Ibid, vol. 2, p. 76; *Cheltenham Free Press*, 20 December 1851.

[143] Solly, *Working Men's Social Clubs*, pp. 22-23.

[144] Solly, *These Eighty Years*, vol. 2, p. 33.

[145] Adams, *Memoirs of a Social Atom*, p. 116.

[146] Solly, *These Eighty Years*, vol. 2, pp. 111, 288-289, 301 & 521.

[147] Ibid, vol. 2, p. 93; Bailey, *Leisure and Class in Victorian England*, p. 109. Led by Maurice, J.M Ludlow, Charles Kingsley and E.V Neale, between 1849 and 1854 the Christian Socialists made fresh attempts at class conciliation by promoting acceptable labour organisations, particularly co-operative producers. In this venture they were joined by a number of leading London Chartists including Gerald Massey, John Bedford Leno and Walter Cooper. Although these initiatives failed, Solly, who appears to have met Walter Cooper at this time, was impressed by their attempts at human fellowship. Solly was subsequently influenced by Maurice's Club and Institute movement, particularly by his ideas on rational recreation. For the Christian Socialist influence on Solly, see *These Eighty Years*, vol. 2, pp. 53-54. For the tensions between the Christian Socialist and the Chartist leaders see M. Finn, *After Chartism*, pp. 153-159; D. Shaw, *Gerald Massey: Chartist, Poet, Radical and Freethinker*, London,1995, pp.3 5-36; O.R. Ashton & S. Roberts, *The Victorian Working Class Writer*, London 1999, chapter 7, particularly pp. 82-83. Solly is not mentioned in P.N. Backstrom, *Christian Socialism and Cooperation in Victorian England*, London, 1974.

[148] Ruston, 'Henry Solly', p. 623.

[149] Although he was the most well known and successful practitioner of his kind in the field, Henry Solly was not the only Unitarian minister involved with the Chartists. Others included William Linwood at Mansfield, Joseph Barker at Leeds, Archibald Browning at Tillicoutry in Scotland and John Gent Brooks in Birmingham. See D. Jones, *Chartism and the Chartists*, London, 1975, pp. 50-53; E. Bushrod, 'The Diary of John Gent Brooks – A Victorian Commentary on Poverty (1844-1854)', *Transactions of the Unitarian Historical Society*, vol. 20, pt.2, 1992, pp. 98-113.

[150] Fladeland, *Abolitionists and Working Class Problems*, p. 127.

[151] E. Yeo, 'Culture and Constraint in Working Class Movements, 1830-1855', in E. & S. Yeo (eds), *Popular Culture and Class Conflict 1590-1914: Explorations in the History of Labour and Leisure*, Brighton, 1981, pp. 154-186.

[152] Ruston, 'The Omnibus Radical', p. 79.

[153] Solly, *James Woodford*, vol. 2, p. 234.

CHAPTER 3

THE ARISTOCRAT OF CHARTISM:
WILLIAM STEPHEN VILLIERS SANKEY (1793-1860)

When the Chartists' first national parliament-like gathering, the General Convention of the Industrious Classes, met in London during the winter of 1839, the Chartist press was given an unprecedented opportunity to introduce a gallery of new faces to a rapidly expanding audience, both in the metropolis and the nation at large. As the proceedings unfolded, reported, as they were, Hansard-style in the columns of the press, both Bronterre O'Brien's *Operative* and William Carpenter's *Charter* augmented their reports and entertained their readers with weekly 'portraits' of delegates. These 'portraits' introduced an impressive range of individuals: from the irascible Salford carpenter-cum-bookseller, R.J. Richardson, and Bradford's Chartist publican, Peter Bussey, to the Newport magistrate, John Frost, and the Birmingham manufacturer, T.C. Salt. One man's background and career must have seemed extraordinary even by these standards: William Stephen Villiers Sankey. Not surprisingly, Sankey attracted a 'portrait' in both series. According to the *Operative*, the Irish-born representative of the Edinburgh and Mid-Lothian Chartists was 'the scholar, the philanthropist and the patriot' among the delegates; to the *Charter* Sankey's 'gentlemanly' appearance pointed to a 'remarkable illustration of the force of truth, in breaking down early and deep-rooted privileges'. Although he was the representative of 'working men' in Edinburgh, the author continued, 'he belongs not to this class'.[1] Both portraits went on to detail a life of privilege: education at universities in three countries; publications in an impressive range of disciplines spanning the Arts and Sciences; and a proud lineage that stemmed back deep into English and Anglo-Irish history linking Cromwell's army and Grattan's parliament. To paraphrase Marx's well known aphorism, the tradition of the dead generations of his own family weighed heavily on this man of exceptional ability.[2]

Surprisingly then the aristocrat of Chartism has become little more than a footnote in the history of the movement.[3] As one of the second lieutenants of Chartism his prominence is cause enough to write about him, but there are other reasons that recommend him as a case study. Although Sankey embraced the cause of the people, both in his native Ireland and in Britain, he never turned his back on his own class. Rather he sought to convince them that their future could only be secured in a democratic Britain. By so doing Sankey anticipated the later attempts of the aristocracy to come to terms with democracy – characterised famously by Carlyle as 'shooting Niagara'[4] – but he was also one of the last of the leisured patricians who had provided the model for public life for previous generations of radicals. As a delegate to the General Convention Sankey was one of the leading Chartists who sought to rally working people in Britain and Ireland to a unified cause; moreover, he was one of the few to use the Convention not only as a forum for debate, but also as an alternative to the House of Commons in all its forms. Perhaps more than any other delegate, Sankey functioned as a representative of those who had 'elected' him to the Chartist parliament. Furthermore, as one of the most prolific writers among the 'friends of the people', Sankey provides a wealth of material for a study of ideas. From his disparate publications (varied in both subject and genre) the historian can piece together the various elements of the complex world view of an intellectual who became a Chartist. This is the more important because opportunities to glimpse into the mind of a Chartist, especially one who was not among the first rank of leaders, are relatively uncommon.

William Stephen Villiers Sankey was born in Dublin in 1793. As noted, his was an ancient family that had taken its place among the aristocracy at the beginning of the twelfth century when military service for the Baron of Warrington, Payanus de Vylers, earned Gerard de Sanki a grant of land to establish an estate near Warrington in Lancashire. According to a privately circulated nineteenth century family history, the line from Gerard to the current family (including the Chartist delegate, although this detail was omitted from the account) was unbroken.[5] In its portrait, the *Charter* listed Sankey's relatives among the more recent ranks of the English aristocracy suggesting that, in the mind of the author at least, the Chartist public might still be susceptible to the traditional forms of deference that characterised the political order they sought to overthrow. Nevertheless, the list was impressive, including, as it did, four peers, two of whom had been Prime Minister: Lords Grey and Melbourne. The *Charter* also pointed to the close connection to the Villiers family that had been renewed when William's grandfather, Matthew Sankey, had married the daughter of John Villiers of Hanbury Hall in Worcestershire. Although the Villiers were a very powerful dynasty that stemmed back beyond the same Payanus de Vylers who had promoted Gerard de Sanki, the connection might have held little more than antiquarian interest except for the fact that most Chartists would have associated the name with William's cousin, Charles Pelham Villiers, the radical MP for Wolverhampton, who had recently earned national notoriety for his role in the parliamentary campaign for a repeal of the Corn Laws.[6]

To understand Sankey the Chartist, however, we must begin by exploring his connection with his place of birth, Ireland, and with a tradition of parliamentary politics that also had its origin there. Sankey's early life revolved around his father's family home in Harcourt Street in the Irish capital, and the Sankey family seat, Coolmore, in Fethard, County Tipperary. Both places contained unmistakable indicators of the relationship between Britain and Ireland. Located in a fashionable quarter of south Dublin, his father's home stood within sight of the symbol of English power in Ireland, Dublin Castle. The power of the Castle was just as evident in Tipperary: Fethard was a market town located about seven miles north of Clonmel that, at the time of Sankey's youth, numbered just under 4000 inhabitants. In economic terms it was known for its two flour mills which were reputed to be in constant operation.[7] In a country with a predominantly agricultural economy the presence of the mills is not surprising. But Ireland had become, in the words of one contemporary, 'England's bread basket',[8] and, like most Irish grain, the flour milled in Fethard was not consumed there: it was exported to England.

Sankey and his father were renowned for their support for Irish independence in one form or another, but their forefathers had first crossed St George's Channel with sword in hand. One of William's best known ancestors, Hieronymous Sankey (known as either Hierome or, more often, Jerome Sankey), had been a fellow of All Souls' College and a Proctor of Oxford University who had famously conferred a meal and an honorary doctorate of law on Oliver Cromwell in 1649.[9] Over dinner Sankey reputedly discussed military strategy with God's Englishman, who promptly recruited his host for a forthcoming expedition to Ireland. During the next three years 'Colonel' Jerome Sankey saw bloody action on many occasions, earning a reputation for his zeal in battle and, after his appointment as a Commissioner, in levying extraordinary taxes and duties on the local populace.[10] Sankey's Irish service earned him extensive grants of property in Tipperary: Fethard, the location of the family seat, was famous for a siege by Cromwell's army in 1650, a fact that was undoubtedly etched deeply in local memory. Irish service also opened the door to politics: in 1654 Sankey was elected as the Member for Tipperary and Waterford. At the election in 1656 he transferred to the English seat of Marlborough (and later Woodstock), and he remained an active member of the so-called 'still' Parliament under the Protectorate, being knighted by Henry Cromwell in 1658.[11] Thereafter Jerome Sankey took little further part in public affairs, retiring to his Irish estates, but his nephew and heir, Richard Sankey, was reputed to have urged Richard Cromwell to 'abdicate' while also remaining vehemently opposed to the Restoration. According to William, who frequently expounded on his family history, Richard Sankey was forced into 'exile' during the brief reign of James II, only to return triumphantly as a coadjutor of William of Orange. This coda allowed William to present his family's seventeenth century history in the best possible light for a radical audience in the 1830s: they had supported the Commonwealth in its republican guise while opposing Cromwellian excess;

moreover, they had opposed the Catholic restoration and actively promoted the Glorious Revolution of 1688, an event that held tremendous significance in the popular versions of British constitutional history upheld by many radicals.[12]

The other feature of his family history that Sankey was keen to emphasise was also commenced by the venerable Jerome in Ireland: parliamentary service. Sankey the Chartist had politics in his blood. 'For five generations – for near two hundred years', he wrote in 1838, 'I number among my ancestors those who were representatives of the people in Parliament, and the defenders of their liberties'.[13] This was politics as a family business on a grand scale; an example worthy of Namier's classic study of parliamentary nepotism at the accession of George III.[14] Most important, in terms of influence, was his father's parliamentary career. William Sankey senior had studied law in Glasgow before returning to Dublin where he built a successful legal practice that led to his appointment as a QC. He was also active in the political struggles of the 1770s and 80s, becoming both a captain in the 'never-to-be-forgotten' Irish Volunteers and an MP in the independent Irish Parliament that they helped to establish in 1782. No amount of creative reconstruction could elevate William Sankey senior to the place in Irish history occupied by his more celebrated Irish 'friends', 'Henry Grattan, the Emmetts, Curran and George Ponsonby' (in fact Sankey did little to attract attention at the time[15]), but he supported Catholic emancipation and, as Feargus O'Connor put it in characteristically blunt language, Sankey was one of those who 'refused to commit suicide by voting for a legislative union with England'.[16] Many Chartists would also have been impressed that William Sankey senior had shared his seat, Philipstown, with O'Connor's uncle, Arthur O'Connor, a venerated leader of the United Irish who spent the last fifty years of his life in exile in France.[17] William junior's attitude to the Union was, as will be discussed later, more complex, but he might have had no opportunity for a career in radical politics at all had his father accepted the offer of a judgeship and a peerage and, like many other members of the Protestant ascendancy, supported the Union.[18]

Notwithstanding his opposition to the Union, William senior fitted easily into the United Kingdom, renewing associations made during his days as a student. For a man of his social standing few doors were closed. Among the wider circle he built up in England one name stands out: William Wilberforce. William senior was a friend and occasional correspondent of the celebrated evangelical: his acquaintance was intimate enough to holiday with Wilberforce during one Whitsuntide recess (accompanied by his son), but not sufficiently important to bring it to the notice of the emancipator's biographers, old or new.[19] Although William junior was critical of the 'hypocrisy' of those who opposed Black slavery while turning a blind eye to the White slavery that afflicted the British working classes, he admired Wilberforce's capacity for sympathy. So taken with Wilberforce was William junior that he wrote a short biography that was published in 1850.[20]

From his predecessors William Stephen Villiers Sankey thus inherited much to boast of, but he also placed emphasis on the importance of his family connection, through marriage, to the republic of Switzerland. While in Paris as a student Sankey met, and later married, Sophia Mary Muloch, daughter of Robert Muloch, Comptroller General of the Stamp Office from Berne, and a close relative of a former *Landermar* of Switzerland. There can be no doubt about the importance of this marriage in two respects. First, Sophia Sankey was clearly a women of ability who was, apparently, little restrained by the conventions that weighed heavily on others of her class.[21] According to the *Charter* Sophia was characterised by a 'sweetness of temper' that made her 'a crown of rejoicing' to her husband, but it also drew attention to her 'solidity of judgement, liveliness of imagination, and ... extraordinary facility in expressing her thoughts and feelings'. Sophia died in 1853 having borne him six children.[22] Secondly, Sankey was clearly proud of this connection to a 'land of liberty' (his words) that would also undoubtedly have appealed to Chartist audiences more generally. After all, many Chartist celebratory toasts included William Tell, a man with a reputation for democracy, and the Manchester Chartists performed 'Hofer, Tell of the Tyrol' as an inspirational play.[23]

The facts of Sankey's family background provide the main elements for the framework for his career. The others were provided by his education. As a fourteen year old protégé William entered Trinity College, Dublin, where his prodigious talent marked him as an exceptional scholar.[24] At the age of eighteen Sankey graduated as a Bachelor of Arts, 'with the highest honours', earning prizes in general literature, science, the classics, and Hebrew, as well as a rare prize for practical astronomy. As an aristocratic younger son he was destined for a 'liberal profession'. Initially, he began to read for the Church, but despite an abiding religiosity (discussed in a later section), Sankey quickly began to harbour doubts about the relationship between the gospel and the political and religious establishment of the day.[25] Here was the genesis of the religious radicalism that suffuses his later writings. As a consequence Sankey redirected his efforts to the study of the law and of medicine, a decision that brought him to the British mainland. At first he attended Edinburgh University, becoming an extraordinary member of the Edinburgh Medical Society, and, subsequently Sankey studied at Cambridge University, gaining a Master of Arts. As noted, he later went to France to attend the University of Paris.[26] In the French capital he became a member of the *Société d'Enseignement Mutuel de France*, the organisation responsible for the rapid spread of the Lancasterian system of mutual instruction in France during the second and third decades of the nineteenth century. Here Sankey made influential friends, including one of the conductors of the *Revue Encyclopedique*, and Edmé-François Jomard, the celebrated archaeologist who had accompanied Napoleon to Egypt and earned international fame for his near-flawless copy of the hieroglyphics on the Rosetta

Stone.[27] Lancasterian schools had many supporters among British radicals and, although there is no evidence that Sankey was involved in the English equivalent, he remained a member of the French society until his death. Moreover, Jomard, the chronicler of the progress of the *Société d'Enseignement Mutuel*, may have fuelled Sankey's interest in philology which would blossom in the early 1830s.[28]

By 1828, at the age of thirty-five, Sankey was living amid the idyllic vistas of rural England in Stockbridge in Hampshire (he called it 'a remote part of England').[29] Whether he practised medicine or the law in Stockbridge is not clear; it is more likely that he had no job as such or, rather, his family wealth meant that he had no need of employment. He later admitted that he had been 'born in the lap of luxury' and it is probable that he did not need to work to produce an income of his own.[30] In this sense Sankey cut a very eighteenth century figure: the leisured gentleman. He was a polymath with the independence to give free reign to his intellect and to dabble in public affairs both at home and abroad. The extent of his intellectual prowess should not be underestimated. An inventory of Sankey's publications as a relatively young man provides a valuable index to what one commentator would later call his 'boundless range of diversified knowledge' and his 'magnificent intellectual power'.[31] His first publications were papers on the Greek language and mythology that appeared in the prestigious *Journal of Science Literature and the Arts* produced by the Royal Institution of Great Britain, which were followed by an essay on the rise of fluids in the thermometer that was published in the proceedings of the Royal Society of Edinburgh.[32] According to the *Charter* the latter had been encouraged by the Secretary of the Society and a leading figure in Edinburgh's flourishing scientific community, David Brewster, whom Sankey had befriended during his sojourn as a student in the Scottish capital.[33]

Sankey published his first pamphlet in 1825 on *The Geometrical Rectification of Any Arc of a Circle*. Resulting from his research in Edinburgh two years previously, this treatise on the 'principles of ultimate and limiting ratios' and the 'curious properties of a Quadratrix' was written for a specialist audience, but it has left no discernible mark on the history of either mathematics or geometry.[34] His next publication, in 1828, represented a total change of subject matter and genre. *Rhymes on Geography and History* was an account of British history up to and including the Roman conquest rendered in poetry. For its author, this represented both an attempt to 'communicate useful knowledge through the medium of verse, as a branch of Mnemonics' (a strategy that he would employ many times in subsequent years), and an intellectual challenge. 'Tied down by the severity of Truth', he wrote in the preface, 'I could not, for a moment, consider myself at liberty to colour facts, much less indulge in fiction'.[35] By delving into the mythical past Sankey was typical of many young intellectuals in an increasingly romantic age,[36] but the poem also provides a glimpse of a very serious individual. 'Deeply impressed with the value of human life, and the awful responsibilities of man', he reassured his readers that he had 'carefully abstained from attempting to describe War and Combat in over charged and glowing language'.[37]

Over the next few years Sankey published two pamphlets which, although copies are no longer extant, suggest from the titles that his principal interest in the early 1830s was philology: an *Essay on the Origin of the Oriental Mode of Writing* and *An Alphabet of Animals*.[38] In 1838 he continued this trend with the publication of *The Porte-Feuille of Science, Literature and Art* – an ambitious collection of philological propositions ranging from suggestions for 'improving the grammatical nomenclature of the Latin tongue' to an opinion on the 'identity of the Syrian and Chaldaean languages'.[39] The preface of this work suggested that Sankey had not finished with philology, indicating that he planned to publish analytic dictionaries of Greek and Latin,[40] but by this time he was already being drawn into radical politics. The study of language was not left completely behind – he later published an analysis of Coronation Oaths and one of his political pamphlets contained an objection to the appellation 'Ultra-Radical' on philological (and botanical) grounds[41] – but there is no doubt that during 1837-8 politics came to occupy a central place in his life. Unlike the eclecticism of his earlier endeavours, over the next three years virtually everything that flowed from Sankey's pen was overtly political in subject matter and polemical in style. In these years he published *The Rights of the Operatives Asserted, Universal Suffrage, The Right of Labour to Protect itself, Popular Control of Hasty Legislation, A Voice for the Operatives,* and two separate works entitled *Thoughts on Currency,*[42] as well as numerous public letters and poems in a range of newspapers.

Like Peter McDouall, Sankey was politicised by observation of the world around him. Having returned to Edinburgh at some point in the mid-1830s, he was appalled by the harsh contrasts that he encountered. As he wrote in a pamphlet published in 1837, he was motivated by 'strongest and warmest feelings of sympathy [for] the lot of the great mass of the people.'[43] The 'gorgeous capital' of the Scots, he lamented, juxtaposed 'extensive' 'apartments' that were 'furnished up to the acmé with all that the refinement of modern luxury has introduced into the … splendours of domestic life', with 'unhealthy abodes' that were 'dark, damp, ill-ventilated', and 'sunk in many instances beneath the level of the street' where 'the light of heaven' could 'only enter indirectly though some grating in the pathway'.[44] Sankey's 'mixture of pain and indignation' was further aroused by a paper read before the British Association (probably McDouall's investigation into Ramsbottom) that showed that the average operative earned 15 shilling per week. How could it be, Sankey mused, that some of the wealthy members of society had an income 12,500 times greater than a common operative?[45] As was the case in some of his other publications, Sankey saw his audience as members of his own class, pressing them to 'take a deeper

interest in the amelioration of the condition of the working classes'. Although
he did not wish to 'discourage' the charitable instincts that were exhibited by
a few among the wealthy classes, he concluded that the only real solution was
not philanthropy but 'UNIVERSAL SUFFRAGE'; only political equality would
guarantee workers 'a fair profit or return for their labour'.[46]

At this time Sankey also got up from his desk and ascended the public
platform. It was a big step into the centre of national radical politics. In
November 1838 a meeting of the Edinburgh and Midlothian Chartists elected
Sankey as their delegate to the General Convention of the Industrious Classes
then due to convene in London. Sankey had been involved in the proceedings of
the democratic movement in the Scottish capital for some months,[47] but he was
by no means its leading figure and, consequently, the decision to elect him has
perplexed at least one previous historian of Scottish Chartism. For Leslie Wright
it was a 'strange choice' that must have been due to the fact that the meeting had
been held in the poorest quarter of the town where Sankey's Irish countrymen
predominated.[48] Contemporary opponents of the Chartists also attacked
the selection. The leading Whig journal, the *Scotsman*, for example, without
acknowledging that Sankey claimed to represent Edinburgh, dismissed him as
a 'physical force bully' engaged in a 'precious farce' in 'some obscure tavern in
London'.[49] Another leading journal, the *Caledonian Mercury*, scoffed at Sankey's
credentials, suggesting that he had about as much connection with Edinburgh as
Sir Robert Peel or Lord John Russell had with Timbuktu. He may have resided
there for the winter, the editor continued, but this counted for naught:[50]

> from the airy eminence of Castle-hill to the slimy bottom of the pond of
> Canonmills, from Arthur's seat to Atholl Crescent, aye, from Libberton to Leith, or
> from Newington to Newhaven, one might have rambled fruitlessly and bootlessly
> inquiring after Mr Sankey.

As will be discussed below, Sankey responded in practical terms by providing a
depth of representation probably exceptional among the Convention delegates,
but in the short term his cause was taken up in the Chartist press. The *Operative*
went on the offensive, attempting to turn a perceived weakness into a virtue by
suggesting that it was a testimony to the discernment of the Edinburgh radicals
and an indication of their fitness for the suffrage that they should elect such
an outstanding representative despite the fact that he was 'alien in blood' and
'unconnected with them in trade'.[51] The *Charter* took almost the opposite view.
Sankey, the editor claimed, had earned the respect of the Edinburgh working
people from his radical principles and his numerous (unspecified) acts of
philanthropy. Moreover, the *Charter* continued, the editor of the *Mercury* 'well
knows that Mr Sankey's connection with Edinburgh is a substantial one, and
of some years standing', but the editor also pointed out that Britain's leading

politicians were not known for their connections to their seat: 'What connection has Lord John Russell with Stroud, or Lord Palmerston with Tiverton'?[52]

Nevertheless, Sankey proved to be a controversial delegate. Those historians that have bothered to notice him at all have, perhaps taking their cue from the *Scotsman*, focused on a perceived inconsistency in his statements, dismissing him as nothing more than a 'good disciple of O'Connor', 'blowing now hot, now cold, over Physical Force'; a man who used bold words, and then 'betrayed a strong disposition to eat them'.[53] Without resorting to the same level of pejorative language, the foremost historian of Chartism in Scotland, Alexander Wilson, also suggests that Sankey 'slipped' from being an open advocate of physical force into what he calls the 'conditional obedience' school among the delegates – those who would not accept the unconditional obedience to the law preached by some Chartists.[54] The charge that Sankey advocated physical force stems from a widely reported speech given at the Crown and Anchor in March, early in the life of the Convention. Sharing the platform with O'Connor, Bronterre O'Brien and England's Marat, George Julian Harney, Sankey warned his audience that even millions of signatures on the National Petition would not carry the Charter, but it was important that the House of Commons understood that they were the signatures of 'fighting men' 'who will not allow any aristocracy, oligarchy, landlords, cotton lords, money lords, or any lords to tyrannise over them any longer'. It may be, as Wright suggests, that these were the sort of 'fighting words' that led to divisions in the Chartist ranks, but several points need to be made to place the speech in a proper context.[55]

Firstly, previous historians have invariably omitted important elements from the speech. Sankey did refer to 'fighting men', but these were 'men who understand their constitutional rights', which alters the sense of his words considerably. Moreover, as even the report in the Whiggish *Morning Chronicle* made clear, Sankey's remark was followed by 'laughter and cheers' suggesting that, from his tone, he was clearly not issuing a blood curdling call for revolution.[56] Despite the note of humour and the reference to the Constitution (discussed later), the full speech did contain the implied (albeit mild) threat of insurrection, but the second point that must be made is that it was a very common form of rhetoric and not only among Chartists. Any student of the Reform Bill agitation well knew the value of what the liberal *Manchester Examiner* later called a 'salutary terrorism' that 'convinces spiritual and temporal Lords that concession is much more safe and more salutary than repression'.[57] Not surprisingly Anti-Corn Law League spokesmen often warned the Parliamentarians that, if they were obstinate in opposing repeal of the Corn Laws, a desperate people would turn against the existing order and force the enactment of the People's Charter.[58]

Thirdly, it must be acknowledged that Sankey was inexperienced: although he was from a political family, he was relatively new to the platform. Nor was he the only Chartist to be carried away by his audience. The most prominent leader of the Anti-Corn Law League, Richard Cobden, informed Joseph Sturge that he would not employ former Chartists because they were too readily 'carried away by their audiences',[59] and Chartists also acknowledged the trait: O'Connor told William Lovett in 1842, 'I don't lead, I am driven by the people', and Thomas Cooper saw the demagogue as 'rather the people's instrument than their director'.[60] Sankey's countryman, Robert Lowery, accounted for this aspect of Chartist oratory in his autobiography:[61]

> speaking consisted of that kind which is ever the most eloquent and impressive to the feelings of the multitude, where speaker and audience are one in feeling and desire. The speaker only gives vent to the hearer's emotions. His words at once find a response in their wishes.

Finally, and most importantly, the charge that Sankey was an advocate of physical force cannot be sustained in the light of his full career. Sankey, who, it will be recalled, worried that his verse might have glorified war, was a consistent 'friend of peace'.[62]

Notwithstanding this controversy, Sankey made two significant contributions to the 1839 Convention. The first related to Ireland. Despite the fact that Daniel O'Connell was nominally one of the authors of the People's Charter, his relationship with the Whig Government and his support for some of its unpopular policies, as well as his long standing feud with O'Connor, had soured relations with a significant section of the immigrant Irish in many British cities and drastically restricted the progress of the movement in Ireland. The first attempt to redress the situation had come in November 1838 when one hundred and ten Radical Associations in England and Scotland (including Edinburgh) had put their names to an Address to the Irish People which identified *exclusive legislation* as the 'same curse which plunders, oppresses, and blights the happiness of both countries … *whether Parliament meet in London or Dublin*', and offered them a union in the struggle against it.[63] The appeal failed. Thus it was against a bleak backdrop that O'Connor put Ireland on the agenda of the Convention in February 1839. In part he sought vindication for the stand he had taken against O'Connell, but the speech also led to the establishment of a committee of ten (including Sankey) charged with considering 'the best means of enlisting the support of the Irish people' which, in turn, led to Chartist 'missionaries' being sent across St George's Channel.[64]

Unwilling to let matters rest there, in April 1839 Sankey issued his own address to the 'Men of Ireland' that was published in several British radical newspapers and widely reported in Ireland. Although it has been ignored by previous historians,[65] it is a document that is worth lingering over. Sankey began by seeking to establish his credentials as an Irish nationalist, addressing them as 'the son of one of the volunteers of Ireland – of one who assisted in winning her independence in 1782 …'.[66] It was a claim acknowledged by both O'Connor and O'Connell. For the former, Sankey was a 'noble Irishman, son of one of the gallant Irish members who refused to commit suicide by voting for a legislative Union with England'; whereas for the Liberator he was 'a moral force Radical Reformer, and a sincere and ardent Repealer'.[67] In part, Sankey used the Address to compare the Charter with a proposal (one of many) mooted by O'Connell to extend the representation of Ireland in the House of Commons to 150 members. Here simple mathematics could be used to buttress a political argument: why embrace O'Connell's plan for 150 ('which is not a *fourth* of the Imperial Parliament'), he asked, when the introduction of equal electoral districts guaranteed by the Charter would give Ireland 219 representatives?[68] Here again Sankey courted controversy. Some Chartists – the leaders of the Birmingham Political Union, for example – opposed the idea of strictly equal constituencies precisely because it would necessitate conceding far greater representation to Ireland which at that time had about one third of the population of the United Kingdom.[69]

Taking the argument a stage further, Sankey sought to respond to the charge that the Chartists were violent men and, in particular, to dispel the sinister connotations that had been placed on the practice of holding meetings by torchlight. 'My friends, as having presided over torch-light meetings', he stated, 'I can assure you there was no attempt at intimidation; no idea of the destruction of property': 'These meetings were held by torch-light, because they were meetings of the working classes, who could not leave their work during the *day*, without suffering a diminution of wages, which, with their scanty earnings they could ill afford'.[70] Of course, Sankey recognised, 'intemperate language had been complained of'. In answering this point we can detect a hint of self-justification given the controversy he had excited weeks earlier:[71]

> no doubt, in the warmth of their feelings, men suffering under wrongs, *or indignant at the wrongs of others*, have used the bold language of Britons, and a servile press may have, by their exaggerations, misrepresentations, and garbled extracts held up the speakers to the condemnations of the timid, or the base attacks of the designing.

Rising to his task Sankey asked with a rhetorical flourish: had not the champions of Catholic Emancipation (including O'Connell) been subjected to the same charge and condemnation 'on account of the inflammable or exciting language, which they unquestionably used'? It was a good point.

Sankey's address also canvassed some general issues which provide important insight into to his attitude to the relationship between Ireland and Britain. Having absolved the Chartists of the charge of violence, he went on the offensive. What were the motives of leaders, he mused, who counselled rejection of the Charter when it offered to Ireland '*more* even than she demands'.[72] In a poetical appeal to Ireland published in January 1841, Sankey expounded on the point more fully[73]

The rich and the noble are seeking
For justice to Ireland, 'tis true;
But their justice, for all their fine speaking,
Will yield but small justice to you.

This was a view that O'Connor would advance on numerous subsequent occasions. Moreover he would go on to draw what seemed to be the obvious conclusion: that without the suffrage, repeal of the Union would be of comparatively little value.[74] At this point, however, O'Connor and Sankey parted company. While O'Connor was prepared to endorse not only repeal, but also the idea of separation, for Sankey the only realistic objective was a just settlement within the context of the British Isles. It had not always been the case, as he explained by reference to a somewhat surprising interpretation of recent Irish history. The problem, as he saw it, lay with the Parliament of 1782 in which his father had served. Instead of 'occupying its time in paltry squabbles as to the commerce between the two countries', Grattan's Parliament 'ought rather to have asserted the independence of the kingdom, in demanding the right of the nation to be represented by its own ambassadors in the different courts of Europe'. Had they done so, Sankey argued, Ireland and England would have been equals, united solely 'by the golden link of the Crown'. Unfortunately, the time for a separate Irish nation had passed, it was no longer feasible in a modern Europe: 'it might be questioned whether these islands would present so strong a barrier to Russian aggression, if dissevered and disunited in policy'.[75]

Concern about Russia was not uncommon among radicals between 1830 and 1860,[76] but if realpolitik dictated that foreign policy and defence be 'united in the hands of an imperial legislature and executive', what was left for an Irish nationalist? The solution, he suggested, was for Ireland to be given control of domestic affairs 'on the principal of federation with Scotland, Wales, [and] the north and south of England'.[77] The significance of this proposal deserves emphasis: it was, in fact, a precocious version of the 'plan' for a political federation of the British Isles popularised by William Sharman Crawford, an Ulsterman and radical Member of the House of Commons, in 1843, which, in turn, anticipated many of the proposals for devolution and 'Home Rule all round' that were to emerge on both sides of the Irish Sea during the second half of the nineteenth century.[78] In particular the notion of dividing England was highly unusual in 1839. Sankey could scarcely disguise his enthusiasm for what was, after all, a scheme that promised less than full national independence to his native land. Here he turned not to O'Connor but to O'Connell; had not the Liberator consented to be called a 'west Briton', he asked? Ever the scholar, Sankey even offered a philological basis for the plan: 'the two islands were known to the Greeks under the *generic appellation* of the *British Isles*'.[79]

Earlier Sankey had outlined a scheme for an even greater devolution of power to Councils of 500 elected by Universal Suffrage in each county. These Councils would 'manage the local business of the District, local taxation &c' as well as vetting 'national legislation', reflecting his commitment to the Chartist practice of local democratic control.[80] Detailed in a pamphlet entitled *Popular Control of Hasty Legislation*, Sankey was attempting to come to terms with the broader question of how 'a regularly organised controlling power may be exercised by the people over the acts of their Representatives'.[81] In common with many radicals (such as James Scholefield, see chapter 5), Sankey had a Cobbett-like suspicion of centralised government, and he complained vociferously of perceived encroachments on individual liberties from passports to the registration of births, deaths and marriages. He was particularly concerned, moreover, by legislation 'smuggled through Parliament' by MPs who refused to represent the wishes of their constituents.[82]

At the Chartist Convention of 1839 Sankey was given the opportunity to practice what he preached. The result was a form of representation that, as noted earlier, was perhaps unique among his fellow delegates. The parallels between the Convention and the House of Commons were many and most of them were unavoidable: from the style and form of the proceedings, to the Hansard-like manner in which the debates were recorded in the press. While some delegates were concerned by the idea that the Convention was becoming an analogue of parliament, other delegates encouraged it. In some cases this led to nothing more than the superficial affectation of MC (Member of the Convention) after their name. In Sankey's case it dictated a way of life. Although Chartists were almost invariably unimpressed when they visited the House of Commons and saw the political elite in action,[83] it is worth making the point that Chartism was based on a recognition of the fundamental importance of Parliament as an institution. Coming from a family with a strong tradition of parliamentary service these attitudes were particularly acute in Sankey.

On the one hand he was a passionate believer in Parliament (properly constituted) calling, in one of his 1838 pamphlets, for the House of Commons to reassert its supremacy over the House of Lords by adopting universal suffrage as a 'declaratory RESOLUTION'.[84] At the same time Sankey was harshly critical of existing MPs. 'With respect to all those who now sit, or have sat in Parliament', he stated bluntly in 1841, 'with the sole and single exception of Feargus O'Connor, I would have no confidence whatever in any of them …'[85] What sort of conduct would have met his high standard? As a Chartist he believed in direct democracy: representatives must not seek to implement their own views, they must represent the views of their constituents. By adopting this position Sankey was flatly rejecting the notion of representation outlined famously in 1774 by a leading Whig Parliamentarian, Edmund Burke. '[Y]our representative owes you, not his industry only, but his judgement', Burke told his constituents in Bristol, 'and he betrays instead of serving you, if he sacrifices it to your opinion'.[86]

By rejecting the prevalent Burkean notion that held representation to be a form of trust, Sankey was doing nothing out of the ordinary for a Chartist; where he did break new ground was in his conception of the role of the parliamentarian as an advocate. Sankey believed that the representative must act as an advocate on behalf of his constituents in their dealings with executive government. In August 1840 Sankey attacked the existing crop of Radical-liberal MPs, insisting that they could be doing more to stop the ill-treatment of Chartist prisoners.[87] Within a couple of months he had apparently decided to do something about it himself, taking up the case of 'one of his constituents', Robert Peddie, a leader among the Edinburgh Chartists who was languishing in Beverley Prison in Yorkshire. Following an approach from Peddie's tenacious wife, Jane Peddie, Sankey used his aristocratic connections to good effect to obtain an interview with the Home Secretary, the Marquis of Normanby. Although, not surprisingly, Sankey's intervention proved to be fruitless, it is significant that he regarded it as his role to intercede on behalf of the Peddies. Aristocratic paternalism slipped easily into democratic advocacy. What is equally significant is that Jane Peddie saw it in the same way.[88]

Ironically, most of Sankey's activities on behalf of his Edinburgh 'constituents' – he consistently referred to them as such during 1839-40 – took place after he had resigned from the Convention. His resignation had come in May 1839, ostensibly as a result of his opposition to the decision to move the proceedings to Birmingham. Once the National Petition had been handed over to Thomas Attwood, the Radical MP for Birmingham, he argued, the principal task of the Convention had been completed. It was an odd stance in the light of subsequent activities on behalf of his 'constituents'. At the time of his resignation, however, Sankey was well aware that his 'constituents' were opposed to the increasingly threatening tone of the proceedings. As he indicated: 'the people of Scotland were too calm, too prudent, and too humane to peril the cause upon bloodshed'.[89] Given his views on representation, it is doubtful that he could have done anything else but resign.

Although Sankey's 'constituents' accepted his resignation, it earned him the ire of O'Connor, who, in September 1839, listed him as one of the 'middle-class' delegates who had deserted the people at their time of need.[90] By this stage Sankey and his family had removed to London, taking up residence in a house in Harwood Street, Camden Town. Despite the brickbat from O'Connor, Sankey remained an active Chartist over the next eighteen months. During this period he published a string of public letters and poems which, taken together with his earlier writings, allow us to delve more deeply into his worldview. The range of issues that fell under his purview was impressive: his public letters were invariably erudite and incisive and, although his muse was sometimes strained and often a little trite, Sankey took poetry as a form of popular communication very seriously, which makes the views it contained all the more interesting to the historian. A number of themes stand out. In December 1839, for example, he wrote to the Lord Chief Justice, Nicholas Tindal, protesting over the use of Scripture during the conduct of the trials of the Chartists then being held at Monmouth.[91] The letter provides a clue as to one of the key components of his public personality. Earlier it was noted that as a young student Sankey was intended for the Church, but he became concerned by what he saw as the insidious relationship between the Church and the State.[92]

Sankey's earlier doubts about the Established Church became entrenched opposition. 'THE TRUTH', he argued, 'refuses to be established, indignantly rejecting every aid wrung by compulsion from the grasp of an unwilling people'.[93] There is no evidence that he formally left the Anglican Church, let alone that he joined any other sect, but, in either case, Christianity remained central to the outlook that he upheld throughout his public life. Sankey provided the most detailed insight into his theology in an address published at Christmas 1840. From this letter, and other writings, it is clear that the Christ that he worshipped was a working man, 'sprung from the ranks of the operatives – the son of a carpenter – a carpenter himself …' 'Working men', he argued, 'you of all men, should be last to renounce the name of Jesus; his glory is your glory; his elevation is the elevation of your order'.[94] Sankey's Christ 'powerfully advocated the rights and the cause of the poor' and 'boldly' 'rebuked the rich'.[95] Moreover, for Sankey, Christ was a democrat who suffered the fate of the Chartists:

> What better proof can we have that he constantly advocated the principles of liberty than this – that the magistrates sent the police to apprehend him – employed spies to entrap him – and, at last, bribed one of his own followers to inform against and betray him.

The true Church, he argued, was composed of 'Operatives – the fishermen and tentmakers', who had elected their office-bearers by 'Universal Suffrage': 'Elevate his cross as the standard of liberty, and invoke his name as the rallying word of freemen'.[96] As is evident from several of the other case studies considered in this volume, this form of radical Christianity had many supporters among the Chartists.

For all that Sankey was committed to Christ the operative, he never stopped preaching to his own class. Like McDouall, Sankey rejected the division favoured by some radicals between the 'productive' and 'unproductive' classes. '[T]he wealthy and the higher grades do toil', he insisted, 'and that in connection with the intensest [sic] labour – that of the mind'.[97] Sankey was no leveller. At the same time, however, he was harshly critical of his own order for their lack of vision. Firstly, as he outlined in an Address to the 'Noblemen, Gentlemen and Middlemen' of England, Scotland and Wales that was published in May 1839, Sankey rejected their opposition to reform based on fear. He offered reassurance. 'On the part of my constituents', he wrote, 'I can truly say that while they seek *their own* rights as men and Britons, they ask not to infringe on *yours* – while they claim the protection of their only property, their labour, they have no idea whatever of robbing you of *your* property'.[98] But if these fears could be assuaged, the real threat was unseen. In an earlier pamphlet Sankey had turned the usual question on its head to great effect: 'You are afraid of the consequences in granting', he noted, 'Are you afraid of no consequences in persisting to deny this privilege?'[99] Moreover, as he wrote in a public letter to the Secretary of State, Lord John Russell, the link between wealth and political privileges was fragile: 'I blush for those of my own order who, possessed of the franchise themselves, value it so little as to peril it upon the contingency of anything so little under their own control as wealth …'[100] Although they rarely came from the mouth of a proud 'aristocrat by birth and education', these views were unexceptional in Chartist circles. What made them significant in Sankey's case, however, was that they were based on an organic view of society and of social hierarchy that, far from being destroyed, would be preserved by universal suffrage: '[I]t would be my sincere desire', he wrote, 'by mutual explanations, to reconcile interests that should be recognised as identified'.[101] It was not until much later in the century that other members of the aristocracy became convinced that their future could be secured in a democratic Britain.[102]

Further examination of Sankey's writings – in particular his poetry – of 1840-41, reveal that while he was concerned about complacency over political rights he cherished a tremendous sense of expectation. His solution to complacency was to attempt to shake it. Take, for example, the bleak opening of 'Ode'(February 1840):[103]

> Men of England, Ye are slaves …
> Though ye boast by land and sea,
> Britons everywhere are free.

Again, in 'Song' (April 1840), he lamented:[104]

> Ye working men of England,
> Who plough your native soil,
> Whose hands have reared her fabrics
> With unabated toil;
> Though your labours clothe her nobles,
> The monarch on the throne,
> Yet bereft, ye are left,
> In slavery to groan …

He was not the only Chartist to take this view. For G.M.W. Reynolds, for example, 'nothing' was 'more disgusting than to hear individuals boast of

English freedom': 'in a word, British freedom is a humbug – a mockery, a delusion and a snare'.[105] But there the similarity with Sankey ended. Whereas Reynolds believed that, far from being the 'envy and admiration of the world', the British Constitution masked a 'vitiated, deficient, and tyrannical ... form of government',[106] Sankey's vision of the future was based on a quest to regain lost rights. At the Convention he had rebuked some of his fellow delegates for invoking the French Revolution when, as far as he was concerned, the Charter was based on a 'the first principles of the original Saxon Constitution'.[107]

With God and history on their side the Chartists could not fail. The last stanza of 'Ode' was full of hope:[108]

> Hark! The stormy tempest raves –
> 'Tis the nation's voice I hear,
> Shouting 'Liberty is near'.

By the end of what had been a year of rebirth for the Chartists, Sankey's 'Rule Britannia' (November 1840) sounded an unequivocally positive note:[109]

> Let Britain's heralds take their stand,
> And loudly through the isle proclaim
> This is the Charter of the land;
> While millions of voices shout the same.
> Hail, Britannia! Britannia's sons are free!
> Suffrage guards their liberty.

It was clear from other poems that he published at this time that Sankey anticipated that the benefits of democracy would be spread far and wide. In 'There's a Hum through the Land' (December 1840) and 'The Chartists' Address to Ireland' (January 1841) he confidently anticipated that the fruits of victory would be shared throughout the British Isles.[110] Nor was his hostility to the revolution in what he called 'frantic, blood-gorged France'[111] indicative of a hostility towards either France or Europe. Far from it; 'all are of one family throughout the earth', he wrote.[112] In 'To the Working Men of Every Clime' (November 1840) Sankey held out the prospect that 'the voice of liberty' would echo throughout Europe:[113]

> Europe's workmen, one and all,
> Rouse ye at your brethren's call,
> Shouting loud from sea to sea,
> Yours will be the victory.

Perhaps Sankey's most novel letter of 1840-41 outlined a plan for a monthly electoral registration fee of 6d. 'Britons!', he urged, 'Do honour to your country and yourselves, and demand that the franchise shall be placed on a footing worthy of the great nation to which you belong'.[114] At a time of economic malaise, Sankey urged consideration of a scheme that could give the Chartists something to bargain with: 'you may be able to offer the minister for finance ... in the midst of his financial embarrassments ... a productive source of revenue to the amount of upwards of a million a year ...'[115] Sankey's plan apparently received no support in the movement, but there were many other Chartist schemes that were rejected during 1840, a time when organisation was at the top of the agenda. The fact that Sankey released it all emphasises his acute sense of independence from the various tendencies within the movement. There was other evidence of this trait. His relationship with William Lovett is a case in point. Sankey and the author of the Charter had much in common including support for the Lancasterian school system.[116] In August 1840 Sankey travelled to Birmingham to congratulate Lovett on his release from prison, and a week later he eulogised the former Secretary of the Convention at a large public dinner in London.[117] Not surprisingly Lovett attempted to recruit Sankey to the National Association mooted in his educational pamphlet, *Chartism: A New Organisation of the People*, but all he got was a sharp rebuff. Your plan, he told Lovett, 'would raise us a knowledge qualification, or a moral qualification, neither of which are legitimate'; 'I totally dissent from the idea that [the people's rights] are to be based upon anything but their birth-right qualification as men'.[118] Notwithstanding his idiosyncrasies, Sankey is also a reminder that the various Chartist factions were not hermetically sealed off from one another. Like many other Chartists Sankey moved easily through the rich and varied culture of Metropolitan radicalism.[119]

This fruitful period of his public life culminated in mid 1841 when he decided to stand for the seat of Marylebone at the general election. Given his attitude to Parliament and his family tradition it is surprising that Sankey had not contested a seat in the House of Commons before this, but his decision came at a time when the Chartist ranks were deeply divided over what policy to pursue. Controversy had been touched off in June when from his prison cell O'Connor had urged Chartists to support the Tories in the coming election. Although his epistle called forth a torrent of criticism from liberals, moderate radicals and from some Chartists, O'Connor's reasoning was quite simple: a Tory victory would put the 'Whigs on the same side of the fence as you': 'if you get a House of Tories you get a good working Whig-Chartist opposition'.[120] Defending his stance a couple of weeks later, O'Connor indicated that, in addition to a tactical judgement, he had also been drawn into the contest from a desire to assist a number of Chartist candidates already in the field, including Henry Vincent, McDouall (see chapter 1), and Sankey, whom he praised as 'open, frank, straightforward, and honourable'.[121] For Sankey the question was not merely tactical: he had no ideological qualms about opposing a Whig. As he told the

Convention two years earlier, although he detested the Tories 'as much as any man can do', the harsh reality was that since 'the Whigs have been in power they have struck more and deeper at the liberties of Englishmen than the Tories'.[122]

Sankey's election address was based on a commitment to support universal suffrage, which was not only 'the only guarantee for the poor' but also, reiterating his earlier contention, 'the best security for the rich'. He also committed himself to vote for a repeal of the New Poor Law Amendment Act. For Sankey, as with many other radicals, this Act summed up the worst features of the 'base, brutal and bloody' Whig administrations that had governed in the decade since the Reform Act: it was 'unconstitutional', 'heartless and tyrannical' and should be repealed.[123] Finally, Sankey offered the electors of Marylebone the sort of direct representation that had characterised his tenure as a Convention delegate: 'Being a resident in the Borough', he argued, 'its Local Interest must necessarily engage my best attention': 'Neither Whig nor Tory, it shall be my proud boast to be, indeed, and in truth, the Representative of the People'.[124]

During the campaign 'spirited meetings' were held every evening by Sankey and his supporters and, perhaps encouraged by his presence, the Tories campaigned harder in what was normally regarded as a quiet seat.[125] Polling itself was characterised by a fierce riot and, according to a leading liberal daily, the *Sun*, by 'greater energy than was ever known in this division of the metropolis'.[126] At the end of counting Sankey had run last in a field of five, receiving a mere 72 votes. He could have not expected otherwise. At the declaration of the poll, Sankey stated that he looked on these few votes 'with pleasure, because he was satisfied that, like himself, they had come forward upon principle'. He was also comforted by the fact that the successful Whigs had had to pledge themselves to more faithfully represent local interests in order to stave his critique of their performance.[127]

Electoral defeat, however, may have been the catalyst for change. In March 1842 Sankey chaired a large public meeting of radicals, Chartists, and other liberals in Marylebone that was aimed at cementing an alliance between supporters of the Charter and repeal of the Corn Laws. From the chair Sankey urged the Chartists to 'stand by their rights and to make no surrender'.[128] This was in line with his previous comments on the campaign against the Corn Laws – up to this point he regarded the question of repeal as a distraction from the more important work of political reform[129] – but, in fact, the comment concealed a fundamental shift in his allegiances. He had always opposed regulation, as part of his broader opposition to government intrusion per se, a point he had made clear in 1837 in a series of reflections on economic policy addressed to the Secretary of the United States Treasury. Using a Greek pseudonym, 'Clavis' (key), Sankey canvassed the possibility of abolishing not only the myriad of laws affecting credit and debt but even currency itself.[130] This pamphlet was a mixture of utopianism, proto-anarchism, and extreme economic liberalism that had excited little interest, but it did put him into close contact with men who would later play important parts in the Anti-Corn Law League in Edinburgh: its publishers, Adam and Charles Black, were stalwarts of the campaign for free trade in Scotland.[131] Thereafter, Sankey appears to have had little direct contact with the Anti-Corn Law League (despite being Villiers' cousin), but at about the same time as the combined meeting of Marylebone radicals, he had begun chairing local meetings of the League, some of which were disrupted by Chartists.[132] In 1842 he also published a lengthy pamphlet on the question of currency reform in which he attacked the monopoly of the Bank of England, a cause cherished by some prominent Leaguers.[133]

During 1842 Sankey also shifted his allegiances within Irish politics. Early in the year he had been courted by the man that Daniel O'Connell called the 'Chief Pacificator of Ireland', Thomas Steele, and by August 1842 Sankey had applied to join the Repeal Association. At a meeting in Conciliation Hall, Dublin, O'Connell himself took the stage to move Sankey's admittance, praising his new recruit for having the political sagacity to turn his back on O'Connor. The application was seconded by Steele who described him as 'an honour to any political society in the world'.[134] By formally joining the ranks of Irish nationalism that had been occupied by his father, Sankey gave his public career a certain symmetry, but, by embracing the 'two Repeals' he effectively ended his career as a Chartist. Not that either the League or the Irish Repeal Association gained much from their new recruit. Although he lived for nearly two more decades, Sankey's public life came to an abrupt halt in 1842. Even his prolific pen fell silent. Apart from a short pamphlet that appeared in 1850, he apparently published nothing after 1842. Whether illness or some other reason brought about the sudden end to his public life at age fifty is unclear. When he died in 1860 (from undisclosed causes) obituary notices in the Metropolitan press recorded the regret of family and friends, but gave no hint of Sankey's brief efflorescence on the national political stage.[135]

Regardless of whether or not Sankey chose to retire in 1842, in one sense the course of popular politics was passing him by. Although some historians have pointed to the persistence of the 'gentleman leader' in nineteenth century radicalism, the scope for aristocratic second lieutenants was surely rapidly closing. As a Bradford Chartist, William Martin, told Feargus O'Connor in 1841, while 'the people' retained their confidence in O'Connor because he was an 'honest aristocrat', 'it was clear now', observed Martin, 'that the people were determined to place confidence in men of their own order'.[136] Nor was Sankey merely another Tory-radical in the mould of Richard Oastler, 'the King of the Factory Children'. What set him apart was his abiding commitment to democracy. For Sankey democracy offered, 'to use the language of the Mathematician', the 'general solution of the great problem of which the others are but particular cases'.[137] At the same time, William Sankey never turned his back on his own class; indeed, his views presaged those of later aristocrats and their supporters who embraced democracy because they saw in it a potential to preserve rather than destroy. It was not until the 1850s that Conservative thinkers began, in the words of one historian, to regard 'the masses as a Tory asset'.[138] Although, he did not live to see it, Sankey's vision of the future was realised in 1867.

Notes

[1] *Charter*, 14 April 1839; *Operative*, 10 March 1839. Although it contains little information about William's life, there is useful information about the early history of the Sankeys on a family website: www.sankey.demon.co.uk.

[2] K. Marx, *The Eighteenth Brumaire of Louis Bonaprate*, 1852, repr. New York, 1975, p. 15.

[3] And often not even that. For example he is not mentioned in either D. Jones, *Chartism and the Chartists*, London, 1975; E. Royle, *Chartism*, London, 1980; D. Thompson, *The Chartists*, London, 1984; or R. Brown, *Chartism*, Cambridge, 1998. In Irish history he is remembered only as a minor poet. See D.J. O'Donoghue, *The Poets of Ireland: A Biographical and Bibliographical Dictionary of Irish Writers of English Verse*, Dublin, 1912, p. 415.

[4] T. Carlyle, 'Shooting Niagara: and After?', 1867 repr. in *Critical and Miscellaneous Essays*, London, 1899, vol. v, pp. 1-48.

[5] *Memorials of the Family of Sankey AD 1207-1880, Printed from the Genealogical Collection of Clement Sankey Best-Gardner of Eaglesbush, Neath*, Swansea, 1880; W. Beaumont, *A History of Sankey*, Warrington, 1889; Sir B. Burke, *A Genealogical and Heraldic History of the Landed Gentry of Ireland*, London, 1912, p. 625. Gerard de Sanki had been a carpenter.

[6] *Charter*, 14 April 1839. For Villiers see 'A Member of the Cobden Club' (ed.) *The Free Trade Speeches Of the Right Hon. Charles Pelham Villiers MP. With a Political Memoir*, London, 1883, 2 vols.

[7] *A Topographical Dictionary of Ireland*, London, 1837, vol. 1, p. 626. It was also known as a great depot for approximately 30,000 barrels of culm produced annually at nearby mines.

[8] Fethard was in the part of the country where the soil and climate were most suited to tillage; in fact grain crops were grown principally (but not exclusively) within a triangle linking Wexford, Dundalk and Cork on the eastern seaboard of Ireland. See K.T. Hoppen, *Ireland Since 1800: Conflict and Conformity*, London, 1989, p. 33; C. Kinealy, *A Death-Dealing Famine: The Great Hunger in Ireland*, London, 1977, p. 33; C. Ó Gráda, *Ireland: A New Economic History, 1780-1939*, Oxford, 1994, pp. 33-4, 120.

[9] *Memorials of the Family of Sankey*, n.p; *History of Sankey*, n.p; *The Letters and Speeches of Oliver Cromwell with elucidations by Thomas Carlyle*, London, 1904, vol. 1, p. 442. Cromwell referred to him as Proctor Zanchy.

[10] *History of Sankey*, n.p.

[11] W.A. Shaw, *The knights of England: a complete record from the earliest time to the present day of the knights of all the orders of chivalry in England, Scotland, and Ireland, and of knights bachelors*, London, 1906, vol. 2, p. 224; *Notes and Queries*, 5 November 1859, p. 383.

[12] W.V.S. Sankey, *The Rights of the Operatives Asserted*, Edinburgh, 1838, p. 21; *Operative*, 10 March 1839.

[13] Sankey, *The Rights of the Operatives Asserted*, p. 21.

[14] Sir L. Namier, *The Structure of Politics at the Ascension of George III*, London, 1961.

[15] He is not mentioned, for example, in S. Gwyne, *Henry Grattan and His Times*, 1939, repr., Westport, 1971 or J. Kelly, *Prelude to Union: Anglo-Irish Politics in the 1780s*, Cork, 1992.

[16] *Charter*, 7 April, 14 April 1839; *Northern Star*, 26 June 1841.

[17] See *Operative*, 10 March 1839. For Arthur O'Connor see the entry by S.H. Palmer in J.O. Baylen & N.J. Gossman (eds), *Biographical Dictionary of Modern British Radicals*, Sussex, 1979, pp. 347-

9.

[18] *Charter*, 7 April, 1839.

[19] There is no mention of William Sankey senior in R. & I. Wilberforce, *The Life or William Wilberforce*, London, 1839, 5 vols; O. Warne, *William Wilberforce and His Times*, London, 1962; R. Furneaux, *William Wilberforce*, London, 1974; or J. Pollock, *Wilberforce*, London, 1977.

[20] Sankey, *The Rights of the Operatives Asserted*, pp. 13-14; W.S.V. Sankey, *The Mission of Sympathy: A Poem in Four Cantos*, London, 1850, pp. 75, 133-5.

[21] *Memorials of the Family of Sankey*, n.p; *Charter*, 14 April 1839. For a discussion of the role of middle-class women in public life in this period see A. Tyrrell, 'Woman's Mission and Pressure Group Politics in Britain (1825-60)', *Bulletin of the John Rylands University Library of Manchester*, vol. 63, no. 1, Autumn 1980, pp. 194-98; P.A. Pickering & A. Tyrrell, *The People's Bread: A History of the Anti-Corn Law League*, London, 2000, chapter 6.

[22] *Charter*, 14 April 1839; *Memorials of the Family of Sankey*, n.p; *Gentleman's Magazine*, April 1853, p. 450. Sankey, however, had conservative views on female suffrage. See conclusion below.

[23] Sankey, *The Rights of the Operatives Asserted*, p. 21; *Chartist Circular*, 28 September 1839; 26 September 1840; D. Jones, *Chartism and the Chartists*, London, 1975, p. 160; P.A. Pickering, *Chartism and the Chartists in Manchester and Salford*, Basingstoke, 1995, pp. 186-7; E. Biagini, *Liberty, Retrenchment and Reform*, Cambridge, 1992, pp. 27, 67-9.

[24] He is not mentioned by the historians of Trinity College. See R.B. McDowell & D.A. Webb, *Trinity College Dublin, 1592-1952, An academic history*, Cambridge, 1982.

[25] *Charter*, 14 April 1839.

[26] Ibid.; *Operative*, 10 March 1839.

[27] *The Times*, 3 December 1860; *Morning Chronicle*, 4 December 1860; *Charter*, 14 April 1839.

[28] See E-F. Jomard, *Progres des ecloes d'enseignement mutuel, en France et dans l'etranger*, Paris, 1819; W. Lovett & J. Collins, *Chartism: A New Organisation of the People*, 1839, repr. New York, 1969, p. 79; R.G. Cowherd, *The Politics of English Dissent*, London, 1959, pp. 38-9.

[29] W.S.V. Sankey, *The Geographical Rectification of Any Arc of the Circle, founded on the principle of ultimate and limiting ratios to which is added an examination of some curious properties of a Quadratrix*, Edinburgh, 1825, p. 3.

[30] W.S.V. Sankey, *A Voice for the Operatives*, Edinburgh, 1837, p. 11. Certainly neither of the Chartist portraits mentioned that he actually did any work.

[31] *Pilot* [Dublin], 2 March 1842; 24 August 1842. See also Sankey, *A Voice for the Operatives*, p. 11.

[32] He was apparently never elected a Fellow of the Society. See H. Frew (ed.), *Index of Fellows of the Royal Society of Edinburgh elected 1783-1984*, Scotland's Cultural Heritage Unit, University of Edinburgh, 1984.

[33] For the Royal Institution see M. Berman, *Social Change and Scientific Organisation: The Royal Institution, 1799-1844*, London, 1978. For Brewster, the 'father of modern optics' and inventor of the kaleidoscope, and the Royal Society see N. Campbell and R.M. Smellie, *The Royal Society of Edinburgh, 1783-1983*, Edinburgh, 1983. Sankey is not mentioned in the memoir of Brewster written by his daughter, Mrs Gordon, *The Home Life of Sir David Brewster*, Edinburgh, 1881.

[34] See A.N. Kolmogorov & A.R. Yushkevich (eds) *Mathematics in the 19th Century*, Basle, 1992; C. Lanczos, *Space through the Ages: The Evolution of Geometrical Ideas from Pythagoras to Hibbert and Einstein*, London, 1970. According to Lanczos, p. 35, the quadratrix was invented in Greece by Hippias of Elis around 425 BC which would explain Sankey's interest.

[35] W.V.S. Sankey, *Rhymes on Geography and History Part 1, illustrated with two coloured maps*, Edinburgh, 1828, p. v.

[36] See, for example, P.A. Pickering, '"Glimpses of Eternal Truth": Chartism, Poetry and the Young H.R. Nicholls', *Labour History*, no. 70, May 1996, pp. 53-70 and chapter 1 above.

[37] Sankey, *Rhymes on Geography*, p. v.

[38] *Charter*, 14 April 1839.

[39] W.V.S. Sankey, *The Port-Feuille of Science, Literature, and Art*, Edinburgh, 1838.

[40] Ibid, frontispiece.

[41] Sankey, *The Rights of the Operatives*, pp. 16-17.

[42] There are apparently no copies of *Universal Suffrage*, or *The Right of Labour to Protect itself* extant. In *Popular Control of Hasty Legislation*, published in 1838, Sankey refers to pamphlet written three years earlier although he does not give its title. We have been unable to identify this work.

[43] Sankey, *A Voice for the Operatives*, p. 3.

[44] Ibid., pp. 3-5.

[45] Ibid., pp. 4, 8.

[46] Ibid., pp. 10-11.

[47] See *Northern Star*, 7 July 1838.

[48] L.C. Wright, *Scottish Chartism*, Edinburgh, 1953, p. 48

[49] *Scotsman*, 20 February 1839.

[50] Cited in *Charter*, 14 April 1839.

[51] *Operative*, 10 March 1839.

[52] *Charter*, 14 April 1839. His defenders might have added that several of Sankey's pamphlets were published in Edinburgh.

[53] Wright, *Scottish Chartism*, p. 48, M. Hovell, *The Chartist Movement*, Manchester, 1918, p. 132.

[54] A. Wilson, *The Chartist Movement in Scotland*, Manchester, 1970, pp. 102-3. See also A. Briggs, *Chartism*, Stroud, 1998, p. 67.

[55] Wright, *Scottish Chartism*, pp. 55-6; *Charter*, 19 March, 24 March 1839.

[56] See *Operative*, 24 March 1839; *Northern Star*, 23 March 1839. The *Star*'s report was, it freely acknowledged, taken from the *Morning Chronicle*.

[57] *Manchester Examiner*, 18 March 1848.

[58] See, for example, *Manchester Times*, 12 February 1842; *Manchester and Salford Advertiser*, 19 March 1842; *McDouall's Chartist and Republican Journal*, 26 June 1841; *Northern Star*, 9 July 1842. Cobden's well known private preference for a force behind the League's respectable facade that would 'frighten the aristocracy' was expressed to J.B. Smith. See MPL, J.B. Smith, Anti-Corn Law League Papers, R. Cobden to Smith, 4 December 1841. Villiers also believed that 'the *brickbat argument* is the only one that our nobles heed'. See L. Brown, 'Chartists and the Anti-Corn Law League', in A. Briggs (ed.), *Chartist Studies*, London, 1959, p. 348; Pickering & Tyrrell, *The People's Bread*, pp. 143-4.

[59] British Library, Ad. MS. 50,131, fol. 46-7 Cobden to Sturge, 7 September 1841. We are grateful to Alex Tyrrell for this reference.

[60] O'Connor cited in A. Briggs, 'The Local Background of Chartism', *Chartist Studies*, p. 10; T. Cooper, *The Life of Thomas Cooper*, 1872, repr. Leicester, 1971, p. 180.

[61] R. Lowery, 'Passages in the Life of a Temperance Lecturer', repr. as B. Harrison & P. Hollis (eds.), *Robert Lowery: Radical and Chartist*, London, 1979, p. 96.

[62] Sankey, *The Rights of the Operatives*, p. 3.

[63] *Northern Star*, 3 November 1838.

[64] *Northern Star*, 23 February 1839.

[65] He is not mentioned in J. Belchem, 'English Working Class Radicalism and the Irish, 1815-1850', *North West Labour History Society Bulletin*, no. 8, 1982-3, pp. 5-18; R. O'Higgins, 'The Irish Influence in the Chartist Movement', *Past and Present*, No. 20, 1961, pp. 83-96; J.H. Treble, 'O'Connor, O'Connell and the Attitudes of Irish Immigrants Towards Chartism in the North of England 1838-48', in J. Butt & I.F. Clarke (eds), *The Victorians and Social Protest*, Newton Abbot, 1973, pp. 33-70; and D. Thompson, 'Ireland and the Irish in English Radicalism before 1850', in J. Epstein & D. Thompson (eds), *The Chartist Experience: Studies in Working-Class Radicalism and Culture, 1830-60*, London, 1982, pp. 120-151.

[66] *Charter*, 7 April 1839.

[67] *Northern Star*, 26 June 1841; *Pilot*, 24 August 1842.

[68] *Charter*, 7 April 1839.

[69] *Charter*, 12 May 1839. Perhaps taking his lead from the offer of the Radical Associations, Sankey

also sought to assure the Irish people of the support of the British: 'My friends, you are much mistaken in supposing that Englishmen, Scotchmen, or Welshmen, are opposed to your rights; that they have no sympathy with your sufferings, or that they cherish a feeling of antipathy towards your country'. As proof of this he pointed to the number of his fellow Convention delegates who were Irish. See *Charter*, 7 April 1839.

[70] *Charter*, 7 April 1839.

[71] Ibid. Emphasis added. In his case it has been historians that have used 'garbled extracts'.

[72] Ibid. Earlier Sankey had predicted that O'Connell would support Chartism. See Sankey, *The Rights of the Operatives*, p. 20.

[73] *Northern Star*, 16 January 1841.

[74] *Charter*, 7 April 1839. See also P.A. Pickering, '"Repeal and the Suffrage": Feargus O'Connor's Irish Mission, 1849-50', in O. R. Ashton, R. Fyson & S. Roberts (eds), *The Chartist Legacy*, Rendlesham, 1999, pp. 119-146.

[75] *Charter*, 7 April 1839.

[76] His address was written at the time of a controversial entente proposal by Palmerston. See Jones *Chartism and the Chartists*, p. 162; R. Shannon, 'David Urquhart and the Foreign Affairs Committees' in P. Hollis (ed.), *Pressure from Without in early Victorian England*, London, 1974, pp. 248-50.

[77] *Charter*, 7 April 1839.

[78] See O. MacDonagh, *The Emancipist: Daniel O'Connell, 1830-1847*, London, 1989, vol. 2, p. 254; F.S.L. Lyons, *Ireland Since the Famine*, London, 1971, pp. 147-151; J.L. Garvin, *The Life of Joseph Chamberlain*, London, 1933, vol. 2, chapter 27, especially pp. 75-7.

[79] *Charter*, 7 April 1839.

[80] Sankey, *The Rights of the Operatives*, p. 15; Pickering, *Chartism and the Chartists in Manchester and Salford*, chapter 2.

[81] W.S.V. Sankey, *Popular Control of Hasty Legislation. To which is subjoined a letter to a Member of Parliament, on the English Bill for the Registration of Births, Marriages and Deaths*, Edinburgh, 1838, p. 3. This idea of a Council based on districts had many later resonances in Irish history from O'Connell's controversial call for a Council of 300 in mid-1843 to the Dáil Éireann itself. See MacDonagh, *The Emancipist*, p. 221; Lyons, *Ireland Since the Famine*, pp. 400-8.

[82] Sankey, *Popular Control of Hasty Legislation*, pp. 3-15.

[83] See Harrison & Hollis (eds), *Robert Lowery*, p. 140. S. Bamford, *Passages in the Life of a Radical*, 1844, repr. Oxford, 1984, pp. 26-8. See also Pickering & Tyrrell, *The People's Bread*, p. 166 for similar attitudes held by Anti-Corn Law Leaguers.

[84] Sankey, *The Rights of the Operatives*, p. 18

[85] *Northern Star*, 6 February 1841.

[86] Quoted in P. Kelly, 'Constituents' instructions to Members of Parliament in the eighteenth century', in C. Jones (ed.), *Party Management in Parliament 1660-1784*, Leicester, 1984, p. 170.

[87] *Northern Star*, 15 August 1840.

[88] *Northern Star*, 28 November 1840; S. Roberts, *Radical Politicians and Poets in Early Victorian Britain*, Lampeter, 1993, p. 65.

[89] J.T. Ward, *Chartism*, London, 1974, p. 118; Wilson, *Chartist Movement in Scotland*, pp. 73-4; *Northern Star*, 15 December 1840.

[90] *Northern Star*, 21 September 1839.

[91] *Northern Liberator*, 20 December 1839.

[92] *Charter*, 14 April 1839. Although he was an Anglican, there was family tradition of dissent. In one of his pamphlets he referred to his father and grandfather being prevented from obtaining an education at either Oxford or Cambridge by the 'religious tests' imposed by the 'southern universities'. See Sankey, *The Rights of the Operatives*, p. 22n.

[93] Sankey, *Popular Control of Hasty Legislation*, p. 9.

[94] *Northern Star*, 26 December 1840.

[95] Ibid.; Sankey, *The Rights of the Operatives*, p. 8.

[96] *Northern Star*, 26 December 1840.

[97] Sankey, *The Rights of the Operatives*, p. 6.

[98] *Charter*, 19 May 1839.

[99] Sankey, *The Rights of the Operatives*, p. 15.

[100] *Northern Liberator*, 6 June 1840. See also Sankey, *A Voice for the Operatives*, p. 11.

[101] *Charter*, 19 May 1839.

[102] See D. Southgate, 'From Disraeli to Law', in Lord Butler (ed.), *The Conservatives: A History from their Origins to 1965*, London, 1977, p. 159.

[103] *Northern Star*, 29 February 1840.

[104] *Northern Star*, 25 April 1840. See also *Cleave's Gazette of Variety*, 2 May 1840.

[105] *Reynolds's Weekly Newspaper*, 12 May 1850.

[106] Ibid, 17 November 1850.

[107] *Northern Star*, 4 May 1839. An ironic comment given his Norman ancestry.

[108] Ibid., 29 February 1840. See also *McDouall's Chartist and Republican Journal*, 19 June 1841.

[109] Ibid., 14 November 1840.

[110] *Northern Liberator*, 19 December 1840; *Northern Star*, 16 January 1841.

[111] Sankey, *The Mission of Sympathy*, p. 71. See also *Popular Control of Hasty Legislation*, pp. 9-10.

[112] Sankey, *Popular Control of Hasty Legislation*, p. 9.

[113] *Northern Star*, 28 November 1840.

[114] *Northern Liberator*, 15 August 1840.

[115] Ibid.

[116] See Lovett & Collins, *Chartism: A New Organisation of the People*, p. 79.

[117] *Northern Star*, 8 August 1840.

[118] Ibid., 17 April 1841. Sankey submitted his own petition for universal suffrage in 1840. See PP. *Reports of the Select Committee of the House of Commons on Public Petitions*, vol. 116, 1840, p. 84.

[119] See Pickering, 'Glimpses of Eternal Truth', pp. 53-70.

[120] *Northern Star*, 19 June 1841.

[121] Ibid., 26 June 1841.

[122] Ibid., 23 March 1839. See also 8 August 1840.

[123] Ibid., 26 June 1841, 2nd Edition.

[124] Ibid.

[125] Ibid.; *Sun*, 1 July 1841.

[126] *Sun*, 1 July 1841; 2 July 1841.

[127] Ibid., 2 July 1841, Evening edition.

[128] *Sheffield Iris*, 5 March 1842.

[129] Sankey, *The Rights of the Operatives*, p. 17.

[130] [W.S.V. Sankey], *Thoughts on the Currency as affecting production, suggested by the late Commercial Crisis &c in a letter addressed to the Honourable the Secretary of the American Treasury*, Edinburgh, 1837, pp. 3-12. He envisaged 'one great mutual co-operation society' that embraced 'all the inhabitants of the earth'.

[131] See *Scotsman*, 23 January 1839; 14 January 1843.

[132] *Pilot*, 2 March 1842.

[133] W.S.V. Sankey, *Thoughts on the Currency*, London, 1842. Despite the same short title, the contents of this pamphlet were different to the earlier one.

[134] *Pilot*, 24 August 1842.

[135] *The Times*, 3 December 1860; *Morning Chronicle*, 4 December 1860.

[136] *Northern Star*, 4 September 1841.

[137] Sankey, *The Rights of Operatives*, p. 17.

[138] See Butler (ed.), *The Conservatives*, p. 159.

CHAPTER 4

THE 'REMARKABLE WORK' OF THE REVEREND BENJAMIN PARSONS (1797-1855)

Had Benjamin Parsons lived in Tyndale's time, (they were born in the same village) he would have been a Bible translator and a Martyr: had William Tyndale lived in these days, he would have been what Benjamin Parsons was – an inflexible nonconformist – an earnest minister of the cross – an advocate of liberty – a Friend of the People.[1]

According to an obituary in the *Eclectic Review*, a journal with a large audience among the Dissenting middle classes in mid-Victorian Britain, Benjamin Parsons 'did remarkable work … in a remarkable way'.[2] Convinced that the Bible was a radical book, Parsons earned a reputation in the nineteenth century as an outspoken gospel preacher, propagandist, teacher and publicist on a wide range of national issues. Despite his local reputation as the 'Oberlin of Gloucestershire' for his philanthropic efforts and educational work,[3] Parson's humanism differed from that of the Alsatian pastor, J. H. Oberlin, because he actively involved himself in radical politics, most notably as a stout defender both of Chartism and the Anti-Corn Law League. At the same time he was indefatigable in his pursuit of temperance, anti-slavery, the abolition of church rates, Sabbatarianism, and international peace. A prolific writer, Parsons published approximately twenty books on various subjects,[4] but he is best known for those that promoted class conciliation in the turbulent 1840s: *The Mental and Moral Dignity of Woman* (1842), *Education, the Birthright of Every Human Being* (1845), and, in eighteen parts, *Tracts for Fustian Jackets and Smock Frocks* (1847-9). Published monthly in penny editions in order to maximise their circulation amongst the working classes, the *Tracts* were strident in tone but unequivocal in their rejection of violence of any kind as a means to achieving political change. If Parsons' views and actions led him, inevitably, into controversy with establishment figures in church and state, they also earned him considerable attention, including two biographies.[5] His *Tracts*, in particular, spread his fame far and wide. At the close of the nineteenth century, Charles Shaw, a Tunstall pottery worker who witnessed the 'Plug Plot' riots of 1842 as a child, recalled being presented with a volume of 'tracts by Benjamin Parsons of Ebley, Stroud' by fellow members of his Mutual Improvement Class. A delighted Shaw noted, as he was about to leave to train as a Methodist minister, that[6]

> They contained some of the most vigorous and sane writings then extant for 'the people', who had just been moved by the great stir produced by 'The People's Charter'.

By contrast, in the twentieth century interest in Parsons virtually disappeared; the most recent work, including a piece by one of the present authors, is unpublished. A fresh assessment is clearly long overdue.[7] This chapter therefore takes a closer look at Parsons' life and times. It seeks to evaluate, in the light of previous writings, the merits of the description offered to readers of the *Eclectic Review*: did Parsons do remarkable work in a remarkable way?

Parsons' early life is crucial to understanding his role as an apostle of class collaboration in the 1840s. He was born in 1797 in the village of Nibley, Gloucestershire, the youngest child in a family of eight. His parents – Thomas and Anna – were both from long-established families in Uley; they were devout Dissenters, followers of George Whitefield and worshippers at Dursley Tabernacle chapel. Parsons, however, was born into a family in crisis, which left a deep impression on his mind whilst growing up. At the time of his birth, an unsuccessful business transaction had plunged his enterprising father, a tenant farmer, into heavy debt. Landed influence and power were both strong and enduring across agricultural Gloucestershire in the nineteenth century. In this particular case it resulted in a 'spiteful and unjust landlord' acting tyrannically by giving Benjamin's father immediate notice to quit.[8] As another farm could not be obtained, all the animals had to be sold off to clear their debts. Parsons thus entered life in a pious family, but living on the edge of poverty. His father managed to make a living of sorts as a turnpike gatekeeper at a toll-house in the parish of Kingscote. At the age of six Benjamin suffered a paralytic seizure through sitting on damp ground which produced a permanent lameness. Two months after this unfortunate incident Parsons' father suddenly collapsed and died, probably as a result of the effects of all the pressures that had conspired to oppress him. Inspired by a religious faith and with financial help from two close family friends – a lawyer's clerk and a doctor's assistant, both drawn from the small town, genteel circle in which they once mixed – Benjamin's mother sent him to the parsonage school at Dursley and then to the grammar school at Wotton-under-Edge. His classical education at the grammar school was cut short, however, by his mother's intervention. She learnt that the headmaster, impressed by Parsons' love of books and intellectual talents, had made plans for him to go up to Oxford, with a view to a career as a classical scholar and to become involved in the Anglican Church. A remarkable sea change then ensued with Benjamin, the would-be academic, entering the world of work as a humble apprentice to a tailor in the village of Frampton-on-Severn. Whilst working as a journeyman his thirst for knowledge of all kinds not unnaturally continued to grow, but the untimely death of his mother when he was only fifteen saw his self-education take a more religious turn. It took several forms: a commitment to an intense and often literal study of Biblical texts; becoming a Sunday School teacher from the age of eighteen; joining the Countess of Huntingdon's Connexion at Rodborough Tabernacle chapel; and engaging in animated debates about the merits of the Scriptures with fellow shop-mates. Parsons' ability to reason and defend his corner in all these activities was doubtless helped by the fact he had assiduously continued a programme of self-education that included polishing his earlier command of Latin.[9]

In 1821, his apprenticeship completed, Parsons came to Stroud, the manufacturing centre for the long established, yet increasingly beleaguered, Gloucestershire cloth industry. Encouraged in particular by the sermons and advice of one of the town's leading Dissenters, the Rev. John Burder of the Independent denomination, Parsons took the momentous decision to become, like others in this volume, a man of the cloth.[10] In September of that year, Parsons exchanged the life of a village craftsman for that of a minister in the Countess of Huntingdon's Connexion. Thus began a career which, if not well paid, was to restore him to a position of middling social standing which his father's misfortunes had jeopardised. Nevertheless, he remained implacably opposed to that society of deference on which his parents had been so economically dependent in Gloucestershire.

As a member of the Huntingdon Connexion Parsons shared in a rich heritage that was important in shaping his later career. A product of the eighteenth century religious revival, Selina, Countess of Huntingdon (1707-1791), became one of the leaders associated with the rise of Calvinistic Methodism.[11] The daughter of a prominent aristocratic family, Selina married Theophilus Hastings, the ninth Earl of Huntingdon, in 1728. At Donnington Park, the family seat in rural Northamptonshire, the Countess displayed a deep concern for the spiritual and social needs of her contemporaries. For example, she took a keen interest in the welfare of all who served on the family estate, and she also earned a reputation for her benevolence towards the poor both in the surrounding countryside and the nearby town of Ashby-de-la-Zouche. The Connexion that she founded seems to have grown by degrees. Her strategy was to appoint evangelical preachers driven from the Church of England as her chaplains, and to build proprietary chapels where they could search for the most effective ways of reaching the people. As part of this strategy, she founded a college for the training of gospel preachers at Trevecca in Breconshire in 1768. In 1779, Countess Huntingdon felt compelled by legal disputes to register her Connexion as a Dissenting body under the Toleration Act. By 1781, her chapels had ceased to be societies within the Church of England and the Connexion became a sect. After the Countess' death in 1791, the ministerial training college was moved to Cheshunt in

Hertfordshire. Here it faithfully retained its philosophy, which, by promoting a more practical Christianity through good works and deeds, became increasingly relevant to the demands of an industrialising society.[12]

Between 1821 and 1825, Parsons trained at Cheshunt College where his embryonic radical ideas began to develop. After occupying a pulpit in the industrialising port of Swansea for nine months in 1825, and following a short stay in the Lancashire mill town of Rochdale, Parsons returned to his native Gloucestershire to the village of Ebley, half way between Stroud and Stonehouse. Here the Countess of Huntingdon's chapel, which was without a minister, had a small, predominantly working-class congregation, financial debts and a building that was crumbling.[13] After a trial period of six weeks, Parsons consented to stay. A ministry of twenty-eight years thus commenced on 26 September 1826; and, although he was to lecture elsewhere in the country from time to time, the Ebley-Stroud axis was the principal scene of his labours for the rest of his life.[14]

From his base at Ebley chapel, Parsons successfully managed to 'reach' the hearts and minds of weavers who toiled in the cloth mills of a 'factory' village that had expanded in the first twenty years of the nineteenth century, in order to meet a renewed demand for its staple product.[15] The range of activities and the kind of provision he made were impressive. The chapel was extensively refurbished and the congregation built up from about twenty to well over one thousand worshippers within the space of a few years.[16] Sunday schools were established to cater for over four hundred children, and a special Sunday class serving the needs of girls and adult females was formed under the supervision of Parsons' wife, Amelia, whom he had married in November 1830. In addition, during 1840 Parsons founded a flourishing British day school for infants that was surrounded by purpose-built playgrounds and gardens; undertook mid-week and evening classes for parents; and, tutored some paying pupils in the parsonage to an advanced standard. Directly as a result of Parsons' endeavours the Ebley chapel also had its own benefit society, literary society, library, debating club, choral group and elocution class.[17]

Parsons' personality played a crucial part in the popularity of these schemes and he unquestionably became something of a cult figure in the community. A man possessed of great natural ability and strength of character, he was fearless in displaying and defending his own particular convictions. In his sermons, orations and addresses this individuality was often expressed in a charismatic style and with a distinct body language which could have an electrifying effect on audiences. According to one local commentator, P. H. Fisher, Parsons' 'complexion was dark, his features irregular but very flexible, his voice powerful; and when excited in speaking his eyes, flashing from beneath his large, black scowling eyebrows, gave fearful effect to his fierce denunciations'. 'In opposing persons or things obnoxious to him', Fisher continued, Parsons was a force to be reckoned with: 'his manner was bold, undaunted, scornful and decisive … and

he employed unsparingly his terrible powers of sarcasm'.[18] Fisher's recollections
also give us a glimpse of a man so supremely confident in his own ability that he
could be arrogant. '[S]ome of his opinions were extreme', Fisher remembered,
and he 'sometimes advanced startling paradoxes, as if for the pleasure of dex-
trously explaining them away'.[19] More often than not, however, he put his skills
to good use; as P.M. Walmsley has stressed, Parsons was a born teacher who
lectured to the people on virtually everything he read.[20] In an accessible form he
would deliver talks on an impressive range of topics from mechanics, chemistry,
and dietetics, to animal physiology, history and geography. Nor did he eschew
controversial topics, such as the French Revolution, the British Constitution
and the Bible as a Radical book, much to the chagrin of the local authorities in
church and state.[21]

Convinced that there could be no real elevation of the people without education, Parsons placed the Ebley British day school at the centre of his teaching
schemes. Here he put into practice his ideas – a mixture of old and new – about
the organisation and content of elementary education. They were also published
in 1845 in the form of a tract, after being submitted in a national competition
on proposals for public education. Although he did not win, his entry, entitled
Education, The Natural Want and Birthright of Every Human Being, was well-
received in Dissenting circles because of its defence of Voluntary principles.[22]
Offering elementary education to all, Parsons' plan won generous praise from
both the *Sunday School Magazine* and the *Congregational Magazine* for its contribution to educational thought, stout rejection of governmental control or
even assistance, and for providing a fillip to Sabbatarianism.[23] Inevitably, some
of Parsons' ideas regarding the organisation of the school and the content of the
curriculum were set in a religious mould; traditional teaching methods, such as
the monitorial system, were also retained. In two respects, however, Parsons was
ahead of his time. Firstly, he believed strongly that the minds of girls were equal
to those of boys and therefore both sexes should be offered the same educational
opportunities at school. Consequently the three Rs, elementary science, geography, music and the Scriptures were taught and tested in mixed classes at Ebley
day school. In 1842 Parsons even backed up these ideas in print with the tract
The Mental and Moral Dignity of Woman. A contemporary advertisement for
this tract, which was reprinted twice before 1856, stated 'In this work the author
argues that the mental powers of women are equal and her moral feelings supe-
rior, to those of men'.[24] The *Eclectic Review* felt that it would 'win for woman,
wherever it is carefully perused, a larger portion of intellectual respect, than she
at present possesses'.[25] Parsons also believed in the teaching of practical subjects
like science, gardening and dietetics, and the provision of play facilities to stimu-
late the imagination, though, as Walmsley notes, on this point the theory was
better than the practice.[26]

Parsons' hostility to a government-controlled education system was indicative of a wider opposition to the state church and the practices that sustained it. In this and other respects, Parsons' career reflected nationwide developments in the rise of combative Dissent.[27] Consequently, like many radical Dissenters including James Scholefield (see chapter 5), Parsons was also involved in the struggle against the payment of church rates to the Anglican establishment. He viewed this contentious tax as both unjust and anti-scriptural, and urged the Anglican hierarchy to adopt the Voluntary principle. 'It seems', he wrote in the sarcastic tone that had impressed Fisher:[28]

> that with all your zeal for the Church, you would do nothing to support your mother, unless put under the necessity of a compulsory rate …There is not a single instance in the New Testament of the Apostles having demanded a compulsory rate for the support or propagation of the Gospel.

Not surprisingly, in 1837 he played an important role in setting up the Stroud Association for the Protection of Liberty, which had links with similar societies in and around London. The Stroud Association drew up a memorial that was presented to Lord John Russell at a time when it was known that the Whig cabinet was preparing a new church rate measure. Russell was left in no doubt about the strength of local feeling. The scheme was abandoned for various reasons,[29] but the fact that Russell was one of the two Whig MPs for the Stroud borough was a point not lost on either the petitioners or the petitioned.[30] Thereafter the payment of church rates was not an acute local issue, being levied only occasionally in certain parishes, and never in Stroud or on Parsons himself.[31] This fact did not prevent Parsons from lending his personal support as a platform speaker to an ambitious anti-church rates campaign organised by a loose alliance of Dissenters and Chartists in neighbouring Cheltenham Spa, where the evangelical Anglican, the Rev. Francis Close, was attempting to enforce their payment.[32]

Parsons' active involvement in politics began in 1833 over the issue of the abolition of slavery. When the notorious pro-slavery campaigner, Peter Borthwick,[33] visited Stroud to mobilise support for the cause, Parsons confronted him in a public debate. According to Stratford, 'the village pastor covered [Borthwick] … with shame and confusion by his strong arguments and vehement denunciations'.[34] The next person to experience Parsons' opposition in this humanitarian work was one of the would-be Stroud MPs, William Hyett of Painswick House, a Whig and leading landowner in the County. Hyett's ambivalence towards the emancipation of the slaves was revealed during the general election campaign of December 1832, the first for the new two member seat of Stroud borough under the terms of the Reform Act. With the help of three other Dissenting ministers in the town, including the Rev. John Burder, Parsons organised a petition of electors which left Hyett in no doubt of where they stood. They also requested Hyett to call upon Lord Althorp to press upon him the need to introduce a comprehensive measure ensuring total emancipation when the Bill was introduced.[35] Parsons was again to the fore in 1838 when the Stroud Anti- Slavery Association decided to memorialise their two MPs (by this time G. P. Scrope and Lord John Russell) for an immediate end to the scheme of compulsory unpaid labour known as the Negro apprenticeship.[36] As Walmsley points out, Russell assured them 'of his regret at this disagreement with government policy, which in fact was reversed in the following year'.[37]

Although Parsons had indicated his support for the Chartists in January 1841 when Henry Vincent published his call for Chartism to become a teetotal creed,[38] Parsons devoted himself primarily to fighting the cause of Corn Law repeal between 1839 and 1846. By the 1840s the long established but relatively small-scale cloth industry around Stroud was well and truly in decline. According to J.C. Symonds,[39] a man who lived in Cheltenham and had specialist knowledge of the industry, by 1842 there were only 77 mills in the Stroud district whereas ten years previously there had been 133.[40] Notwithstanding their good reputation as factory paternalists and active Nonconformist laymen in their village communities, the leading employers – the Marlings, Stantons, Playnes and J. W. Partridge – were under siege.[41] Faced with fierce competition from the West Riding of Yorkshire, they were introducing power looms, undertaking rationalisation schemes and reducing the size of the workforce in their mills in order to survive. All this took place against a background of frequent depression in the cloth trade and poverty and unrest among the men. The cash nexus, property distinctions, and increased political cohesion displayed by the employers, led to considerable class bitterness and animosity in the 1840s. Whereas the employers believed that the repeal of the Corn Laws was the only effective remedy for the wholesale revival of trade, with few exceptions,[42] the weavers were equally convinced that only the enactment of the People's Charter would ensure their long term future.[43] Predictably, Parsons entered the fray determined to help employers and workers alike.[44] In the opinion of A. W. Paulton, an Anti-Corn Law League lecturer who was on a tour of the West Country in December 1841, the flourishing state of the agitation in and around Stroud was 'owing to the zeal of the ministers, Messrs Parsons and Burder'.[45] By this time the manufacturers appear to have left most of the public campaigning to a handful of Dissenting ministers in Stroud. As in many parts of the country, these men of God turned the campaign for repeal into a moral crusade. Parsons was pre-eminent in the local struggle: he is reputed to have said that he never looked upon repeal as a 'merely civil and political question', but 'one of justice and therefore religion'.[46] Unlike the Leaguers in Manchester who enthusiastically enlisted new technology to aid their campaign, Parsons' methods were old-fashioned, but equally effective:[47]

On his pony, 'Dobin', he trotted to the towns and villages around him; and by mingled argument and fact, pathos and wit, aroused the people to demand, as their right, free trade in bread.

Before long Parsons' prominence led him onto a larger stage. Parsons was among a select group of Dissenting ministers chosen to represent the Stroud and Ebley Associations at national conferences of the Anti-Corn Law League, including the Manchester Convocation of Ministers in August 1841. At this most stage-managed of events Parsons was invited to move one of the conference resolutions, which was an indication of his standing in the eyes of the League hierarchy.[48] Six months later, along with Burder, Parsons attended the League's 'Great Meeting' in London at the Crown and Anchor, where he was elected to its executive committee.[49] After his return, Parsons wrote a letter to the League's newspaper, the *Anti-Bread Tax Circular*, proposing a national boycott of excisable articles,[50] and by the beginning of 1843 he had become a member of the influential General Committee of the Great League Fund.[51] Parsons' exertions in fund-raising at a local level were soon apparent: in that year when the League's national target was £50,000, the small Stroudwater district raised £274; a year later when goal of the Great Fund was raised to £100,000, the amount subscribed from Parsons' district was doubled to £550.[52] Parsons had the satisfaction, too, of successfully bringing pressure to bear on the local MPs. In 1837 both G.P. Scrope and Lord John Russell had not voted in the division on the Corn Laws; by 1843, Scrope and W. H. Stanton, who had replaced Russell, were firmly committed to the agitation. One important result was that both could be relied upon to support local petitions to parliament and memorials to the Queen demanding 'immediate and total repeal'.[53] In 1846, after repeal had been achieved Parsons delivered his last speech on the subject at a celebration meeting held in Ebley. It finished with one of those humorous illustrations that he could so well engage in with his audience:[54]

> I was sitting in my study, some time since; the window was up, and I could hear all that passed below it; my children had just been burying in childish amusement a cat. They had made a mock coffin for it, had dug a grave, had covered it: when, just as they were leaving, one of the youngest cried out, 'Oh, we have just forgot something!' What was that? 'Why, we have forgot to cry over it'. We have buried the Corn Laws, but we have forgot to cry over them.

One of the most striking feature of the local Anti-Corn Law League campaign was its positive relationship with the Stroudwater Chartists. Apart from occasional confrontations in 1841 and 1843,[55] elements within both movements appear to have tried to find common ground in the struggle against 'monopoly' and 'Old Corruption'. At the first Anti-Corn Law meeting in Stroud in January 1839, for example, although the repeal of the Corn Laws was prioritised, platform resolutions calling for the enactment of the secret ballot and an extension of the franchise were also passed.[56] A formal agreement between the two movements was in fact momentarily cemented in January 1842. According to Walmsley, the motion that was passed on that occasion had been skilfully drafted:[57]

> While this meeting most unequivocally denounces the iniquity of the Corn Laws, it cannot forget that unjust laws have sprung out of a monopoly of legislation, and is therefore of the opinion that the selfishness of monopoly cannot be overcome until all classes of the people are fully, fairly and equally represented in the House of Commons.

Parsons undoubtedly played a key role in trying to unite the two movements . A number of reasons can be suggested as to why this was the case. First, Chartism was strong in Ebley. By 1839, it had a branch membership of about one hundred weavers and village craftsmen, drawn from among those in the community whom Parsons worked with and respected.[58] Secondly, by his speeches and actions over several years Parsons appeared to be in tune with the needs of both his congregation and other workers in the district. As early as 1833, for example, he had been made an honorary member of the Stroud Friendly Institution, a self-help group set up by the town's workers to protect their needs in times of sickness.[59] From the pulpit, too, he had earned a reputation as a political preacher with outspoken views in opposition to the privileges of the aristocracy, the hypocrisy of the Anglican Church, the inappropriateness of the New Poor Law of 1834, and the levying of church rates.[60] Perhaps the most influential factor that led him to advance the cause of inter class co-operation was his energetic support of temperance. According to Stratford, Parsons 'saw its power to benefit the working classes, and he laboured to bring them under its influence'.[61] Parsons earned considerable respect amongst working men by his temperance convictions. Unlike some other Dissenting ministers in Stroud, he laid stress not only on moral concerns, but also on practical issues. These included personal health benefits, the application of science to improved diet (a belief he shared with Peter McDouall), and the need to re-direct disposable income saved from alcohol into boosting home demand for agricultural and manufacturing products.[62] All these arguments were expounded in his book, *Anti-Bacchus*, that was published in 1840; it was considered to be one of the most powerful publications of its kind on the damage caused by intoxicating drinks.[63]

Henry Vincent's teetotal initiative and Joseph Sturge's Complete Suffrage Union, both of which aimed more or less explicitly at promoting class conciliation, attracted considerable support in the West Country. Following the publication of Vincent's teetotal manifesto, a Democratic Teetotal Society was formed in Stroud early in January 1841,[64] and, according to R.G. Gammage, Sturge's conference plans were also well received.[65] Parsons himself responded positively to these developments. For one thing, he admired both men: Vincent he regarded as 'the most eloquent advocate of the people's rights';[66] whereas Sturge was nothing less than a 'real friend of the people'.[67] All three, too, had much in common: they were engaged in what they saw as a broadly based radical crusade against privilege, ignorance, 'beer and superstition'.[68] One tangible result of their combined influence was the formation of a politically inspired Society of Rechabites in Stroud in 1841.[69] Despite growing divisions within the national leadership, according to a report in the *Cheltenham Free Press*, members of this society hailed both O'Connor's *Northern Star* and Vincent's *National Vindicator* as 'guides to the lovers of freedom', an attitude that was undoubtedly encouraged in regular addresses by Parsons.[70] Another result was a more formal effort at inter-class cooperation. Aided by Rev. Burder in Stroud and Rev. J. Watts, a Baptist minister at Wotton-under-Edge, Parsons put into effect Sturge's plan for a 'cordial union' between the Repealers and the Chartists in Wotton, where it functioned under the careful eye of Watts, who acted as secretary.[71]

Shortly after his return from the Manchester Convocation of Ministers in August 1841, Parsons felt it necessary to prioritise his commitment to repeal, but he indicated that this preference simply resulted from the fact that 'he wanted more time to think about the Charter'.[72] This decision may also help explain why he only became more actively involved in the activities of Sturge's Complete Suffrage Union from the Autumn of 1843 onwards.

Although the Complete Suffrage movement went into widespread decline after the failure of the December 1842 conference, the situation in Gloucestershire provided something of a contrast over the next two years. Encouraged by lectures from visiting leaders, including Henry Vincent, R. K. Philp, Thomas Beggs and Joseph Sturge himself, Parsons continued promoting the Complete Suffrage cause and building up trust between Chartist elements and influential radical middle-class sympathisers in the County. Among the latter were Burder in Stroud, Symonds in Cheltenham Spa, and Samuel Bowly in Gloucester. Parsons helped ensure that tracts were circulated, lecture evenings organised and publicised, and even a Complete Suffrage almanac was made available.[73] From Ebley, Cirencester and Tewkesbury, where Parsons was active in this work of reconciliation, the *Cheltenham Free Press* was able to report in September 1843 that the 'best feelings between the classes prevail in these towns'.[74] It was a short step to Chartism proper.

Signs that Parsons had thought about the Charter long enough soon occurred. For the local Chartists 1843 was a year of relative decline,[75] but in May 1844 John Harris, the Stroud representative at a West of England Chartist delegate meeting, reported that a Chartist revival had recently taken place in the district 'on account of assistance rendered them by several Dissenting ministers'.[76] Almost certainly Parsons played a part in bringing about this rejuvenation and, following the repeal of the Corn Laws in June 1846, Chartism became his next great crusade. At annual sermons for the members of both the Ebley Sunday and Day schools in 1846 he outlined his core beliefs about the universal brotherhood of man, the democratic character of the gospel of Jesus Christ, and the aristocratic character of 'false religion'.[77] Late in March 1848, as the Chartist mass protest across the country gathered momentum, Parsons gave his unequivocal support to the activities of the re-constituted Stroud branch of the National Charter Association. At a public meeting attended by over five hundred people, including significantly some sympathetic shopkeepers and 'one or two woollen manufacturers', Parsons led the way. He openly pledged his support for the People's Charter, signed the National Petition, and seconded the resolution that led to the reappointment of well-respected and long serving branch officers. Significantly, too, the latter group arranged to hold future meetings not in a public house, but in one of the member's Coffee Rooms.[78] According to the report in the *Northern Star*:[79]

> the meeting was considered the best ever held in Stroud upon the question of the Charter. Signatures to the Petition are hourly increasing, and we hope by Saturday to number 3,000.

Undoubtedly Parsons' very public declaration of support at the meeting had provided a significant fillip to the movement.

By far his most significant contribution to the Chartist cause was his publication, between October 1847 and February 1849, of the monthly penny tracts addressed to the *Fustian Jackets and Smock Frocks*. The earliest bound edition, containing the first three – 'The State of the Polls, Masters and Men at the [1847] Election' and 'The Bible and the Six Points of the Charter' (in two parts) – appeared simultaneously in London and Stroud late in October 1847. The complete edition, which contained another fifteen lively pieces, was published in London in the spring of 1849. Among those of immediate interest to the Chartists were 'Radicalism an Essential Doctrine of Christianity', 'A Few Words for the Chartists – The Working Classes the Best Reformers', 'The Queen, the Aristocracy, and the People', and 'Physical Force and Moral Force'.[80]

The *Tracts* are a testimony to Parsons' genius as a publicist and polemicist. At one level they reveal his unique relationship with his large congregation, which he estimated at 'not less than a thousand' and 'mostly operatives' in social composition,[81] but he had a broader audience of working people in mind. The title of the *Tracts*, he explained in the first number, was a calculated gesture:[82]

> I address you as the Fustian Jackets and Frock Smocks of the neighbourhood, not only to compliment you on your useful and respectable garb, but, because from some observation on society, I have learnt that you have among you the largest amount of common sense.

As noted previously, the fustian cloth of everyday working-class life was an unmistakable symbol of class which reflected a new found working-class consciousness in popular radicalism that had been forged in the bitter experiences of the 1830s. For Chartists, Feargus O'Connor had imbued fustian with special significance by addressing his famous weekly epistles in the *Northern Star* to the 'fustian jackets, blistered hands and unshorn chins'.[83] Although Parsons did not claim that he was a working man, as O'Connor sometimes did, his gesture of supplication was equally significant as a recognition of the sentiments and expectations of working people, even in the towns and villages of rural England.[84] For Parsons, like William Sankey, honouring the common man had a religious dimension: 'From Genesis to Revelations', he argued 'we have denunciations against the ungodliness of the rich and at the same time the most tender sympathy towards the poor ... yet good men are excluded from the polls and parliament because they do not possess certain amounts of riches'.[85] Unlike Sankey, however, Parsons reserved his strongest criticisms for those near the top of society: 'We only demand that the lords shall not rob us of our property, destroy the majesty of the laws or the monarch, nor impoverish and ruin the land of our fathers'.[86] If the readers of the *Tracts* were offered an uncomplicated and uncompromising view of the world, it was one that, coming from the mouth of a former Leaguer and Complete Suffragist, helped to prepare the ground for the mid-Victorian consensus.[87] In Parsons' hands fustian was transformed from a symbol that seemed to promise class confrontation, to a token of the potential for class cooperation on a more equitable basis.

Not surprisingly, a common theme in the *Tracts* was the religious basis of radicalism, and it was this case that attracted a reviewer in the *Northern Star* who quoted a lengthy extract from 'The Bible and the Six Points of the Charter' that is worth lingering over. Parsons began by asking a rhetorical question that was dripping with cynicism:

> [I]s there a dissenting minister in the country so lost to shame as to say that he has any man in his congregation beyond the age of *twenty-one* who is unfit to vote or a member of parliament? If such a spiritual prodigy can be found, then the sooner he quits the pulpit the better. To be the professed enlightener of a congregation and to have so far neglected his duty as to have men under his charge who are too ignorant or wicked to be trusted with the franchise, is a reproach which few men will be ready to avow.

Rising to his task Parsons turned his attention specifically to the Church of England:

> if we believe the Bishops and Clergy, matters are ten thousand times better there; for all persons baptised by these successors of the Apostles are, the catechism asserts, 'made members of Christ, children of God, and inheritors of the Kingdom of Heaven' ... To say that 'a member of Christ, a child of God, and an inheritor of the Kingdom of Heaven', is too ignorant or too wicked to be entrusted with the franchise, is a libel on the Clergy, on the Church, and on Christianity.

For a veteran opponent of church rates one conclusion suggested itself: 'If the masses are not fit for the Suffrage, then in the name of justice what have the over-paid Clergy been doing with their time?' Parsons' peroration, however, contained a message that was more broadly applicable: 'Every Clergymen to be consistent must be an advocate for the Extension of the Suffrage. To deny its constitutional character would prove him ignorant of the political rights of man: to deny its equity would convict him of being unacquainted with the first principles of Christian rectitude ...'[88] Democratic institutions were also, Parsons pointed out in another *Tract*, more conducive to international peace, which would, in turn, lead to reduced expenditure on national defence.[89] Again this was based on a religious conviction of mankind's 'natural equality and fraternity': 'God has made of one blood all nations of men for to dwell on the face of all the earth ... The minister of religion who denies this is an infidel'.[90]

Since the People's Charter was sanctioned by the word of God, Parsons preached that it was man's sacred duty to agitate until 'this great principle became the law of the land'.[91] For all the depth of his conviction, however, he never advocated other than moral force. Following the events of 10 April in London in 1848 when some Chartists contemplated the use of force in the face of parliament's rejection of the last National Petition, Parsons urged his Chartist friends to pursue change only by peaceful means:[92]

> Do it by moral means alone. Not a pike, a blunderbuss, a brick-bat, or a match, must be found in your hands. In physical force your opponents are mightier than you, but in moral force you are ten thousand times stronger than they. The best way to prove that you deserve your rights, is to show that you respect the rights of others, and that you will not redress even a wrong by revenge, but by reason and justice alone. Your manner ought to demonstrate that *Fustian Jackets and Smock Frocks* have no connection with rudeness or vulgarity.

Despite the injunction to 'moral means' Parsons' *Tracts* shocked many people. The liberally inclined *Eclectic Review* felt, on balance, that in relation to the masses his zeal had led him 'into something very like the pernicious flattery of their prejudices and pride, which characterises the common herd of demagogues'. As a consequence, the editor felt, Parsons had 'injured his usefulness with the working people themselves, by descending too frequently to the vulgar arts which constitute almost the only claim of popular leaders to distinction'.[93] The *Nonconformist* was less circumspect: 'earnestness of purpose, vigour of thought and freshness of language', it observed, 'have secured for each deserved popularity'.[94] Not surprisingly, the *Tracts* attracted fulsome praise in the columns of the *Northern Star*. According to one of its reviewers, Parsons was to be in every way encouraged, because of his 'noble efforts for the emancipation of the millions and the establishment of those principles of public equity, without which the *preaching* of Christianity is but a mockery'.[95] The fustian jackets and frock smocks to whom Parsons paid homage no doubt agreed.

The *Star* followed its favourable review by advertising the *Tracts* as recommended reading, and notifying its readers of a series of lectures on 'The Brotherhood of Man', which Parsons was scheduled to give at the Zion Chapel in Whitechapel, London, commencing on 14 May 1848.[96] Between 1848 and 1850, Parsons continued to support fresh initiatives aimed at cross class collaboration between Chartists and sympathetic middle class radicals. He gave his backing both to Joseph Hume's ' Little Charter' agitation during 1848 and to Joshua Walmsley's National Parliamentary and Financial Reform Association in 1850.[97] Parsons' standing in the community was further strengthened by his involvement in the provincial activities of the British Peace Society. The local leader was the veteran of numerous radical campaigns, Samuel Bowly of Cirencester. By 1849, Bowly too had joined Parsons in identifying with the Chartists' cause. One of the most striking public examples of inter class cooperation occurred in January 1849 when both Parsons and Bowly joined the Cheltenham Chartists at a Peace Society meeting in the Cheltenham Town Hall to hear Richard Cobden lecture on the 'merits of arbitration and not war'.[98] Parsons was not a national leader of the campaign, but his close relationship with Bowly – a Sturge ally – locates him, not surprisingly, on the radical wing of the movement.[99]

Beyond Chartism, Parsons was also involved in a number of campaigns at the end of the 1840s and in the early 1850s. For example, when the Jewish Disabilities Bill was being considered at Westminster during 1848, he preached in favour of equal rights for Jews.[100] Most of his efforts were aimed at improving the condition of the working classes and, as always, religion and politics were inextricably linked. For example, his strong views on maintaining the sanctity of the Sabbath stemmed from the fact that he regarded it as 'the Poor Man's Property'.[101] This conviction even led him to write to the Earl of Derby in 1853 opposing the opening of the Crystal Palace on Sundays.[102] Locally, he took an active part in opposing the enclosure of Selsley Common, which he regarded as a 'People's Park'.[103] In language reminiscent of the kind used by the radical William Cobbett in the 1820s and 30s, Parsons reminded the aristocracy in 1852 that:[104]

> There is scarcely a law on our statute book which is more iniquitous than the law respecting enclosures. It is brimful of the old aristocratic injustice which framed the Corn Laws and which seems always to proceed on the principle that the poor must be robbed to enrich the rich.

Parsons saw himself, too, as the defender of working-class self-help in education. He therefore resisted any and every attempt at involvement on the part of the state. So strongly did he feel about this particular issue in the late 1840s that it led him to fall out publicly with two former Anti-Corn Law League allies. The civil servant Jelinger Symonds and the Stroud MP, W. H. Stanton, were both in favour of the extension of the state's role in elementary education. The general election campaign of 1847 afforded one opportunity to show his displeasure. Parsons attacked Symonds for his lack of political credibility as a prospective parliamentary candidate;[105] and against Stanton he unsuccessfully backed a third Liberal candidate in the actual contest for Stroud borough.[106]

By the spring of 1854 Parsons' health began to fail. In the summer of that year his Ebley friends made plans to present him with a testimonial for his enforced retirement. On 1 August nearly 1,400 people assembled at a tea party given in his honour in the chapel grounds. In addition to a 'purse of three hundred sovereigns', Parsons received £100 that was raised on the day; he was also given a Bible and stand. At the same ceremony his wife was presented with her husband's portrait. All the donations were, according to Stratford, 'honour to whom honour was due, and it was rendered by men of all classes and conditions'.[107] Parsons died six months later on 10 January 1855 aged 58 years and he was buried in his own chapel graveyard. On 23 September 1857 a granite obelisk was erected by public subscription over his grave and a marble monument, suitably inscribed as a record to his wide-ranging philanthropy, was placed in his old pulpit.[108]

Benjamin Parsons undoubtedly played a leading role in community politics and public activity in nineteenth century Gloucestershire. In many ways he was a natural leader. Gifted intellectually and with considerable oratorical skills, Parsons was able to help the weaker members of society precisely because he had been plunged into and experienced poverty himself. It left an indelible mark on his mind and he never forgot his humble roots. The opportunity of renewed social mobility – moving from lowly artisan to esteemed clergyman – only served to reinforce a personal belief in the power of the Bible as a radical book and that his life's mission was to bring about, on earth, the brotherhood of man. For Parsons, free trade and Chartism were both sanctioned by God and founded in natural justice. He also played a pivotal role in working-class educational and temperance schemes that sought to create a culture of respectability and self-reliance. Such activities found common ground with Henry Vincent's teetotal initiative of 1841 and Joseph Sturge's Complete Suffrage Union overtures of 1842. Parsons' involvement helps explain why inter-class contacts were more common in the manufacturing towns of Gloucestershire, than was the case in other centres up and down the country.

Towards the end of his life Parsons described himself as 'a Radical, but I am only a Conservative Radical'.[109] What he meant was that he was an old-fashioned radical: for all the genuine sympathy he displayed towards the plight of working men and women, he lacked an ability to shift his analysis of society's wrongs from that of 'Old Corruption' to one focused on the fraud and force used by a union of both land and industrial capital. His support for the men of business in the Gloucestershire cloth trade was unquestioning, and he worked tirelessly for their free trade cause before turning to help the Chartists. In his Ebley Day school and Sunday school, Parsons was in some ways an old-style paternalist. 'The only power I wish the people to have is that of intelligence, and strict and rigid morality,' he once remarked.[110] Although the curriculum and organisation of his school reflected current practice, the playgrounds, gardens, and the attitude to female education were revolutionary.[111]

For all his shortcomings, Parsons inspired trust amongst the working class. They looked up to him and respected his authority. Ultimately, it was through his involvement that Chartism became acceptable to the influential manufacturers and his fellow Dissenting ministers in Stroud and Ebley. In the wake of his public act of accession in 1848, support grew significantly and signatures to the National Petition appeared in their thousands. Parsons' nineteenth century biographer, Edwin Paxton Hood, who disliked the Chartist leaders, believed that by his political actions in the district, Parsons had 'in some measure' counteracted 'the wickedness and vice of Feargus O' Connor and his miserable band of simple dupes and ambitious knaves'.[112] It was a conclusion that left so much unsaid. Although class cooperation always remained at the top of his agenda, he embraced the 'fustian jackets and frock smocks' on their own terms by promoting moral and political reform without condescension and, by so doing, he anticipated important aspects of the mid-Victorian consensus. The *Eclectic Review* was correct: Parsons 'did remarkable work in a remarkable way'. His friend and colleague, the Rev. John Burder, provided another perceptive verdict on the nature and extent of Parsons' influence over the people:

> Valuable as those conservators of public peace are (the police force), a moral police is best of all. Such are ministers of Religion. To such a moral police has Stroud been mainly indebted for its quiet in times of distress and alarm … and of that moral police Benjamin Parsons may fairly be considered as having been a chief captain.[113]

Notes

[1] J. Stratford, *Benjamin Parsons, The Friend of the People*, Cirencester, 1864, and repr. in Stratford's *Good and Great Men of Gloucestershire: a series of biographical sketches with a brief history of the County*, Cirencester, 1867.

[2] *Eclectic Review*, November 1856. Parsons' nineteenth century biography, Edwin Paxton Hood, wrote for *Eclectic Review*.

[3] Stratford, *Benjamin Parsons*, p. 6; L. Stephens & S. Lee (eds), *Dictionary of National Biography*, Oxford, 1921, vol. xv, pp. 397-398.

[4] According to the *Dictionary of National Biography*, Parsons published thirteen books and pamphlets, but Hood listed twenty. See also P. M. Walmsley, 'Political, Religious and Social Aspects of Stroud Parliamentary Borough, 1830- 52', M. Litt. University of Bristol, 1990, p. 152.

[5] Hood's biography, published in London in 1856, is still the only comprehensive work available. Despite its hagiographic tendencies, it is certainly no work of fiction in its assessment. Eight years after Hood's authoritative work, Joseph Stratford wrote his short piece that was primarily intended to serve the interests of readers in Gloucestershire. About the same time the temperance historian and biographer, P. T. Winskill, attributed Parsons' achievements to the fact that he was an 'old

style Radical' See E. Paxton Hood (ed.), *The Earnest Minister: a Record of the Life and Selections from Posthumous and other Writings of the Rev. Benjamin Parsons of Ebley, Gloucestershire*, London, 1856; P. T. Winskill, *The Temperance Movement and its Workers*, London, 1893, pp. 217-218; and Winskill's *Temperance Standard Bearers of the Nineteenth Century*, vols. 1-2, Liverpool, 1897, p. 304. See also P. H. Fisher, *Notes and Recollections of Stroud*, Gloucester, 1871, pp. 50-53.

[6] C. Shaw, *When I was a Child*, 1903, repr., Sussex, 1977, p. 228.

[7] Apart from an entry in the *Dictionary of National Biography* in 1921, Parsons has featured in only three published scholarly works. In 1916 H. U. Faulkner made passing reference to him as an important 'political preacher' in his *Chartism and the Churches*, 1916, repr. London, 1970. Many years later Brian Harrison recalled Parsons' involvement in good causes, both in *Drink and the Victorians*, Pittsburgh, 1971, and *The Dictionary of Temperance Biography*, London, 1973. The only two studies relating specifically to the life of Benjamin Parsons that have been written in the last one hundred years are unpublished. See O.R. Ashton, 'Radicalism and Chartism in Gloucestershire, 1832-1847', Unpublished PhD thesis, University of Birmingham, 1980, particularly pp. 98-100, pp. 271-280, & pp. 319-322; Walmsley 'Political, Religious and Social Aspects of Stroud Parliamentary Borough', chapters 10, 11, & 13. Parsons' role as a Chartist in Ebley is briefly referred to by Paul Pickering in 'And Your Petitioners &c. Chartist Petitioning in Popular Politics 1838-48', *English Historical Review*, vol. cxvi, no. 466, April, 2001, p. 374.

[8] Stratford, *Benjamin Parsons, The Friend of the People*, pp. 3 & p. 12.

[9] *Dictionary of National Biography*, vol. xv, p. 393.

[10] See Winskill, *Temperance Standard Bearers*, p. 172.

[11] E. Royle, *Modern Britain. A Social History*, London, 1997, pp. 295-296.

[12] G. W. Kirby, *The Elect Lady*, London, 1972, revised 1990, with commendation by Rev. Dr A. Skevington Wood on http://www.cofhconnexion.org.uk/electlady.html, p. 37.

[13] Walmsley, 'Political, Religious and Social Aspects of Stroud Parliamentary Borough', p. 150.

[14] Stratford, *Benjamin Parsons*, pp. 6-11.

[15] Walmsley, 'Political, Religious and Social Aspects of Stroud Parliamentary Borough', p. 151.

[16] Winskill, *The Temperance Movement and its Workers*, p. 217.

[17] Hood (ed.), *The Earnest Minister*, pp. 52-53, 67-72.

[18] Fisher, *Notes and Recollections of Stroud*, p. 53.

[19] Ibid.

[20] Walmsley, 'Political, Religious and Social Aspects of Stroud Parliamentary Borough', p. 153.

[21] Hood (ed.) *The Earnest Minister*, p. 67.

[22] B. Parsons, *Education. The Natural Want and Birthright of Every Human Being, Or Education as it is and as it ought to be , and the only Scriptural Preparation for the Millennium*, 1845, repr, London, 1850, n.p.

[23] Ibid.

[24] Gloucester City Library, HC3.8: Advertisement for *The Mental and Moral Dignity of Woman*.

[25] *Eclectic Review*, November 1842.

[26] Walmsley, 'Political, Religious and Social Aspects of Stroud Parliamentary Borough', p. 154.

[27] We are grateful to Alex Tyrrell for this point.

[28] Hood (ed.), *The Earnest Minister*, pp. 282-283.

[29] Walmsley, 'Political, Religious and Social Aspects of Stroud Parliamentary Borough', p. 165.

[30] W. R. Williams, *The Parliamentary History of the County of Gloucester, 1213-1898*, Hereford, 1898, pp. 225-226. Russell was first elected, unopposed, in May 1835, and then re-elected in 1837, along with G. P. Scrope.

[31] Ibid.

[32] *Cheltenham Free Press*, 13 December 1845. The speakers were: Benjamin Parsons, William Hollis, John Goding and Samuel Charles Harper. See also J. Goding, *Norman's History of Cheltenham*, Cheltenham, 1863, p. 572. The combined opposition reached its peak in March 1847. See also the chapter on Henry Solly in this volume.

[33] *Dictionary of National Biography*, vol. ii, p. 871. Borthwick's pro-slavery meetings were fre-

quently interrupted or broken up by the intervention of Sam Bowly, who followed him around on his tour of Gloucestershire in 1833. Borthwick became an MP briefly for Evesham in 1837; later in life he became editor of the *Morning Post*.

[34] Stratford, *Benjamin Parsons*, p. 9.

[35] Walmsley, 'Political, Religious and Social Aspects of Stroud Parliamentary Borough', p. 164.

[36] Winskill, *The Temperance Movement and its Workers*, p. 127.

[37] Walmsley, 'Political, Religious and Social Aspects of Stroud Parliamentary Borough', pp. 165-166.

[38] See *Cheltenham Free Press*, 2 January 1841. See also 12 December 1840; B. Harrison, 'Teetotal Chartism', *History*, 1973, pp. 193-217, particularly p. 201.

[39] Jelinger Symonds was an Assistant Commissioner for the south of Scotland on the Commission of Inquiry into the condition of Handloom Weavers, 1840. He was also a leading authority on elementary and technical education. For an outline of his career, see Goding, *Norman's History of Cheltenham*, p. 481.

[40] *Cheltenham Free Press*, 22 January 1842.

[41] J. De L. Mann, *The Cloth Industry in the West of England*, Oxford, 1971, p. 105.

[42] T. Excell, *A Sketch of the Circumstances which Providentially led to the Repeal of the Corn and Animal Laws*, 1847, repr. Dursley, 1903. Excell was one of the weavers' leaders in Gloucestershire in the 1820s and 1830s but he was not involved in Chartism.

[43] *Place Papers*, 34,245A, Letter 68 from Thomas Farr, Chartist, of Stroud, 21 Feb.1839. Farr wrote 'Almost all the master manufacturers are Whigs and staunch supporters of that insidious tyrant Russell ... The middle classes here, as elsewhere, have had their attention engrossed by the Corn Law question and imagine the repeal of these laws will be their salvation'.

[44] Stratford, *Benjamin Parsons, The Friend of the People*, p. 9.

[45] *Anti-Bread Tax Circular*, 30 December 1841.

[46] Walmsley, 'Political, Religious and Social Aspects of Stroud Parliamentary Borough', p. 173.

[47] Stratford, *Benjamin Parsons*, p. 9. For the League see P. A. Pickering & A. Tyrrell, *The People's Bread: A History of the Anti-Corn Law League*, Leicester, 2000, chapter 1.

[48] *Report Of The Conference Of Ministers Of Ministers Of All Denominations On The Corn Laws, Held In Manchester, August 17th, 18th, And 20th, 1841. With A Digest Of The Documents Contributed During The Conference*, Manchester, 1841, pp. 5-18; *Anti-Bread Tax Circular*, 26 August 1841.

[49] *Anti-Bread Tax Circular*, 10 February, 24 February 1842.

[50] Walmsley, 'Political, Religious and Social Aspects of Stroud Parliamentary Borough', p. 174.

[51] *Anti-Bread Tax Circular*, 17 January 1843.

[52] *Cheltenham Free Press*, 27 January 1844.

[53] Hood (ed.), *The Earnest Minister*, pp. 269-270. See also *Cheltenham Examiner*, 15 March 1843; *Cheltenham Free Press*, 18 March 1843. Colonel T.P. Thompson, the veteran radical, and R. R. Moore, a League lecturer, spoke. Scrope and Stanton were sent a petition signed by 2,000 people.

[54] Stratford, *Benjamin Parsons*, p. 9.

[55] *Gloucester Journal*, 22 May 1841; *Anti-Bread Tax Circular*, 21 April 1843. For reports of the only two instances of public confrontation between the Leaguers and the Chartists.

[56] Walmsley, 'Political, Religious and Social Aspects of Stroud Parliamentary Borough', p. 178.

[57] Ibid., pp. 179-180.

[58] *Place Papers*, 34,245A, Letter 68 from Thomas Farr, Chartist. Farr indicated that the Chartist numbers were steadily increasing with 90 members in Stroud and 100 in Ebley.

[59] Gloucester Library: Rules and Regulations of Stroud Friendly Institution, Stroud, 1833. Burder was also an honorary member.

[60] Hood (ed.), *The Earnest Minister*, pp. 251-256, 269-271.

[61] Stratford, *Benjamin Parsons*, p. 9.

[62] Hood (ed.), *The Earnest Minister*, pp. 314-317; Harrison, *Drink and the Victorians*, p. 368.

[63] Stratford, *Benjamin Parsons*, p. 9.

[64] *Northern Star*, 2 January 1841.

[65] R.G. Gammage, *History of the Chartist Movement, 1837-1854*, 1854, repr. New York, 1969, p. 198.

[66] B. Parsons, *Tract for Fustian Jackets*, London, 1849, No. 3, 'The Bible and the Six Points of the Charter', p. 19.

[67] Ibid., no.3, 'State of the Polls, Masters and Men at Elections' (1847), p. 5.

[68] *English Chartist Circular*, vol. 1, no.17, p. 68. See also B. Harrison, 'Teetotal Chartism', p. 201.

[69] *Northern Star*, 14 August 1841.

[70] *Cheltenham Free Press*, 4 June 1842.

[71] Ashton, 'Radicalism and Chartism in Gloucestershire', pp. 177 & 211. One result of this union was the election of Bronterre O'Brien as their delegate to the Complete Suffrage Union conference in Birmingham in December 1842

[72] *Cheltenham Free Press*, 30 October 1841.

[73] Based on reports of Complete Suffrage activity in the *Cheltenham Free Press*, 3 December 1842, 23 September 1843, 14 October 1843, 23 December 1843, 13 January 1844.

[74] Ibid., 23 September 1843.

[75] *Northern Star*, 12 August 1843.

[76] Ibid, 11 May 1844.

[77] Walmsley, 'Political, Religious and Social Aspects of Stroud Parliamentary Borough', p. 156.

[78] *Northern Star*, 8 April 1848.

[79] Ibid.

[80] The full list also included: 'Goody Goody, or State Education a National Insult'; 'The Chief of the Slaughter-Men and our National Defences'; 'The Knife and not the Sword, or Civilisation versus War and Desolation'; 'The Radicalism of Moses'; 'The Shaking of the Nations and the Downfall of Tyranny'; 'The Powers that be'; 'Who are the Lewd Fellows of the Baser Sort?'; 'A Few Words for the French'; 'The Potato Blight, And How to Prevent it'. For this book we have consulted the set in the Dorothy Thompson Special Collection at Staffordshire University. All have recently been reprinted in G. Claeys (ed.), *The Chartist Movement in Britain 1836-1850*, London, 2001, vol. 4.

[81] Parsons, 'The Bible and the Six Points of the Charter', p. 17.

[82] Parsons, 'The State of the Polls, or Masters and Men at the Election', p. 2.

[83] For O'Connor's first use of the expression see *Northern Star*, 24 February 1838.

[84] For the significance of fustian see P. A. Pickering, 'Class Without Words: Symbolic Communication in the Chartist Movement', *Past and Present*, no. 112, August 1986, pp. 144-162.

[85] Parsons, ' The Bible and the Six Points of the Charter', p. 22.

[86] Parsons, ' The Queen, the Aristocracy, and the People', p. 11; Stratford, *Benjamin Parsons*, p. 13.

[87] For Livesey see Pickering & Tyrrell, *The People's Bread*, pp. 153-4.

[88] *Northern Star*, 23 October 1847.

[89] Parsons, 'The Chief of the Slaughter-Men and our National Defences', p. 11.

[90] Parsons, 'The Radicalism of Moses', p. 3.

[91] Parsons, 'The Chief of the Slaughter-Men and our National Defences', p. 1.

[92] Parsons, 'The State of the Polls, or Masters and Men at the Election', p. 9; Stratford, *Benjamin Parsons*, p. 10.

[93] *Eclectic Review*, November 1856.

[94] *Nonconformist*, 22 March 1848.

[95] *Northern Star*, 23 October 1847.

[96] Ibid., 6 May 1848, 1 July 1848.

[97] *Cheltenham Free Press*, 17 June 1848; 25 May 1850

[98] Ibid., 3 February 1849.

[99] See A. Tyrrell, *Joseph Sturge and the Moral Radical Party in Early Victorian Britain*, London, 1987, pp. 166, 168 & 193; Harrison, *Dictionary of Temperance Biography*, p. 13. Parsons' respect for Bowly was made clear in his Tract No. 10: 'That distinguished philanthropist and christian, Mr.

Samuel Bowly, whose character stands so deservedly high throughout the city and the county of Gloucester, was lately called upon to defend himself for having attended a meeting of the operatives that he might give them the aid of his counsel. The religious people were almost in hysterics on the subject; some seemed ready to faint'. See Parsons, 'A Few Words for the Chartists – The Working Classes the Best Reformers', p. 8; Ashton, 'Radicalism and Chartism in Gloucestershire', pp. 296-297. Parsons is not mentioned by Martin Ceadel, *The Origins of War Prevention: The British Peace Movement and International Relations, 1730-1854*, Oxford, 1996.

[100] Walmsley, 'Political, Religious and Social Aspects of Stroud Parliamentary Borough', p. 163.
[101] Stratford, *Benjamin Parsons*, p. 11.
[102] B. Parsons, *A Letter to the Earl of Derby on the Cruelty and Injustice of opening the Crystal Palace on the Sabbath*, London, 1853.
[103] Ibid., p. 157.
[104] Hood (ed.), *The Earnest Minister*, pp. 253-254.
[105] Gloucester Record Office: Letter from Jelinger Symonds to Benjamin Parsons on the Election at Stroud, Stroud, 1847, pp. 1-10.
[106] Walmsley, 'Political, Religious and Social Aspects of Stroud Parliamentary Borough', p. 167. See also Williams, *The Parliamentary History of the County of Gloucestershire*, p. 226: W. H. Stanton (Liberal) 563; G. P. Scrope (Liberal) 541; Merryweather Turner (Liberal) 176. Parsons also wrote a 2d pamphlet at the time, *The Unconstitutional Character of the Government Plan of Education*, London, 1847.
[107] Stratford, *Benjamin Parsons*, p. 11.
[108] Ibid., p. 14.
[109] Ibid., p. 13.
[110] Ibid.
[111] In emphasising this we are taking a different view to Walmsley, 'Political, Religious and Social Aspects of Stroud Parliamentary Borough', p. 154.
[112] Hood (ed.), *The Earnest Minister*, pp. 271 & 288.
[113] Ibid., pp. 405-408. Extract from a letter by Burder to Hood, Clifton, 5 April 1856.

CHAPTER 5

'THE CHAPLAIN OF THE MANCHESTER CHARTISTS'[1]: THE REVEREND JAMES SCHOLEFIELD (1790-1855)

17 August 1842, was a busy day in the life of the Reverend James Scholefield. Amidst the turmoil and confusion of the 'Plug Plot' riots that had brought the factories of Manchester and Salford to a standstill for over a week,[2] his religious institution in Ancoats became the focal point of national Chartist politics. About a mile and a half from the centre of Manchester, Scholefield's 'Round Chapel' in Every Street was located on the fringe of working-class Ancoats in the fork between Great Ancoats Street and the River Medlock.[3] The Chapel was a 'commodious' structure with a substantial basement often referred to by contemporaries as the 'School Room'.[4] Attached to the Chapel by covered passageways were two buildings: overlooking the Medlock at the rear, was a building known as the 'Surgery' or 'Apothecary' and, on the west side, there was a two storey dwelling house where Scholefield lived with his five surviving children.[5] Surrounding these buildings was Scholefield's privately owned cemetery covering an area of three or four acres, where untold numbers of Mancunians were buried for over three decades after the establishment of his Chapel in the early 1820s. Part of the cemetery under a window of his home was reserved as Scholefield's family plot where he had buried his wife, Charlotte, and his three youngest children in the space of four months during 1835.[6] In August 1842, however, by far the most prominent feature in this landscape was the nearly completed Monument to Henry Hunt, the leader of the previous generation of radicals. Located in the portion of the burial ground facing Every Street and standing some thirty feet in height, the Hunt Monument was constructed of stone and consisted of a 'plain, neat pyramidal shaft, springing from a square pedestal' and supporting a statue of Hunt. Underneath the obelisk were 'spacious vaults … intended as the depositories of the remains of those who shall distinguish themselves in promoting the principles advocated by the late Henry Hunt'.[7] On 17 August, not only was Scholefield host to this symbolic tribute to a past champion of freedom, but also to a National Chartist Conference attended by the man reputed to be 'Hunt's successor', Feargus O'Connor.

At nine o'clock on the morning of the 17th, under the watchful eye of the Manchester police, about forty Chartist delegates joined O'Connor in the Chapel

for the commencement of the deliberations.[8] Scholefield was not an official delegate to the Conference, but he was thoroughly involved in the proceedings. On
the previous evening, for example, he had attended a Tea Party in commemora-
tion of the 23rd Anniversary of the massacre of Peterloo as O'Connor's '*locum
tenens*'. There he had apologised for the absence of O'Connor and the delegates
and had begged 'immediate leave of absence for himself' to join them in discussions on matters of 'national importance'.[9] No one doubted his right to be
present. While the delegates deliberated in his Chapel on 17 August, the level of
Scholefield's participation in the proceedings was only reduced by a host of other
tasks that demanded his attention. As 'one of those who had taken upon himself
the benevolent office of providing for a part of the grievously distressed population' during this, the worst economic depression of the nineteenth century, he
was also occupied 'distributing soup tickets to the starving poor who crowded
his house'.[10] It was also indicative of his sympathies that he had reluctantly been
obliged to turn down an approach for the use of his premises on that day by
the body that had nominal control over the 'Plug Plot' strikers – the Trades'
Delegates Conference.[11] Meanwhile, in the basement under the Chapel, his day
school proceeded uninterrupted. Adding to the pressure on him, Scholefield
had 'no less than four funerals to celebrate in the burial ground attached to his
premises' and, interspersed between the performance of these rites of passage,
he was 'busily engaged in his surgery' tending to the physical needs of 'several
patients' that came to consult him on that day.[12]

The 1842 Conference highlights Scholefield's importance as a figure in
Manchester Chartism and the Hunt Monument is a testimony to the continuity
of his career in local radical politics from Peterloo to the early 1850s.[13] His other
activities that day provide a small sample of the variety of his public concerns,
which made him a well known figure as a preacher, writer, teacher, philanthropist, surgeon, vegetarian, teetotaller and municipal politician. Scholefield was an
important local leader and on this level the need to study him is self evident,[14]
but his significance was greater even than his local reputation. Firstly, his career
underscores the importance of the role of what Max Weber called 'charismatic
authority' in community life,[15] especially amidst the harsh reality of the nineteenth century city. At a time when Frederick Engels found the doors of houses
in working-class Manchester barricaded against grim modernity, here was a
man whose door was never closed, and whose vision of a better world could
be seen despite the smoke and grime that pervaded the industrial landscape.[16]
Scholefield's congregation was not large, even by the standards of the day – in
1851 the *Census* enumerators recorded 334 worshipers at the Round Chapel[17]
– and his chosen sect, the Bible Christians of Manchester and Salford, were often
confused with the Methodist sect of the same name, but these are poor indicators of his influence.[18] Like Benjamin Parsons, Scholefield was what we would
nowadays call a cult-figure. Among his congregation and beyond it he inspired

an extraordinary degree of devotion that reflected both a widespread appreciation of his philanthropy, and a belief in his almost mystical powers of healing.
We only have to think of John Wesley to recall how potent the mix of faith and
medicine could be. At the same time, Scholefield exemplifies the importance
of practical reform in nineteenth century radicalism, combining, as he did, a
Cobbett-like opposition to taxation and central government with a pragmatic
concern for roads and refuse. Here was a man who was not afraid to get mud
on his boots. Finally, Scholefield's visiting card presented him as the 'Rev. Dr.
Scholefield V.D.M. [*Verbi Dei Minister* – Preacher of God's Word]'. This self-
adopted public image highlights the centrality of religion in his life, which, in
turn, makes his career an ideal case study of the development and influence of
religious forms of radicalism in the age of the Chartists.[19]

Scholefield was born in 1790 at Colne Bridge, near Huddersfield in Yorkshire,
the son of Daniel and Rebecca Scholefield. Of his early childhood, education and
his formative religious influences, no information has yet come to light. During
the long eighteenth century Colne Bridge had never been more than a tiny ham-
let renowned for a local forge which had operated since the early 1600s.[20] The
nature of Daniel Scholefield's employment is not known, but his son, clergyman though he was, identified himself as a working man. Discounting his rise
in social standing, in 1841 Scholefield told a meeting of local Chartists 'that the
character of a labouring man was the greatest honour he could possess'; he was
'a working man like themselves' who 'at times wore fustian'.[21] It was a gesture of
supplication and respect similar to those of O'Connor and Parsons (see chapter 4),
but the lingering image of Scholefield is very different: the preacher, the healer, the
friend of the people, was immediately recognisable amidst the squalor of working-
class Manchester by his distinctive orange cassock.[22]

Around the time of Scholefield's birth the Colne Bridge forge closed; whether
this precipitated the family move to Manchester (or whether James moved by
himself) is not clear. What is known is that he had removed to Manchester by
1809 when, as a nineteen-year-old youth, he participated in the Conference that
heralded the formation of a new sect: the Bible Christians. It was the defining
moment of his life. The sect began as a vehicle of one man, William Cowherd,
who had himself come to Manchester in the late 1780s to fill the position of
Curate at St. John's Church of England in Deansgate. It was here that Cowherd
first became acquainted with the writings of the Swedish theologian, Emanuel
Swedenborg. The Rector at St. John's, John Clowes, had long been a devotee of
Swedenborgian doctrine, but he did not favour the formation of an independent
sect. In this he differed from his enthusiastic Curate who, in 1792, resigned from
St. John's and laid the foundation stone of a Swedenborgian Chapel in Peter
Street. Cowherd officiated at Peter Street until 1800 when, in response to dis-
sension that had arisen in his congregation, he moved to establish Manchester's
second Swedenborgian Chapel – known as Christ Church – in King Street,

Salford. Cowherd continued to preach within the Swedenborgian fold for nine years until 1809 when, following further disputation, he oversaw the formation of the schismatic sect.[23]

From this time onward Scholefield assisted Cowherd as Deacon of the King Street Chapel. In 1815, following the establishment of a second Chapel near the Cavalry Barracks in Hulme, Scholefield participated in the running of both Chapels. By this stage he been ordained by his idiosyncratic mentor. After Cowherd's death in 1816, the future of the Church rested largely in his hands and in those of other founding members such as Joseph Brotherton, future MP for Salford.[24] In 1818 Scholefield assumed control of the Hulme Chapel, whilst Brotherton, whom Scholefield had ordained, assumed the main responsibility for King Street. Scholefield continued to officiate at Hulme until 1823 when 'differences arose among the members' which led to the foundation, at his own expense, of the Round Chapel in Ancoats, where he preached until his death in 1855.[25]

Presented in this way, the facts of Scholefield's religious history provide little insight into the nature of his beliefs, but, as E.P. Thompson reminded us in his seminal *Making of the English Working Class*, during the 1790s the Swedenborgian Church of the New Jerusalem prepared artisans 'for more in-tellectual and mystical millennarial beliefs'.[26] Certainly Swedenborgians and, as their name suggests, Bible Christians set great store by the Bible which was deemed to be the literal word of God: the declaration from the 1809 Conference insisted that Bible Christian theology was 'grounded on the literal expression of sacred scripture'.[27] This implies a rigid scriptural fundamentalism that is entirely misleading: it was the process by which the Bible was to be read and interpreted which set them apart from orthodox Christianity.

Swedenborg's doctrine of 'correspondence' – the inter-relationship between physical and spiritual existence – allowed man, he argued, 'to enter intellectu-ally into the mysteries of faith'.[28] If the revelation of 'correspondence' earned Swedenborg the title of mystic, it also accommodated a rationalist element of his theology. Before he turned to religious inquiry, Swedenborg had achieved emi-nence as a scientist – during the early 1700s he published treatises on mathemat-ics, geology, cosmology, chemistry, physics, mineralogy and planetary theory.[29] Through his concept of 'correspondence' the Bible was open to re-interpreta-tion for its 'true' meaning and, crucially, could be reconciled with the findings of natural science. The story of Adam and Eve, for example, was considered allegorical: a description of the spiritual development of man and therefore not in contradiction with eighteenth century scientific theories on the origin of the species.[30] In Britain, Swedenborg's reconciliation of science and faith in a form of allegorical Christianity became part of a wider tradition which, as J.F.C. Harrison has written, offered intellectuals 'a rational, non-credal religion which did not offend their scientific interests'.[31]

The Bible Christians can be located firmly within this tradition of religious rationalism. Like many individuals in late eighteenth and early nineteenth century Britain, Cowherd shared Swedenborg's passion for scientific and technical inquiry: he 'dabbled in physic' and was known as a Doctor; he studied practical chemistry and astronomy using the dome of the King Street Chapel as an observatory and laboratory.[32] Natural science was more than a hobby, it was part and parcel of religious observance. According to one commentator in 1815, the form of public worship adopted by the Bible Christians 'consists chiefly in reading a portion of the Scriptures which are elucidated by the reading [and] bringing forth the phenomena of nature in support of the truth of them'.[33] 'We do not really *believe*', Cowherd wrote, 'what we can not rationally *understand*'.[34]

The importance of scientific inquiry was also reflected in an interest in education: in 1819, for example, during Scholefield's period as Minister, a group of Bible Christians established a Sunday school and an association called the Hulme Philosophical Society in connection with Christ Church. According to local recollection, the Philosophical Society was the earliest 'institution in this country for the dissemination of scientific knowledge' but, rather, it is important to see the Hulme Society as typical of a proliferation of similar groups devoted to scientific education that peppered Britain at this time.[35] Throughout his career Scholefield maintained an active involvement in scientific and general education: during the early 1820s he toured various parts of Lancashire lecturing to societies known as Philosophical Enquiring Christians and, later, his Round Chapel in Ancoats housed a Sunday school and separate day schools for boys and girls which were run by his son and daughter respectively. A survey in 1835 showed that the three Bible Christian Sunday Schools in Manchester and Salford catered for about 500 children. By 1840 Scholefield's Every Street Sunday School alone catered for 482 scholars. In the late 1830s, the Round Chapel also served as a branch lecture room of the Manchester Parthenon (an organisation intended to be a 'working man's university') and, later in the 1840s, Scholefield was involved in the controversial Lancashire Public Schools Association that sought to promote elementary education free from sectarian controversy and the control of the Church of England.[36]

Scholefield's work in the educational field was a continuation of the pioneering efforts of his mentor. Established in about 1800 under the ambitious title of the Salford Grammar School and Academy of Sciences, Cowherd's school was reputed to be the earliest Sunday School in the Manchester and Salford area.[37] It was here that Scholefield was educated. In addition to the study of theology and natural science including medicine, the liberal education he received in this institution is captured in a description of the Academy's annual speech day in 1811. The young Scholefield's contribution was to present an address on 'Cruelty to Animals',[38] and to participate in a performance of Horace's 'Secular Ode' rendered in Latin, and Homer's 'Achilles Shield' in the original Greek.[39] The apparent richness of his education was also evident in his subsequent writings which touched on subjects as diverse as Malthus' theory of 'Surplus Population' and the chemical properties of the grape.[40]

Later in life Scholefield stated that he had 'not been brought up in the school of sectarianism and bigotry',[41] but, if anything, this was an understatement of his experience. The cornerstone of his education with its emphasis on scientific inquiry as a mechanism for scriptural interpretation was the encouragement of independent thought and religious heterodoxy. The Bible Christians adhered to the intellectual process of rational inquiry implicit in Swedenborg's doctrine of 'correspondence', although in other respects they deviated from mainstream followers of the Swedish theologian. Cowherd's secession from the Church of the New Jerusalem was due, ostensibly, to his decision to impose a strict rule of total abstinence from animal food and intoxicating liquor on his congregation which orthodox Swedenborgians considered a pernicious doctrine.[42] This was – and remained in local consideration – the most distinctive feature of the new sect,[43] but there were other organisational and theological differences which led to schism. Although Cowherd did not sever his ties to the Manchester Swedenborgians, his move to King Street in 1800 was his response to what he felt was a lack of intellectual freedom.[44] By 1809 he had 'refused to place Swedenborg's writings on a level claimed by some of his followers' and he feared the establishment of a 'new ecclesiastical hierarchy'. As the Declaration of 1809 made clear, the new sect accepted Swedenborg 'as an interpreter of singular power, but his writings were not held to be otherwise authoritative'.[45] The great 'interpreter' had provided the intellectual process for rational theological inquiry. With this obvious indebtedness to Swedenborg, Cowherd subsequently set out his own theological interpretation in a seven hundred page volume entitled *Facts Authentic in Science and Religion: Designed to Illustrate a New Translation of the Bible* that was posthumously published in parts between 1818 and 1820.

For the same reason we cannot see Scholefield simply as the successor to Cowherd's particular views. Cowherd's distrust of 'ecclesiastical hierarchy', characteristic of many schismatic groups which resisted the transition from 'sect' to a more formalised denomination, was enshrined in the heterodox Declaration which heralded the formation of the Bible Christians:[46]

> they did not form a sectarian church under any particular denomination from man; that they wished to be simple *Bible Christians*; that they held all doctrines, but not all the ideas, of all the Christian sects – so far as they are respectively grounded on the literal expression of sacred scripture ...

This attitude was a central part of Scholefield's religious heritage. As early as 1820 he stated: 'I am not attached to any sect in particular. I and my flock conform ourselves to the scriptures, and act according to them'.[47] It was a declaration of independence. Just as Cowherd's endeavours had led him to new understandings, it was inevitable that Scholefield would apply the same intellectual process to arrive at his own revelations. Although he was often referred to as a 'Cowherdite', Scholefield was, in his own words, an advocate for the 'exercise of reason in the vigorous mind'.[48] After his move to Ancoats in 1823 Scholefield's intellectual independence was enhanced by his social independence. As the owner of his own Chapel in a small schismatic sect he was not responsible to a Church bureaucracy and, in theological matters, was pretty much a law unto himself. He was not, however, without responsibility. In 1821 he had married Charlotte Walker, and the following year the first of their eight children was born. Not surprisingly, the child was named William.[49]

Some three decades after William Cowherd's resignation from the Church of England, the Bible Christians had travelled an enormous distance from orthodox Anglicanism to the very edge of Christianity. While Swedenborgians and Bible Christians adhered to the doctrine of the supreme divinity of Jesus Christ, their denial of the Holy Trinity placed them closer to deism. For many individuals an allegorical form of Christianity, such as that offered by Swedenborg, was part of an intellectual progression that led to deism and on to secularism.[50] One of Scholefield's flock at the Hulme Chapel, Rowland Detrosier, is a good example. Under Scholefield's guidance Detrosier had preached in the Bible Christian faith during the 1820s, but he later seceded to found a Society for Universal Benevolence on explicitly deist principles and, shortly afterwards, under the influence of Richard Carlile and Robert Taylor, 'the Devil's Chaplain', joined the ranks of infidelity.[51] That Scholefield did not take these final steps mattered little from a contemporary Anglican point of view. Reports of Scholefield's 'blasphemous discourses', for example, convinced one indignant Stockport Magistrate to write to the Home Office to insist that he be reported to the Society for the Suppression of Vice. 'His scoffing and reviling of some of the passages of the New Testament', the Magistrate continued, 'are not to be borne by Christians'.[52] Nor was Carlile himself convinced that Scholefield was not an infidel after all:[53]

> the sect of Bible Christians is so mixed up with infidelity, or made up with infidels, that it is to me incomprehensible, unless I may be allowed to suppose that they are all infidels, and that they consider their pretended Christianity to be a useful expediency for the undermining of other forms of Christianity. Such was the inference I drew from such conversation as I had with Mr Scholefield.

Magistrates had due cause to fear Scholefield: in early nineteenth century Britain, his mix of heterodox theology and rationalism was a potentially volatile one. Although he did not go as far as Carlile, who enlisted the 'assistance of MEN OF SCIENCE' to demonstrate that all religion was 'a species of madness',[54] Scholefield employed the intellectual process of rational inquiry, known as zeteticism, to offer a radically deviant alternative to Anglican orthodoxy. By challenging Anglican hegemony Scholefield was threatening the entire social order

that rested on the notion of 'Church and King'. Even a by-product of his rational
religion, the promotion of education, was regarded as subversive. The Tory elite
had long been opposed to the spread of even the most basic education among
the working classes (even reading, it was argued, enabled the people to read sedition[55]), so it is not difficult to understand why they reacted with horror when
the Bible Christians advertised their educational institutions as, in Detrosier's
words, 'the UNIVERSITIES OF THE POOR'. Attending scientific lectures in the
Round Chapel that were 'peculiarly suited to the working classes' could only end
in tears.[56] Not surprisingly, the local opposition to the first Government grant
for education in 1833 was led by Reverend Hugh Stowell, Rector of an Anglican
Church in Salford, who was renowned as an arch-Evangelical and later a strident
critic of Chartism and Owenism.[57]

There was never any doubt that Scholefield would bring 'all those lights which
are furnished to him' to bear elsewhere in society; his religion was a public one.
On many occasions during his public life, Scholefield explained his actions according to a notion of duty to the public good. In 1820, for example, he argued
that it was his duty to 'encourage every institution which is calculated to promote the instruction of youth and the welfare of society'. Twenty years later his
view had not changed. In January 1840 Scholefield explained to a meeting organised to support Chartists arrested for rioting in Newport during the crisis of
1839 that he acted 'from a sense of duty'. He had, he insisted, 'sacrificed private
feeling and interest to public good'.[58] This notion of civic duty and self-sacrifice
was an attitude strongly encouraged by Swedenborg. In *Heaven and its Wonders,
and Hell: From Things Heard and Seen*, Swedenborg had argued that 'spiritual
life finds its fields of action in moral and civil life, because spiritual life consists
in willing well, and moral and civil life in doing well...'[59]

Swedenborg's injunction was echoed in a stanza of Scholefield's 1841 edition
of *Select Hymns for the Use of Bible Christians*, which were 'calculated to cherish
more fully a spirit of true devotion, candid opinion and mutual benevolence':[60]

> For his [God's] own sake, no duty can he ask,
> The Common Welfare is our only task.

Many of Scholefield's activities – his participation in the Temperance Movement
and the Vegetarian Society for instance – were identified with particular tenets
of his religious creed, but Swedenborg's ideal that 'the life of religion is to do
good'[61] was reflected in every cause he championed. For him religion was never
a narrowly circumscribed form of ecclesiastical practice; it was a commitment to
the transformation of society. In early nineteenth century Britain such an aspiration, defined by reason and heterodoxy, marked him as a dangerous man.

Scholefield's public career abounded with good causes. In January 1840 he
presided at the annual dinner of the Manchester Temperance Society, a posi-

tion which reflected an involvement with the organised temperance movement stretching back at least a decade. When, in 1809, Cowherd insisted that Bible Christians renounce intoxicating drink, they probably became Britain's earliest total abstainers and, as early as 1832, a Manchester newspaper carried notices of temperance meetings in Every Street. By 1835 the flourishing Every Street branch of the Manchester and Salford Temperance Society inserted a tribute in the press:[62]

> The Committee bear the most honourable testimony in favour of the well known liberality and zeal of their patron – the Rev. J. Scholefield, to whom the greatest praise is due for his labour in this good cause.

In December 1840 Scholefield was among the first Manchester Chartists to support the Total Abstinence pledge recommended by Chartists associated with the London Working Men's Association, and he remained one of the most vigorous Chartist opponents of the 'tap room society'. 'No government can long withstand', he stressed to readers of the *Star*, 'the just claims of a people who have had the courage to conquer their own vices'. Ever ready to give lofty sentiments a practical help along, Scholefield accompanied this epistle with an 'excellent' recipe for 'Ginger beer'.[63] The road to spiritual and political redemption could have humble beginnings.

Temperance was only one among a number of moral and philanthropic reforms that attracted his patronage. Scholefield's extensive activity in the field of education was another, as was his participation in the Manchester Vegetarian Society during the mid 1840s.[64] Other 'good causes' that formed part of Scholefield's circle of reforms were his role, during the 1820s and '30s, as Administrator of the Bible Christian Building Society – a collective self-help organisation designed to enable 'each member to purchase or build a dwelling house' and, during the 1840s, his participation in the campaigns for a Ten Hour Working Day and to provide Manchester with recreational parks.[65] Later in the 1840s Scholefield was a director and principal shareholder in the Chartist building society that constructed the 'People's Hall' in Heyrod Street, Ancoats.[66] His lifelong interest in the productive capacity of agriculture and land reclamation, led to his involvement in various attempts to relocate urban workers on the land: from a local scheme to establish a colony on the inhospitable marshes of nearby Chat Moss, to a local branch of the Chartist National Land Company during the mid-1840s.[67] A similar objective led him to support one of the Freehold Land Societies that proliferated in the Midlands and across the north of England in the late 1840s and early 1850s.[68]

Scholefield's concern for the welfare of the labouring poor was further evident in his extensive practice as an apothecary, doctor and surgeon.[69] Scholefield earned his reputation as a 'popular quack doctor' during the cholera epidemic of the early 1830s, when he was noted for his successful treatment of many sufferers in the squalid cellars of Ancoats. As one commentator recalled, this reputation endured throughout the 1830s: 'Patients from all the country round used to apply to him, and he had the reputation for curing the ailments of many who had been given up by the regular practitioner.'[70] Although it was only 'advertised by the million tongues of the common people', Scholefield's patented mixture – 'known all over the town and beyond its boundaries as Scholefield's Bottle' – was exceptionally popular on account of its supposed healing properties and was still sold in Ancoats as late as 1904.[71] In one sense Scholefield can simply be dismissed as a quack with an 'unofficial' training in medicine. In another sense, however, he fitted into popular culture. At a time when Robert Southey said there was a 'cunning man' in every town Scholefield, whether he knew it or not, is likely to have been seen in this way. As F.B. Smith has written, 'in 1830 medicine was the *métier* of outsiders'.[72]

Whatever its origin, Scholefield's medical reputation contributed to his prominent local standing and it further emphasised his philanthropy. Although one commentator recalled that 'the shillings came in as thick as drops of rain in a thunder shower', Scholefield was reputed to have given away as many bottles of his famous mixture as he sold.[73] Part of his social mission also involved the provision of poor relief. During the harsh winter of 1839-40 Scholefield began assisting the Parish Churchwardens by visiting the dwellings of the distressed and distributing food vouchers to the needy and, on several occasions during this period, he publicly defended the expenditure incurred by the Churchwardens in the administration of poor relief against attacks from local Whigs.[74] As we have seen, at a time of extreme hardship on Conference Day in 1842, Scholefield was still performing this 'benevolent office'. Referring to these activities, his defence attorney stated in Court in 1843 that 'benevolence ... [had] always formed a conspicuous part of his character ...', but Scholefield's charitable activities with the Churchwardens also highlighted his radicalism.[75] By the 1834 Poor Law Amendment Act, the Whig government had sought to replace the existing system of Parish relief with a centrally controlled Workhouse system. During the 1830s the attempted introduction of this new system had met with fierce resistance, especially in the north of England. In Manchester the bitter struggle for control of poor relief raged into the 1840s and, in this context, Scholefield's actions were not only highly controversial, they also constituted active defiance of the law.[76] It was a 'no holds barred' contest as far as he was concerned and he persisted in his opposition to the 'Whig starvation law' long after others had given up. In 1841-42 he even nominated his own list of candidates for election as Poor Law Commissioners in the hope of disrupting the new system. It mattered little to him that he earned the ire of the oracle of Manchester liberalism, the *Manchester Guardian*, which berated him for causing 'a good deal of inconvenience' and involving 'the ratepayers in needless expense'. Dismissing the

Guardian as a newspaper that was 'ever ready to publish anything that is said or written against me', Scholefield continued to play a watchdog role, most notably in a case when he appeared in court on behalf of women who had been flogged following a riot in the workhouse.[77]

It is not surprising to find that political radicalism also formed a significant part of Scholefield's circle of reforms. Although Swedenborgians do not appear to have incorporated radical political doctrine in their theology, Swedenborg was reputed to have been a sharp critic of social and economic injustice and Cowherd was said to have freely encouraged political radicalism among the Bible Christians.[78] Scholefield took this aspect of his religious inheritance to an obvious conclusion by inextricably weaving radical politics into the fabric of his religion. For him, Christ was the defender of 'truth, justice' and 'PEACE'; the enemy of 'Sectarianism', 'Bigotry', 'Superstition', 'Tyranny and Oppression'; a friend to the poor and the most vehement advocate in 'the cause of liberty'.[79] Scholefield's radical version of 'true' Christianity, which he summarised as 'the comfortable, liberal doctrines of the genuine Gospel',[80] found its expression in his multifarious career as a reformer: for him radical politics was God's work. As he put it: 'When ... a government is incurably bad, cursed are the hands that hold up, and blessed are the hands that pull down!'[81]

Many early nineteenth century Nonconformists whose religious views were far less extreme than Scholefield's, also embraced forms of religious radicalism. Undoubtedly this transition was aided by the deep-seated hatred of the Church of England as the cruel ally of a corrupt and tyrannical government. Other denominations that had aligned themselves with the established order were similarly despised. While this induced many working men to flee the churches for the ranks of Owenism and other forms of infidelity, there were many others who, as 'radical Christians', were prepared to contest the spiritual hegemony of the churches and for whom the cause of radicalism was sanctioned in the Scriptures.[82] In South Lancashire the feelings of bitterness and contempt were deepened because of the complicity of the Anglican Church in the Massacre of Peterloo in August 1819. But when, on the first Sunday after the massacre, the doors of the Anglican Sunday schools were barred to all children sporting radical insignia – green ribbons and white hats – the doors of Scholefield's Sunday school were thrown open in a gesture of defiance specifically to cater for children such as these.[83] And whereas many local Anglican clergyman (and some conservative Nonconformist ministers) signed a 'Loyal Address' applauding the actions of the Yeomanry Cavalry, Scholefield joined many hundreds of his fellow townsmen as a signatory of a 'Declaration of Protest' against 'the unexpected and unnecessary violence' with which the meeting had been attacked.[84] And, when one over-zealous Methodist preacher published a 'Patriotic Sermon' which emphasised the thirteenth Chapter of Romans – 'Let every soul be subject unto the higher powers' – it was Scholefield who took up his pen to proclaim the

Bible as the ultimate source of radical inspiration:[85]

> For all the Books that ever were written, none ever flew so full in the face of oppression, and pleaded for justice, mercy and truth, so boldly and repeatedly, as the Bible. In short the Bible is the Book of all books in the World, considering its inspiration and its doctrines, as eminently worthy of being entitled – RIGHTS OF MAN!

Scholefield's pamphlet also illustrated the breadth of his radicalism. Operating from the premise that he was 'an advocate for that Sacred Book, in opposition to those who pervert and abuse its meaning', Scholefield roundly condemned the society in which 'rich men by their wicked and oppressive systems make you Beggars, and then hate you and despise you for being Beggars!...' Poverty and distress were not the responsibility of 'the benevolent creator of the Universe', he wrote, they were caused by 'the ambition of the nobility' who had been prosecuting an 'unjust and expensive war to suppress a neighbouring nation struggling for freedom'. The 'chains of Sectarian superstition and Political slavery ...' had been forged by 'the tax eaters, the blood sucking pensioners, placemen, Boroughmongers and the whole host of Corruptionists ... preying upon the vitals of the country'. Interwoven with this 'Old Corruption' analysis Scholefield made a plea for 'true' religion:[86]

> What have Sydney, Hampden and Locke, done or said, with such effect, in the cause of liberty, and in favour of the mass of mankind, as Jesus Christ? Let all the friends of liberty and man, be lovers of HIM; and let not their zeal for reforming the corruptions of Christianity, caused by Statesmen wishing to render it subservient of political views, lead them to renounce the comfortable, liberal doctrines of genuine Gospel.

As early as January 1817 he had been noted by the Home Office as an 'Ultra-Radical Huntite', but after Peterloo he developed even closer ties with the popular radical movement. In October 1819, he announced the commencement of a subscription fund 'for the Benefit of the Unfortunate Sufferers' at Peterloo, that would be collected after Sunday service at his Chapel.[87] Having witnessed the massacre, he appeared as a defence witness at the trial of Henry Hunt in March 1820. Under cross-examination he admitted that he had 'written for several newspapers' including two articles – under the pseudonym 'S' – for the radical *Manchester Observer*, edited by his friend James Wroe.[88] Following Wroe's arrest for seditious libel on the Prince of Wales in February 1820, Scholefield's Chapel in Hulme became a subscription point for a relief fund known as the 'Friends of Mr Wroe'.[89] By the second half of 1820 the unpopular Prince (know to radicals as 'the Pig of Pall Mall') had become King, and he soon presented his many opponents with fresh grounds to attack him when he sought to divorce and depose his Queen, Caroline of Brunswick. Radicals grasped the opportunity with relish. First among the 'Friends of Queen Caroline' in Hulme was James Scholefield who preached sermons for her deliverance. Scholefield also toured other Lancashire towns lecturing on Caroline's plight.[90]

By the second anniversary of Peterloo in August 1821 Scholefield's reputation for radicalism had spread well beyond Lancashire. From his prison cell at Ilchester Gaol, Hunt recounted to the 'Radical Reformers of Great Britain' a report he had received of a commemorative procession that had culminated at Christ Church in Hulme, 'where the Reverend Mr. Scholefield christened nine children by the name of HENRY HUNT':[91]

> Mr Scholefield then delivered a most admirable discourse to one of the most crowded audiences that ever honoured a place of worship. His text was, most appropriately, the whole of the 94th Psalm. I understand it was a most able and impressive sermon, and caused his hearers to be bathed in tears. For the good of the public I hope he will print it.

Scholefield's choice of text for this occasion demonstrates the ease with which the Bible could be made to serve the purpose of radicalism – to mark the anniversary of Peterloo the Scriptures offered radicals a stirring call for vengeance:[92]

> O Lord God, to whom vengeance belongeth;
> O God, to whom vengeance belongeth, shew thyself.
> Lift up thyself, thou judge of the earth:
> render a reward to the proud.
> Lord, how long shall the wicked,
> how long shall the wicked triumph?
> How long shall they utter and speak hard things?
> and all the workers of iniquity boast themselves?
> They break in pieces thy people, O Lord,
> and afflict thine heritage.
> They slay the widow and the stranger,
> and murder the fatherless.

At a public dinner on the following Monday, the radicals of Manchester toasted Scholefield and 'the nine young Radical Christians who were christened Henry Hunt'. A pattern had been set. By September 1822, a nervous magistrate warned the Home Office that Scholefield had lost none of the popularity among Hunt's followers that he had gained in 1819 and that 'the disaffected of the lower orders' still made up the majority of his congregation.[93]

Scholefield's commitment to popular radicalism continued into the 1830s and through the Chartist years. In 1833 Scholefield and other radicals participated in crucial public meetings which denied the Anglican Church in Manchester a rate for the first time.[94] Following Hunt's death, in March 1835 a meeting of the 'Radical Reformers of Manchester' was held in his Chapel from which emerged the determination to erect a monument to Hunt's memory. Later that year when Feargus O'Connor, as a representative of the London Radical Association on his first tour of the north, addressed the inaugural meeting of the Manchester Radical Association it was Scholefield who 'came forward and congratulated Mr O'Connor on his appearance in Manchester and wished him success'. At this time Scholefield established a firm friendship with the man who was to be the most popular leader of the Chartist movement.[95]

Scholefield's activities as a Manchester Chartist between 1838 and the Conference in 1842 were varied. He owed the title, 'Chaplain of the Manchester Chartists' (O'Connor was alleged to have bestowed it upon him) firstly, to the position of prominence that he occupied in many of the major episodes in the local history of the movement. When there was a public meeting to chair, a dinner to preside over, a repast to bless, a political sermon to preach, or a comrade to bury, Scholefield was almost invariably the first choice of the Manchester Chartists.[96] It was not always easy work: in March 1842, at a lecture by O'Connor at the Hall of Science, Scholefield began the evening as the Chartist nominee for Chairman and ended up with a black eye and loose teeth when a heated dispute erupted into open violence between the Chartists and a group of Irish Repealers.[97] Making light of his injuries gained 'for the sake of the people's cause' Scholefield rejected potential criticism of his battered appearance with characteristic ebullience: 'I have more reason to glory in them than to be ashamed'.[98] There were also rewarding days for the Chaplain of the Manchester Chartists. Scholefield's injuries had barely healed by the time he joined O'Connor and 'some other individuals of note among the Chartists' in a parade that culminated in the grounds of his Chapel to lay the foundation stone of the Hunt Monument. Towards the end of the proceedings, a member of the Monument Committee 'moved a vote of thanks and gratitude to the Rev. J. Scholefield for his exertions to procure the erection of this monument'. The real honour for Scholefield on that day, however, had come earlier when he was invited to read the lengthy inscription to the vast assemblage before it was sealed, along with other memorials, in the time capsule.[99]

Interspersed between these periodic engagements when Scholefield was called upon to head the public actions of the Manchester Chartists was a constant stream of internal meetings, from the local branch, which often met under his roof, to the executive Council of the Manchester Political Union, which he served on during 1838-9.[100] In addition to regular meetings, Scholefield also made some contributions to the plethora of committees and sub-committees that were an integral part of the structure of Manchester Chartism. During December 1839, for example, he assisted the committee responsible for the Stephens Defence

Fund by opening his Chapel every Sunday as a subscription point.[101] His main contribution to committee work, however, was made to the Hunt Monument Committee. Scholefield's part in the erection of the Monument began with a meeting in his Chapel shortly after Hunt's death in 1835. After this time, the coffers of the subscription fund rose steadily from the contributions of radicals throughout the north of England, but, by late 1838 there was some concern about the future of the project. The *Northern Star*, for example, reported the disquiet of the Ashton radicals who wanted to know 'what had become of the money' they had subscribed.[102] Only after Scholefield's intervention in August 1840 did the project proceed towards completion. At this time, monthly subscribers' meetings were commenced in his Chapel and he donated a plot in his cemetery as a site for the monument. After October 1840, as Treasurer and subsequently President of the Committee, he assumed responsibility for the subscription fund. From then until well into the 1840s the Committee occupied a regular place in his Chartist activities.[103]

Scarcely a day could have gone past when Scholefield did not have some Chartist business to attend to. During August and September of 1839, for example, Scholefield joined many Manchester Chartists in supporting the veteran radical Colonel Perronet Thompson's campaign in the Parliamentary by-election for the borough of Manchester. Scholefield took a prominent position in several public meetings, introducing the 'Chartist Colonel' to electors and using his undoubted eloquence to question opposing candidates.[104] At the nomination it was the Tory candidate, Sir George Murray, who felt the full force of Scholefield's wrath. In quick succession he fired questions at Murray on a range of issues: would he support amendments to the New Poor Law 'to make it more agreeable to the feelings of humanity and the wants of society'; would he vote for a 'tax on machinery, in order to give pensions to those who were disabled by the working of such machinery'; would he ensure that poor law commissioners were 'medical men' appointed 'by some local authority'; would he support demands that government ministers be dismissed 'on the grounds that they had brought the colonies to open rebellion, and also had caused disaffection in this country'?[105] In a few staccato sentences Scholefield had touched upon all the elements of his world-view: his religiously inspired concern for common humanity; his lingering fear of the erosion of local control; his festering anger over the physical consequences of urban industrialism; and his search for practical solutions. The attack on the hapless Murray followed an angry exchange with the Boroughreeve, John Brooks, who was a prominent supporter of the liberal candidate and, as a consequence, his intervention emphasised his independence. Here was the charismatic leader defending his followers and smiting their opponents with full dramaturgical effect.[106]

Scholefield's political activism is further emphasised by an examination of his extensive contribution to 'municipal Chartism'. Scholefield had first been elected to the ranks of the Manchester Police Commission in 1833 and he served a full term retiring in 1836.[107] Late in 1838 he participated in the fierce resistance to the introduction of a Charter of Incorporation under which local power was taken from the Police Commission and given to a new Borough Council. Characteristically his Chapel served as the central meeting place in the radical election campaign for the New Cross Ward in the newly created Council. It is important to note, however, that Scholefield opposed Incorporation not as a defender of the old system – there was a £16 franchise for the appointment of a Commissioner of Police – but on the grounds that it was a reform that did not go far enough. Thus, when at the end of 1839 he and his longstanding friend and ally, James Wroe, stood as candidates for election in both the Police Commission and the new Borough Council, the main plank of their campaign was 'Universal Suffrage in *local* as well as General Government' by means of extensive reform of the Municipal Corporations Act 'so that every ratepayer should have a vote in the election of Councillors'.[108] At the same time they promised a practical application of their Chartist principles: not only would they resign 'at any time that a majority of burgesses may require it', but also they would take up issues raised by their constituents in Council and attend any constituent meetings to give explanations of their conduct or receive instructions.[109] It was a standard of representation that William Sankey and many other Chartists would have approved of.

Scholefield's bid for election to Council was unsuccessful on this occasion, but he was eventually elected in 1847 and served New Cross Ward until 1853.[110] Characteristic of his sense of public duty, Scholefield assiduously attended all but six meetings during his six years of office.[111] Scholefield was re-elected to the ranks of the Police Commissioners in 1839 where he served until 1842. As a local politician Scholefield did not articulate grandiose schemes of urban reconstruction of the sort made famous by Joseph Chamberlain later in the nineteenth century. Like William Cobbett and other popular radicals of the day he associated taxation with 'Old Corruption'. It was, he told a Chartist meeting, 'the Goliath of despots', an 'all devouring monster' that was 'extending its baleful and destructive effects over every department of society'. As a consequence, Scholefield was opposed to giving local government either the power or the revenue for reform on a grand scale.[112] Thus his support as an Police Commissioner and subsequently as a local councillor was for projects of an immediate, practical, and piecemeal kind – paving streets, installing sewers, erecting street lights – while maintaining a vigilant eye on the level of taxation. In November 1840, for example, when his colleagues on the Police Commission turned the meeting into a squabble over the exercise of their patronage in selecting the members of the Board of Directors of the Gas Company that they controlled, Scholefield sharply rebuked them: why, he demanded, were they not discussing the repairs to Pinmill bridge that had not been carried out?[113] Nearly a decade later the forum and many of the faces had changed, but the agenda had not. When, at a time of severe economic hardship in February 1848, some Councillors proposed a salary increase for the Clerk of Committees, Scholefield indignantly dwelt 'on the condition of the poorer ratepayers and small shopkeepers' in a vain attempt to block it.[114]

Shortly after the end of his second term as a Police Commissioner, Scholefield found himself on the other end of the legal process, facing a trial for his role in the 1842 Chartist Conference. According to his own estimation, Scholefield's defence at Lancaster in 1843 cost him £150 which sorely tested both his financial well-being and his relationship with O'Connor which was not fully repaired until 1846.[115] Scholefield's dispute with O'Connor, however, did nothing to lessen his reputation as a 'notorious Chartist'.[116] Such characterisations do not adequately convey the breadth of his radicalism. His active political life after Peterloo exhibited a development of the ideas in his pamphlet in 1819 into a radical ideology that encompassed a great deal more than the Six Points of political reform represented by the People's Charter. During these years, from numerous different platforms, Scholefield indicated his opposition to everything from persecution in Ireland, the 'political State Church', 'tithes of every description', and 'a standing Army', to 'all internal taxes, whether direct or indirect', 'a ponderous debt', the New Poor Law, and the Corn Laws.[117] Although he mistrusted some of the leaders of the Anti-Corn-Law League, Scholefield was a firm advocate of repeal and retained tentative links with the organised Anti-Corn-Law movement: in February 1840, for example, he was invited to be the guest speaker at an Operative Anti-Corn-Law Association Tea Party and, in August 1841, he attended the League's National Conference of Ministers of All Denominations on the Corn Laws in Manchester. Unlike either Henry Solly or Benjamin Parsons who, in different ways, played prominent roles in the Conference, Scholefield remained uncharacteristically silent throughout.[118]

For Scholefield the League Conference was the first step on the road to accepting the liberal embrace, but there were obstacles still to be overcome. When the campaign to provide Manchester with public parks by public subscription got under way in 1844 it seemed to, simultaneously, hold out the possibility of class cooperation on what one commentator called a 'broad neutral ground'. The initial signs were promising. The campaign drew support across a wide spectrum from moderate Tories and Whig grandees to Cobdenite liberals and O'Connorite Chartists. When the Chartists nominated Scholefield and Abel Heywood, a veteran radical, to represent them on the steering committee that was dominated by Leaguers, however, they were bluntly rebuffed. The ground for cooperation was not yet broad enough; separate middle and working class subscriptions were collected.[119]

By 1851 the situation had changed. In September Scholefield became a founding member of the Manchester branch of the Parliamentary and Financial

Reform Association, an organisation that embraced the twin objectives of an extension of the suffrage and a cut in government spending as a prelude to a reduction in taxation.[120] Although the programme was unexceptional, the organisation was contentious because it was the successful product of an alliance between middle- and working-class radicals. In Manchester the formation of the Parliamentary and Financial Reform Association was in many ways the final twist in the long-running split in the ranks of Chartism that had led George Julian Harney, the editor of the *Northern Star*, to remark that he 'would rather be hanged in London than die a natural death in Manchester'.[121] For Scholefield the poisonous atmosphere that afflicted the local movement was a bitter pill: at one meeting in November 1850 he was even hissed at when he attempted to speak, something that would have been unthinkable during the previous thirty years.[122] Throughout these troubled times he remained a close friend and supporter of Feargus O'Connor, but in political terms Scholefield's support for the Parliamentary and Financial Reform Association signalled, as with other local Chartists, a transition to the ranks of nineteenth century liberalism. It was also a reflection of a commitment to practical reform that did little to dent his popularity in working-class Ancoats which remained 'second to none': 'The people felt that his sympathy for them was genuine', recalled one commentator, 'and that his expression of it was prudent as well as courageous'.[123]

The extraordinary variety of Scholefield's public career lends it an apparent lack of cohesion: the administrator of the Bible Christian Building Society in the 1820s seems to bear little obvious relation to the Parliamentary and Financial Reformer of the 1850s. But these activities, like all his 'good causes', were component parts of a campaign for social transformation that drew inspiration from a common source: his radical version of 'true' Christianity. The unity of Scholefield's public life was built into the bricks and mortar of his religious institution in Ancoats. On his death bed, Scholefield was alleged to have advised his daughters: 'Make what use you can of the Chapel, girls. Use it for a circus if you can, after all it's round. It has served its' turn as a Chapel'.[124] It had served as the centre of a great deal more: from Sunday School and lecture hall to Chartist Conference room and Radical Electors' Association; from temperance meeting place and poor relief centre to apothecary and surgery. Giving evidence in Court in 1843, Richard Beswick, Chief Superintendent of the Manchester Police, stated in passing that there were five or six different entrances to Scholefield's Chapel and its adjoining buildings.[125] Contemporaries who wished to catch Scholefield in one of his many guises, literally only needed to know which door to approach: one for medicine, another for education, and another for politics. The Chartist historian cannot be this selective and only inquire after the politician. Because it was the same man behind all the doors to the Round Chapel, Scholefield's participation in Chartism cannot be isolated from the remainder of his public life. Scholefield's commitment to the cause of universal suffrage originated in the Peterloo era, but was only one facet of his radical ideology. By the time the People's Charter was published in 1838, Scholefield had collected more causes under the rubric of radicalism and his ideology was, if anything, more broadly based. All his 'good causes' – from Chartism to vegetarianism – were linked together by his 'religious motivation' towards active participation in 'moral and civil life' and in his radical interpretation of the 'comfortable, liberal doctrines of genuine Gospel'. His activities were combined without a sense of priority over many years and in his day to day experience. On the day of the Conference in 1842 when discussions of crucial importance to the Chartists were taking place under his roof, the Chaplain of the Manchester Chartists also had the sick to heal, the dead to bury, mourners to comfort, children to teach, and the poor to feed. The performance of all these 'duties' was God's work.

Notes

[1] P. Wentworth, 'The Chaplain of the Manchester Chartists', *Middleton Guardian*, 29 March 1890. According to Wentworth this title was conferred on Scholefield by Feargus O'Connor. Paul Pickering has previously written about Scholefield in an unpublished thesis and in an article co-written by Alex Tyrrell. See P.A. Pickering, 'The Fustian Jackets: Aspects of the Chartist Movement in Manchester and Salford to 1842', Unpublished PhD thesis, LaTrobe University, 1992, chapter 9; P.A. Pickering & A. Tyrrell, '"In the Thickest of the Fight": The Reverend James Scholefield (1790-1855) and the Bible Christians of Manchester and Salford', *Albion*, vol. 26, no. 3, 1994, pp. 461-482. The present chapter draws upon the thesis and the joint article.

[2] *Manchester Courier*, 18 August 1842. See also M. Jenkins, *The General Strike of 1842*, London, 1980; F.C. Mather, 'The General Strike of 1842: A Study in Leadership, Organisation and the Treat of Revolution during the Plug Plot Disturbances', in R. Quinault & J. Stevenson (eds), *Popular Protest and Public Order*, New York, 1974, pp. 115-40.

[3] Although Scholefield's Chapel was most often referred too as the 'Round Chapel' or the 'Every Street Chapel' (and less frequently as the 'Beefsteak Chapel' – a slight against the vegetarianism practised by the congregation) it was officially denoted 'Christ Church'. See: Manchester Public Library (MPL), Local History Library (LHL), Biography Index: *Manchester Guardian*, 13 December 1934; [B. Love], *Manchester As it is: or, Notices of the Institutions, Manufactures, Commerce, Railways Etc, of the Metropolis of Manufactures*, 1839, repr. Manchester, 1971, p. 57.

[4] *Manchester Times*, 1 December 1838; *Manchester and Salford Advertiser*, 17 November 1838; 5 October 1839.

[5] F. O'Connor (ed.), *The Trial of Feargus O'Connor Esq., and Fifty-Eight Others at Lancaster on a Charge of Sedition, Conspiracy, Tumult and Riot*, 1843, repr. New York, 1970, pp. 110-11, 155. See also N. Roberts, 'Sixty Years of Service', *Manchester University Settlement Diamond Jubilee 1895 – 1955: Souvenir Brochure*, Manchester, 1955, p. 3.

[6] *Manchester and Salford Advertiser*, 4 November 1837; O'Connor, *Trial*, pp. 110-11; P. Wentworth, 'Every Street Beef Steak Chapel and Burial Ground', *Middleton Guardian*, 5 April, 1890; Ms, *Register of Christ Church, Every Street, Manchester*, MPL, Archives Department, p. 1.

[7] *Manchester Times*, 26 March 1842; *British Statesman*, 2 April 1842. See also: W. Harrison, 'Monument to Henry Hunt', *Proceedings of the Lancashire and Cheshire Antiquarian Society*, vol. 7, 1889, p. 325. For an engraving of the monument see *Northern Star*, 20 August 1842 [2nd Edition]. The Monument was not finally completed until at least 1844; Chartists were buried in the 'Patriot's Vault' into the 1850s. See *Northern Star* 24 August 1844; *People's Paper* 23 September 1854.

[8] O'Connor, *Trial*, pp. 115-16.

[9] *Manchester Courier*, 20 August 1842; *Manchester Times*, 20 August 1842. According to Thomas Cooper, the Leicester Chartist, the secret discussions also took place in the Chapel. See: T. Cooper, *The Life of Thomas Cooper*, 1872, repr. Leicester, 1971, p. 207. Out of these discussions came the famous 'Executive Address' supporting the general strike which, together with the Conference itself, eventually led to the arrest of O'Connor and fifty-eight others including Scholefield and his eldest son William. A copy of the Address is in HO 45/249c fol. 218.

[10] O'Connor, *Trial*, p. 208.

[11] *Manchester Times*, 20 August 1842.

[12] Scholefield's defence against the charge of conspiracy was that he was busily engaged in other ways. Thus, the details of his activities on 17 August in this paragraph are drawn largely from O'Connor, *Trial*, p. 208. See also *Manchester and Salford Advertiser*, 8 October 1842.

[13] One Chartist historian to emphasise long and diverse careers is Dorothy Thompson. See 'Notes on Aspects of Chartist Leadership', *Bulletin of the Society for the Study of Labour History*, no. 15, 1967, p. 27; D. Thompson, 'Chartism as a Historical Subject', *Bulletin of the Society for the Study of Labour History*, no. 20, 1970, pp. 10-1. See also S. Roberts, *Radical Politicians and Poets in Early Victorian Britain*, Lampeter, 1993; I. Prothero, *Artisans and Politics in Early Nineteenth Century London: John Gast and His Times*, London, 1979; A. Tyrrell, *Joseph Sturge and the Moral Radical Party in Early Victorian Britain*, London, 1987.

[14] Scholefield's contribution to Chartism has been noted by a number of historians – with one even describing him as the man who held the local movement together – but there has been relatively little detailed consideration of his political career. See D. Jones, *Chartism and the Chartists*, London, 1975, p. 53. For other passing references see M. Hovell, *The Chartist Movement*, Manchester, 1918, p. 261; F.C. Mather, 'The Government and the Chartists', in A. Briggs (ed.), *Chartist Studies*, London, 1959, p. 391; J. Epstein, *The Lion of Freedom*, London, 1982, p. 66; A. Jenkin, 'Chartism and the Trade Unions', in L.M. Munby (ed.), *The Luddites and other essays*, London, 1971, p. 84; E. Royle & J. Walvin, *English Radicals and Reformers 1760-1848*, Lexington, 1982, pp. 127, 161; D. Thompson, *The Chartists*, London, 1984, pp. 168-9. In Donald Read's essay on Manchester Chartism Scholefield is mentioned once as 'Scholfield [sic], a local Chartist leader', and in their short article on Manchester Chartism Edmund and Ruth Frow fail to notice him at all. Surprisingly there is no reference to him in Eileen Yeo's writings on Chartism and Religion. See D. Read, 'Chartism in Manchester', in Briggs (ed.), *Chartist Studies*, p. 57; E. & R. Frow, *Chartism in Manchester 1838-1858*, Manchester, 1980; E. Yeo, 'Christianity and Chartist Struggle 1838-1842', *Past and Present*, no. 91, May, 1981, pp. 109-39; E. Yeo, 'Chartist religious belief and the theology of liberation', in J. Obelkevich, L. Roper & R. Samuel (eds), *Disciplines of Faith: Studies in Religion, Politics and Patriarchy*, London, 1987, pp. 410-421. The most recent book on this subject by Eileen Groth Lyon only notices Scholefield in passing. See *Politicians and the Pulpit: Christian Radicalism in Britain form the Fall of the Bastille to the Disintegration of Chartism*, Aldershot, 1999, p. 199. See also P.A. Pickering, *Chartism and the Chartists in Manchester and Salford*, Basingstoke, 1995.

[15] See H.H. Gerth & C. Wright Mills (eds), *From Max Weber: Essays in Sociology*, London, 1974 edition, pp. 245-250.

[16] F. Engels, *The Condition of the Working Class in England*, 1845, repr. Moscow, 1977, p 58.

[17] See *PP. 1851 Census: Great Britain, Report and Tables on Religious Worship, England and Wales, Accounts and Papers*, (33), vol. LXXXIX, 1852-3, pp. ccix, 95.

[18] This fundamental error was made by the Census enumerators and historians who have replicated it include H.U. Faulkner, *Chartism and the Churches: A Study in Democracy*, 1916 repr. London, 1970, p. 90 & R.W. Wearmouth, *Some Working Class Movements of the Nineteenth Century*, London, 1963, pp. 191-2. For the history of the Bible Christians see W.E.A. Axon, *A History of the Bible Christian Church Salford*, Manchester, 1909; W.R. Ward, 'Swedenborgianism: Heresy, Schism or Religious Protest?', in D. Baker (ed.), *Schism, Heresy and Religious Protest*, Cambridge, 1972, pp. 303-9; P. J. Lineham, 'Restoring Man's Creative Power: the Theosophy of the Bible Christians of Salford', in W.J. Sheils (ed.), *The Church and Healing*, Oxford, 1982; Pickering & Tyrrell, '"In the Thickest of the Fight"', pp. 461-482. The Bible Christians were probably Britain's

earliest advocates of total abstinence, but, although they have been noticed by historians of the temperance movement, Scholefield's role has not been mentioned. Similarly, although Scholefield spent over a decade in local government, his name does not appear in Redford's massive three volume study. See A. Redford, *History of Local Government in Manchester*, 3 vols., London, 1950; N. Longmate, *The Water-Drinkers*, London, 1968, p. 38; B. Harrison, *Drink and the Victorians, The Temperance Question in England 1815-1872*, London, 1971, pp. 100, 164, 225-6. Most notably there is no reference to Scholefield in Brian Harrison's article, 'Teetotal Chartism', *History*, vol. 58, 1973, pp. 193-217.

[19] 'Scholefield's Visiting Card', MPL, Print Collection, Ace. 58395, n.d. For the importance of personality – 'how people represent themselves to themselves and to one another' – see: C. Geertz, 'On the Nature of Anthropological Understanding', *American Scientist*, vol. 63, no. 1, Jan-Feb, 1975, p. 48.

[20] See G. Redmonds, *The Heirs of Woodsome and other essays in local history*, Huddersfield, 1982, pp. 36-42.

[21] *Northern Star*, 2 October 1841.

[22] Ibid., 9 April 1842 [2nd edition].

[23] The details of Cowherd's early life and career in Manchester have been compiled from numerous sources: J.T. Slugg, *Reminiscences of Manchester Fifty Years Ago*, 1881, repr. Shannon, 1971, p. 192; [anon], *A Description of Manchester and Salford Containing Some Account of their Antiquaries, Public Buildings*, Manchester, 1815, pp. 136-7; W.E.A. Axon, *The Annals of Manchester*, Manchester, 1886, pp. 120, 128, 140-1; W.E.A. Axon, *Handbook of the Public Libraries of Manchester and Salford*, Manchester, 1887, pp. 38-9; W.E.A. Axon, *A History*, p. 17-22; J. Aston, *A Picture of Manchester* ,1816, repr. Manchester, 1969, p. 103-4; *Dictionary of National Biography*, vol. IV, pp. 1303-4. The 1809 schism is covered briefly by Cowherd's adversary, Robert Hindmarsh, in his *The Rise and Progress of the New Jerusalem Church in England, America and Other Parts*, London, 1861, p. 190. In subsequent 'official' histories of the Swedenborgian Church – for example, G. Trobridge, *Swedenborg: His Life and Teaching*, 1907, repr. London, 1974 – Cowherd's contribution is not mentioned at all.

[24] For Brotherton's career see F. Boase, *Modern English Biography*, London, 1965, vol. 1, p. 423; M. Stenton, *Who's Who of British Members of Parliament 1832-1885*, London, 1976, vol. 1, p. 50; *Dictionary of National Biography*, vol. 2, p. 1354; Axon, *A History*, pp. 41-50.

[25] For Scholefield's biographical and religious details see: *Ms, Register*; Boase, *Modern English Biography*, vol. 3, p. 439; MPL, LHL, Biography Index: *Manchester Evening News*, Notes and Queries, 15 December 1883; Axon, *A History*, passim.; Slugg, *Reminiscences*, p. 192-4.

[26] E.P. Thompson, *The Making of the English Working Class*, London, 1980, p. 53.

[27] 1809 Declaration quoted in: J. Scholefield (ed.), *Select Hymns for the Use of Bible Christians by the Late Rev, W, Cowherd* (7th Edition), Manchester, 1841, p. vi. See also MPL, LHL, *Newspaper Cuttings*, vol. 2, p. 40.

[28] Cited in: G. Trobridge, *Swedenborg*, p. 128. See also pp. 174-85.

[29] I. Jonsson, *Emanuel Swedenborg*, New York, 1971, pp. 22-33.

[30] Trobridge, *Swedenborg*, pp. 158-60.

[31] J.F.C. Harrison, *Robert Owen and the Owenites in Britain and America*, London, 1969, p. 251.

[32] Axon, *Handbook*, p. 41; *A History* , p. 25.

[33] [anon], *A Description of Manchester*, p. 136-7; E.T. Craig, 'Socialism in England: Historical Reminiscences', *American Socialist*, 13 December 1887. See also: *Lion*, 16 May 1828; G.A. Williams, *Rowland Detrosier: A Working Class Infidel 1800-1834*, York, 1965, pp. 9-13.

[34] W. Cowherd, *Facts Authentic In Science and Religion Designed To Illustrate A New Translation Of The Bible*, Manchester, 1818, pp. i-iii. See also Axon, *A History*, p. 25; *Handbook*, p. 41.

[35] MPL, LHL, Newspaper Cuttings: *Manchester City News*, Notes and Queries, 2 November, 1878, 5 January 1884, 16 January 1906; Axon, *Annals*, pp. 157-8; *A History*, pp. 81-2. See also B. Simon, *The Two Nations and the Educational Structure 1780-1870*, London, 1974.

[36] HO 40/17 fols. 330-1, Eckersly to HO, 1 August 1822; HO 40/17 fol. 336, Norris to HO,

September 1822 (we are indebted to Iain McCalman for the references to the Home Office papers, 1817-1822, used in this chapter); *Manchester Times*, 1 December 1838; 13 June 1840; *Manchester and Salford Advertiser*, 8 December 1838; O'Connor (ed.), *Trial*, p. 308; *Manchester Guardian*, 9 November 1850. See also M. Goffin (ed.), *The Diaries of Absalom Watkin: A Manchester Man 1787-1861*, Stroud, 1993, pp. 293-4.

[37] MPL, LHL, *Newspaper Cuttings*, vol. 1, p. 82; Slugg, *Reminiscences*, pp. 192-3.

[38] Richard Reed's colleague, the Chartist W.E. Adams, was a great campaigner against cruelty to animals. See O.R. Ashton, *W.E. Adams: Chartist, Radical and Journalist (1832-1906)*, Tyne and Wear, 1991, pp. 137-9.

[39] Axon, *A History*, pp. 33-34. As E.P. Thompson has argued, there is a need for caution when dealing with evidence such as this – an impressive list of titles might as easily represent eclectic dabbling as rigorous intellectual achievement. See: E.P. Thompson, 'On History, Sociology and Historical Relevance', *British Journal of Sociology*, September 1976, pp. 394-5.

[40] For Scholefield's articles see *Manchester Observer*, 2 October 1819; *Star of Temperance: A Weekly Publication for the Diffusion of Temperance Information*, 14 May 1836. According to Axon: 'In the thirties he [Scholefield] published a number of separate sermons and lectures in which such topics as the Creation, [and] Noah's Flood were dealt with from the Bible Christian standpoint. In a twelve page pamphlet printed at Manchester in 1832, he ventured into the flowery field of poetry. His 'Odes to the Sun and Moon, in which are shown the unchangeableness of Deity', are two didactic poems in blank verse of very respectable quality', *A History*, p. 58. In addition, Scholefield edited *A System of Vegetable Cookery as Used by the Society of Bible Christians* (1839); *Letters on Religious Subjects* (1840-1); and *Select Hymns*. See also: *Vegetarian Messenger*, July 1851.

[41] *Northern Star*, 16 March 1839.

[42] Axon, *A History*, p. 31.

[43] MPL, LHL, Newspaper Cuttings: *Manchester Weekly Times*, 14 November 1890; J.T. Slugg, *Reminiscences*, p. 195. Vegetarianism also earned the Bible Christians a certain amount of derision. The Chapels were often referred to as 'Beef-steak Chapels' and for Joseph Brotherton, at the time that he was an aspiring MP for Salford, his diet was a regular object of humour. See the 'The Butcher – The Beef – and the Broth-erton' published in *The Squib: Being A Satire on Passing Events in Lancashire*, 1 September 1832.

[44] Axon, *Handbook*, p. 39.

[45] Axon, *A History*, pp. 27, 32; *Dictionary of National Biography*, vol. IV, pp. 1303-4.

[46] Scholefield, (ed.), *Select Hymns*, p. iv.

[47] *The Trial of Henry Hunt, Esq., for an alleged Conspiracy to Overturn the Government &c, by Threats of Arms before Mr, Justice Bavley and a Special Jury at the York Lent Assizes, 1820*, London, 1820, p. 255.

[48] J. Scholefield, *Remarks on the Sermon Adapted to the State of the Times Preached by the Rev, John Stephens in the Methodist Chapel, Oldham Street, Manchester*, Manchester, 1819, p. 23.

[49] See *Lion*, 16 May 1828. As Wentworth recalled: 'Scholefield was himself so good and so popular that even the most bigoted religionists feared to denounce the doctrine he taught'. See *Middleton Guardian*, 5 April 1890.

[50] Trobridge, *Swedenborg*, p. 129; Harrison, *The Second Coming*, pp. 72-4. The general point regarding the 'stepping stones' that led away from the Anglican Church to 'secularism or indifference' is drawn from H. Perkin, *The Origins of Modern English Society 1780-1880*, London, 1981, pp. 203f.

[51] See: R. Detrosier, *A Form of Public Worship on the Principles of Pure Deism as Used on the First Sunday in every month at the Chapel of the Society of Universal Benevolence*, Manchester, 1827; E. Royle, *Victorian Infidels: The Origins of the British Secularist Movement. 1791-1866*, Manchester, 1974, pp. 39, 309-10; G.A. Williams, *Detrosier*, pp. 9-13; R. Glen, *Urban Workers in the Early Industrial Revolution*, London, 1984, p. 269; MPL, LHL, Newspaper Cuttings, vol. IV, p. 67, vol. X, p. 30. For Carlile and Taylor see I. McCalman, 'Popular Radicalism and Freethought in Early Nineteenth Century England: A Study of Richard Carlile and his Followers, 1815-1832,'

Unpublished MA thesis, Australian National University, 1975.

[52] HO 40/10 fol. 337 Lloyd to HO, 28 December 1820. See also R. Southey, *Letters from England*, 1807, repr. London, 1981, p. 380. Through the fictional eyes of a traveller from Catholic Spain, Southey gave an interesting account of a Swedenborgian sermon: 'I have never in any other heretical meeting heard heresy so loudly insisted upon'.

[53] *Lion*, 16 May 1828. See also 1 February 1828. Scholefield was clearly not amused by Carlile's allegations as he later replied to Carlile, 'I shall not condescend to notice anything more that you may either say, write or do'. See *Lion*, 17 July 1829.

[54] Cited in B. Simon, *The Radical Tradition in Education in Britain*, London, 1972, pp. 116-17.

[55] Simon, *The Two Nations*, p. 132.

[56] Cited in Williams, *Detrosier*, p. 8; *Manchester Times*, 1 December 1838

[57] See E. Royle, *Radical Politics 1790-1900: Religion and Unbelief*, London, 1979, p. 8; [B. Love], *Manchester As it Is*, p. 48; Axon, *Annals*, p. 296.

[58] Scholefield, *Remarks*, p. 23; *Manchester and Salford Advertiser*, 1 February 1840.

[59] E. Swedenborg, *Heaven and its Wonders, and Hell: From Things Heard and Seen*, 1757, repr. London, 1909, pp.290, 298.

[60] Scholefield (ed.), *Select Hymns*, p. 111, Hymn 83.

[61] Cited in Trobridge, *Swedenborg*, p. 128.

[62] *Manchester and Salford Advertiser*, 11 January 1840; *Poor Man's Advocate and People's Library*, 4 February 1832; *Star of Temperance*, 24 October 1835; 30 April 1836. See also: *Manchester and Salford Temperance Journal*, 18 June 1836; 30 July 1836.

[63] *Northern Star*, 5 December 1840; *British Statesman*, 6 August 1842.

[64] See *Vegetarian Messenger*, September 1849; July 1850; July 1851; July 1852; November 1852; Axon, *A History*, p. 52. The model of a 'circle' of interlocking moral and philanthropic reforms that we have employed in reference to Scholefield is drawn from A. Tyrrell, 'Personality in Politics: The National Complete Suffrage Union and Pressure Group Politics in Early Victorian Britain', *Journal of Religious History*, vol. 12, no. 4, 1983, pp. 382-400.

[65] MPL, Archives Department: Ms. *Mortgage by Demise – Trustees of the Bible Christian Building Society*, 1822, MC1576; Ms. *Attested Copy of the Rules and Regulations to be observed by Members of the Bible Christian society for building Dwelling houses established at the Academy, King Street Salford on the twenty ninth day of October One thousand Eight hundred and twenty one*, 1834, MC1578; *Manchester Times*, 20 April 1844; 10 August 1844.

[66] *Northern Star*, 27 March 1841; 18 April 1846; 25 July 1846.

[67] See *Manchester Observer*, 23 September 1819; *Northern Star*, 4 December 1841; 15 November 1845; 31 July 1847; *Vegetarian Messenger*, July 1851; Pickering, *Chartism and the Chartists*, pp. 116-120.

[68] *Freeholder*, 2 June 1851.

[69] This 'good cause' was also a source of income. Because the seats in the Round Chapel were free and Scholefield did not levy a stipend from his congregation, he lived off the proceeds from the cemetery and his medical practice.

[70] Slugg, *Reminiscences*, pp. 55, 193-4; *Middleton Guardian*, 12 April 1890. See also *Lion*, 16 May 1828. Cowherd enjoyed a similar renown as a doctor. See Axon, *A History*, p. 25.

[71] *Middleton Guardian*, 12 April 1890; MPL, LHL, Biography Index: *Manchester City News*, Notes and Queries, 12 March 1904.

[72] Southey, *Letters*, pp. 295-7; F.B. Smith, *The People's Health 1830-1910*, Aldershot, 1993, p. 346. The 'cunning men' of early nineteenth century Britain were, perhaps, an echo of a far older tradition in popular culture. See K. Thomas, *Religion and the Decline of Magic*, London, 1971, pp. 209-301, for a discussion of this tradition in sixteenth and seventeenth century England.

[73] *Middleton Guardian*, 12 April 1890; *Northern Star*, 8 July 1843.

[74] *Manchester Times*, 25 April 1840; *Manchester and Salford Advertiser*, 1 February 1840; 29 February 1840; 25 April 1840.

[75] O'Connor (ed.), *Trial*, p. 204.

[76] For examples see: *Manchester and Salford Advertiser*, 4 March 1837; 10 February 1838; HO 52/46 fols. 197-9, Churchwardens to HO, November 1840.

[77] *Manchester and Salford Advertiser*, 19 March 1842; 23 April 1842; *Manchester Guardian*, 16 March 1842; 20 April 1842.

[78] Jonsson, *Swedenborg*, p. 24; *Dictionary of National Biography*, vol. IV, p. 1303. See also: Ward, 'Heresy', p. 307.

[79] Scholefield, *Remarks*, passim. See also *Northern Star*, 2 April 1842.

[80] Scholefield, *Remarks*, p. 16.

[81] Ibid., p. 11.

[82] See E. Royle, *Radical Politics*, p. 9-10; E. Yeo, 'Christianity in Chartist Struggle', pp. ll0f.

[83] MPL, LHL, Biography Index: *Manchester City News*, Notes and Queries, 15 December 1883; Axon, *A History.*, p. 80. See also Ward, 'Heresy', p. 307.

[84] *Manchester Observer*, 11 September 1819.

[85] *The Bible*, King James Edition, Romans, 13:1-2; Scholefield, *Remarks*, p. 8. See also Ward, *Religion and Society*, pp. 94-5. Ironically the Methodist preacher was John Stephens, father of Joseph Raynor Stephens. We are grateful to Ted Royle for bringing this to our attention.

[86] Scholefield, *Remarks*, pp. 8, 11, 12, 16, 18. See also *Manchester Observer*, 24 July 1819; 4 March 1820.

[87] HO 42/158 Report of R.F., January 1817; *Manchester Observer*, 2 October 1819.

[88] *The Trial of Henry Hunt*, p. 255; Walmsley, *Peterloo*, p. 409n. For Wroe see Pickering, *Chartism and the Chartists*, pp. 209-10.

[89] *Manchester Observer*, 11 March 1820.

[90] *Manchester Observer*, 5 December 1820; 16 December 1820. See also 26 August 1820; 25 November 1820.

[91] H. Hunt, *[Letters] To the Radical Reformers, Male and Female, of England, Ireland, and Scotland*, 25 August 1821, pp. 20-1.

[92] *The Bible*, King James Edition, Psalm 94: 1-6.

[93] Hunt, *[Letters]* , p. 22; HO 40/17 fol. 336, J. Norms to HO, September 1822.

[94] Ward, *Religion and Society*, pp. 179-80.

[95] MPL, LHL, Handbill: 'A Monument to the Memory of H. Hunt Esq.', 1835; *Poor Man's Guardian*, 26 September 1835; *Manchester Times*, 11 April 1835; 19 December 1835; O'Connor, (ed.), *Trial*, p. 289.

[96] For examples see: *Manchester and Salford Advertiser*, 9 June 1838; 29 September 1838; 20 October 1838; 16 March 1839; 1 February 1840; *Northern Star*, 16 March 1839; 22 August 1840; *Manchester Times*, 22 August 1840; 2 October 1841; HO 40/54 fol. 861, Handbill, December 1840; HO 45/43 fol. 58, Wemyss to Phillips, 15 August 1841. See also: *Anti-Corn Law Circular*, 25 March 1841.

[97] HO 40/269 fol. 31, Wemyss to Phillips, 23 February 1842; *Manchester Times*, 12 March 1842; *Northern Star*, 12 March 1842; N. McCord, *The Anti-Corn Law League 1838-1846*, London, 1968, p. 103.

[98] *Northern Star*, 2 April 1842.

[99] *Manchester Times*, 26 March 1842; *British Statesman*, 2 April 1842; *Northern Star*, 2 April 1842.

[100] *Manchester and Salford Advertiser*, 20 October 1838. See also Pickering, *Chartism and the Chartists*, chapter 2.

[101] *Northern Star*, 14 December 1839. Scholefield's Chapel was a collection point for good causes for 30 years; from the Peterloo Victims Fund in 1819 to the Chartist Widows and Childrens' Fund in 1846. See *Manchester Observer*, 2 October 1819; *Northern Star*, 31 January 1846.

[102] *Northern Star*, 17 November 1838.

[103] *Manchester and Salford Advertiser*, 29 August 1840; O'Connor (ed.), *Trial*, p. 107; *Northern Star*, 24 August 1844.

[104] *Manchester and Salford Advertiser*, 7 September 1839; Supplement, 7 September 1839; *Manchester Chronicle and Salford Standard*, Extraordinary, 4 September 1839.

[105] *Manchester and Salford Advertiser*, 7 September 1839.

[106] Sociologists note that Charismatic leadership is typical of 'world-rejecting' cults. See T. Robbins, *Cults, Converts and Charisma: The Sociology of New Religious Movements*, London, 1988, pp. 116-121, 188 & *passim*.

[107] *Manchester Guardian*, 2 November 1833.

[108] HO 52/42 fol. 111, Poster, December 1839; *Manchester and Salford Advertiser*, 5 October 1839. For earlier Chartist opposition to Incorporation in which Scholefield participated see *inter alia Manchester and Salford Advertiser*, 13 January 1838, 10 February 1838, 15 September 1838, 3 November 1838, 17 November 1838, 1 December 1838, 22 December 1838; *Manchester Times*, 20 January 1838; *Manchester Guardian*, 10 February 1838; *Champion and Weekly Herald*, 2 December 1838, 9 December 1838.

[109] *Manchester and Salford Advertiser*, 12 October 1839.

[110] *Northern Star*, 13 November 1847.

[111] MPL, LHL, Biography Index: *Chronicle of the City Council 1838-1877*.

[112] *British Statesman*, 6 August 1842.

[113] *Manchester Times*, 7 November 1840.

[114] *Manchester Guardian*, 26 February 1848.

[115] *Northern Star*, 1 April 1843; 25 July 1846.

[116] Slugg, *Reminiscences*, pp. 55, 193-4; *Northern Star*, 1 April 1843 8 July 1843; 23 November 1850; 27 September 1851.

[117] See for example HO 45/249c fol. 48, Shaw to Phillips, 29 June 1842; *Manchester Times*, 21 December 1839; 20 March 1841; 22 May 1841; *Manchester and Salford Advertiser*, 12 October 1839; 1 February 1840; *Northern Star*, 29 February 1840; *British Statesman*, 6 August 1842. Scholefield supported a property tax, 'an efficient Factory Bill', and a 'searching and vigorous enquiry ...into every branch of the public expenditure'.

[118] *Manchester and Salford Advertiser*, 15 February 1840; *Report on the Conference of Ministers of All Denominations on the Corn Laws, held in Manchester, 17th, 18th, 19th and 20th 1841 with a Digest of Documents contributed during the Conference*, Manchester, 1841, pp. 5-18.

[119] See *Manchester Times*, 3 August 1844; 10 August 1844; 31 August 1844; 14 September 1844; 28 September 1844; 11 January 1845; 1 February 1845; 12 July 1845. See also T. Wyborn, 'Parks for the People: The Development of Public Parks in Manchester, c. 1830-1860,' *Working Papers in Economic and Social History*, no. 29, University of Manchester, 1994, pp. 1-23. Wyborn does not note the rebuff of the Chartists. Paul Pickering has work in progress on this campaign.

[120] *Northern Star*, 27 September 1851.

[121] G.J. Harney to F. Engels, 16 December 1850, in F.G. & R.M. Black (eds), *The Harney Papers*, Assen, 1969, p. 260.

[122] *Northern Star*, 23 November 1850.

[123] *Middleton Guardian*, 12 April 1890. See also *Northern Star*, 18 July 1846 [2nd Edition]. Scholefield's popularity was noted in other local recollections. See Slugg, *Reminiscences*, p. 55; MPL, LHL, Biography Index: *Manchester Guardian*, 13 December 1934.

[124] Cited in Roberts, 'Sixty Years of Service', p. 3.

[125] O'Connor (ed.), *Trial*, p. 111.

CHAPTER 6

'A NEWSPAPER GENIUS'[1]: RICHARD BAGNALL REED
(1831-1908)

For many weeks I watched the *Newcastle (W) Chronicle* with growing impatience for evidence that the men of Tyneside are not behind their fellow-countrymen in 'demonstrating' their earnest desire for the franchise, and as earnest a resolution to break down the barriers that for so long kept them outside the pale of the Constitution.... As it was, I had to 'nurse my wrath' until at length came the *Chronicle* of November 10th, bringing the glad tidings that Newcastle was again 'to the fore'; that the first step had been taken to summon the Northern Reform League from its sleep. I congratulate you. My heart is moved when I see the old names linking the past to the present: *your own*, Richard Ayre, Gregson, Watson, Kane, Reed, and others. (G.J. Harney to W.E. Adams, 1866).[2]

Richard Bagnall Reed was a chainmaker at the village forge in Winlaton, County Durham, who came to wield considerable power both in numerous campaigns for radical reform out of doors, and behind the manager's desk of one of Britain's most important regional newspapers, the *Newcastle Daily Chronicle*. It is well known that Reed owed his remarkable social mobility and subsequent influence to Joseph Cowen junior, the Tyneside industrialist and newspaper baron who was hailed as the 'Tribune of the North' by a generation of working-class radicals in the North East.[3] Plucked by Cowen from relative obscurity in the late 1850s, Reed could be dismissed as little more than a cipher who bathed in the reflected glory of his friend and patron, but to do so would be wrong. Certainly in the early days there was a master-pupil relationship between them, since Reed lacked Cowen's experience,[4] but over time Reed came into his own and, like his fellow worker, W. E. Adams, enjoyed considerable freedom of action in determining the shape and content of the *Chronicle*.[5] Reed was his own man, a fact that was recognised by Cowen himself.[6]

Cowen was right: Reed took part in almost every phase of working-class political activity on Tyneside from the last years of Chartism to the rise of the Reform League. His influence was also felt in other ways: he actively supported trade unions, co-operatives, mechanics' institutes, working men's societies in the form of Freemasonry, and the struggles of those enduring harsher regimes on the Continent. Tributes to Reed's career were many and varied. His colleague, W. E. Adams, the ex-Chartist and disciple of Mazzini, paid tribute to

Reed's untiring political zeal;[7] Karl Blind, the German revolutionary who was arrested in 1848 and subsequently came to live in England, considered him a close friend in view of his clandestine work on behalf of political refugees;[8] G.J. Holyoake, the renowned radical and secularist, respected Reed's skills as a radical journalist;[9] and Richard Fynes, one of the mine workers' leaders in the North East, acknowledged the debt his members owed to Reed as a political educator and campaigner who, among other things, contributed to the election of Thomas Burt for Morpeth in 1874.[10]

Reed has attracted some attention from historians. His high profile role as Secretary of the Northern Reform Union (1857-1862), for example, has been considered in Colin Muris's study of that provincial reform movement.[11] Reed's genius and enterprise as a radical pressman have been stressed in Maurice Milne's valuable entry in the *Dictionary of Labour Biography*, which was the first general outline of Reed's life and career.[12] More recently, Nigel Todd and Joan Hugman, in their respective studies of Joseph Cowen junior, have highlighted the contribution Reed made to Cowen's 'militant democracy'.[13] More needs to be done. The present chapter attempts to build on existing work by exploring sources which do not appear to have been used hitherto.[14] It will argue that Reed's Chartist-inspired radicalism did not lead him easily into supporting the mid-Victorian Liberal consensus. On the lecture platform, in the columns of the press, and in his secretarial work for working-class self-improvement societies, Reed was instrumental in providing the radical cutting edge that was characteristic of provincial Liberalism.

Richard Bagnall Reed was born in 1831 to a family of political activists in the village of Winlaton, County Durham. All his forebears were village craftsmen – blacksmiths and specialist chainmakers – who had worked for or were associated with a compact and illustrious body of workers known as 'Crowley's Crew'. The 'Crew' took their name from and gave allegiance to Sir Ambrose Crowley and his descendants who, from 1690 until 1815, made Winlaton a prosperous manufacturing centre for a wide range of metal goods.[15] The Crowleys owed much of their success to the fact that they were industrial paternalists of a Tory persuasion: they won the respect and political loyalty of their workforce because they paid high wages, introduced a system of social security that included sickness benefits and offered pensions for widows.[16] Moreover, as part of their civilised and stable regime, they also encouraged their workforce to take some control of their own lives through the setting up of Friendly Societies and working men's Freemasonry orders. Both Reed's and Cowen's grandfathers were foremen blacksmiths who became prominent figures from the 1760s onwards in one of these self-help groups which the Crowleys had appropriately named the Lodge of Industry.[17] Reed continued the tradition of working-class self-improvement when he became a member of the Lodge in 1865.[18]

By the time of Reed's birth in 1831 only the memory of the Crowley 'ethos' remained, the ironworks having closed in 1816 due to an inability to compete with more efficient centres located nearer to the Tyne and the new railway network.[19] The consequences of this closure had been far-reaching. Wages for the village craftsmen fell by 1840 to less than 10 shillings per week; there was considerable social distress; and, as owner-paternalism vanished, the great cordiality which had once existed was replaced by what one commentator called a 'class feeling which was bitter and rife' between the embattled smiths and chainmakers and a dwindling band of hard-hearted employers.[20] Consequently, as Joan Hugman has shown, the politics of deference engendered by the Crowleys' Tory paternalism was replaced by an extremely class conscious Chartism that was 'firmly rooted in a profound sense of injustice and fuelled by a nostalgic desire to recapture a seemingly halcyon past'.[21]

In the face of poverty and conscious of the limitations of their existing self-help groups, skilled workers like Richard Reed's father, John, made Winlaton one of the most enthusiastic centres for the cause of Chartism in the North East.[22] There can be no doubting that the depth of class antagonism fuelled the violence associated with Newcastle Chartism in 1839.[23] No evidence has been unearthed to suggest that Reed's father was directly involved in making pikes and caltrops, but we do know that he became a close friend of England's Marat, G.J. Harney, the delegate for Newcastle, who was a leading exponent of physical force at the first Chartist Convention in 1839. On visits to Winlaton to address the local ironworkers, Harney lodged with, amongst others, the Reed family in their humble dwelling in the village.[24] Given the economic dislocation caused by the closure of Crowleys, there was almost certainly a meeting of minds between Reed senior and the young firebrand. Like Harney, John Reed did not trust the middle classes and was strongly opposed to any joint effort or compromise at this time. While Harney's oratory was taking 'Winlaton by storm',[25] Richard Bagnall Reed was an impressionable seven year old. There is no direct evidence that the passionate Harney influenced the young Reed in the intimacy of his own home, but in adult life their paths often crossed and, despite Harney's departure for America in 1863, they remained life-long friends.

Apart from what he learned at his parents' table, as a child Reed received only a rudimentary education, the most important outcome of which appears to have been his rejection of the clergy's attempts at indoctrination.[26] Although he appears to have remained a member of the Church of England, unlike others in this book religion appears to have played little role in Reed's life. Apprenticed to the trade of a blacksmith, he specialised in the branch of chainmaking. With encouragement from his parents, Reed used his spare time to educate himself at the village library (established 1819) and by regular attendance at the Winlaton Literary and Mechanics' Institute (founded 1847).[27] According to one report, the chief delight of his leisure time as a young man was researching 'questions of a political character' in the Institute's reading room.[28] Encouraged by the political education he received here and in his parents' home, Reed began to emerge in the 1850s as the classic village politician. In 1851, at the fourth anniversary of the founding of the Winlaton Mechanics' Institute by Joseph Cowen junior, for example, Reed delivered an address on the theme of 'Civilisation-may it reign victorious in every clime'.[29] In the same year he was made the Institute's librarian, a position that brought him into a working relationship with Cowen, who was secretary, for the first time.[30] Shortly afterwards Reed also became active in the local Chainmakers' Union branch which gave him his first taste of journalism as an occasional contributor of editorials to its newspaper, the *Chainmakers' Journal*.[31] This work sharpened Reed's sense of working-class solidarity and helped to widen his political horizons across the North East. Among the trade union and Chartist contacts he now established, two stand out: John Kane, leader of the Ironworkers' Union,[32] and Martin Jude, formerly at the head of the Miners' Association in the early 1840s, and by the mid 1850s, a Chartist publican in central Newcastle.[33] Due to ailing health Jude was unable to give his best to the cause of labour, but he undoubtedly had an important influence on Reed: when he died in August 1860 the most appreciative tribute came, not from his former comrades among the miners but in the *Chainmakers' Journal*.[34]

Reed's first association with Chartism began in a small way, but it probably helped shape his political thinking and subsequent involvement as an activist in the movement. In January 1854, the family's name was on a printed list of agents approved by Cowen for the sale of his new ultra radical periodical, the monthly *Northern Tribune*.[35] Under Harney's editorship, the *Tribune* contained a range of material which was deliberately aimed at widening the appeal of a Newcastle brand of radicalism under Cowen's distinct and forward-looking style of leadership. Interspersed between articles on local history, science and literature, were pieces outlining republicanism as an ideal form of government, reports on foreign affairs, particularly the progress of European nationalist movements and their heroes, as well as proposals for a renewed campaign for universal suffrage. Significantly, the latter were sometimes explicitly aimed at including 'men who can forget their differences'.[36] Cowen's subtle shift of position reflected the lesson he learned from 1848: that universal suffrage could not be gained without the cooperation of enlightened elements among the middle classes.[37] There was little evidence of this mellowing, however, in Cowen's next venture on Tyneside, the National Republican Brotherhood, in which Reed became an active member. Much to middle-class dismay, the Brotherhood grafted Mazzinian republican ideals of citizenship and virtue onto the demand for the Six Points of the People's Charter.[38] Reed does not appear to have mellowed by this stage. Moving a toast at a Brotherhood dinner in the Blaydon Mechanics' Institute, he boldly anticipated the 'glorious time when Kings and oppressors shall be overthrown and the republic established – democratic and universal'.[39] Other evidence, from his outspoken admiration for the United States of America, overt hostility to the

English aristocracy, and support for the abolition of the Game Laws,[40] suggests that Reed had come to cherish deep republican convictions, even if he later kept them in the closet.

The third aspect to Reed's introduction to late Chartism related to foreign affairs. As Joan Hugman has revealed, Reed became a member of the Newcastle-upon-Tyne Foreign Affairs Committee, which Cowen and Harney had set up in November 1854 following widespread concern about the conduct of the war in the Crimea.[41] There is no evidence to suggest that Reed was anything other than a passive member of the group. In a number of respects, however, its activities and gatherings afforded him a unique opportunity to learn more about foreign affairs and to mix with other members of the Committee, whose social background was very different from his own. As he later demonstrated, Reed learned a great deal about foreign affairs during the two years that the Foreign Affairs Committee met. From a variety of sources, we know that members were kept informed on a range of issues from the expansionist plans of Napoleon III, who had seized power in December 1851, to the work being carried out both overtly and covertly on behalf of oppressed nationalities across Europe.[42] The high point for the radical patriots in Newcastle at this time was the warm reception afforded Garibaldi when he came to stay with Cowen at Stella Hall, Blaydon, for three weeks in March 1854. Although Reed is not recorded as being present at the ceremony on Garibaldi's ship in Shields' harbour, when the committee members presented the revered General with a number of momentos, he would almost certainly have known about the occasion from reading the detailed account in the *Northern Tribune*.[43]

Membership of the Foreign Affairs Committee also helped Reed's radical political apprenticeship by bringing him into contact with several important middle-class radicals. As a number of historians of radicalism in the North East have pointed out, one of the striking features of Newcastle Chartism was its appeal to lower middle-class professional men and the 'shopocracy' who, between them, 'gave as much support and leadership as the working class'.[44] Reed now brushed shoulders with an older generation of radical middle-class men including the President of the Committee, Charles Attwood, an ironmaster, Dr John Fife, an eminent surgeon in the Newcastle region, another surgeon, Dr Skelton, and two shopkeepers, Thomas Gregson and J. T. Gilmour. Some of these men had taken part in the earliest Chartist initiatives of 1839; all were active in the cause of either Hungarian, Polish or Italian independence. As well as consolidating ties with Jude, Kane and Harney, membership of the Foreign Affairs Committee also helped Reed to meet a new generation of Chartist leaders such as James Brown and William Hunter. Reed fully appreciated the importance of the nexus encompassed by the Foreign Affairs Committee when he was mobilising support for the Northern Reform Union's electoral campaigns between 1858 and 1862. In the short term, the Committee gave

Newcastle Chartism new vitality and respectability;[45] it also served to underline
Reed's credibility and potential.

Like many Chartists, Reed's interest in both foreign and domestic affairs found
a new outlet in 1858 in what became known as the Orsini affair. What began in
January 1858 as an attempt by an Italian émigré, Felice Orsini, to assassinate
Louis Napoleon on the way to the opera in London, became a major domestic
crisis when a compliant Prime Minister, Palmerston, appeared to follow the
dictates of the French Foreign Ministry by embarking on a reactionary crusade.
Simultaneously, Palmerston's government introduced a Conspiracy-to-Murder
Bill, initiated a campaign of persecution of radicals and their press, and placed
many exiles under police surveillance.[46] The subsequent prosecutions fell on four
leading supporters of Orsini in England: Dr Simon Bernard and Thomas Allsop,
who were both alleged to have manufactured the bombs, Edward Truelove,
who had published W. E. Adams's polemical pamphlet, *Tyrannicide*, which
made out a case in favour of assassinating the French Emperor, and Stanislaus
Tchorzewski, a Polish bookseller, who sold all things hostile to Bonaparte.
In Newcastle, like elsewhere in the country, indignation at the government's
response was considerable. It seemed as though nothing less than the freedom
of the press and the liberty of the subject were now at stake. The leading national
journal of the later Chartists, the *People's Paper*, identified Reed as particularly
active in Newcastle in relation to this affair.[47] At the Chartist Institute in Nun
Street, Reed was one of a number who spoke out against the 'Press Prosecutions'.
Given his knowledge of foreign affairs, a self-confident Reed not only spoke 'in
strong terms about the conduct of "Napoleon the Little"', but also, according to
the report in the *People's Paper*, 'condemned the base and perfidious conduct
of the British Government for playing lackey to Napoleon'.[48] The rejection of
the Conspiracy-to-Murder Bill by Parliament (in the previous February), the
acquittal of Bernard at the Old Bailey in mid April and the abandonment of the
state prosecutions against Truelove and Tchorzewski only a month later must
surely have delighted Reed, who vehemently opposed any attempt by the state at
circumscribing civil liberties.

Prior to his involvement in the Orsini affair Reed had become involved in a
new political reform movement that arguably represented his most important
contribution to public life: the Northern Reform Union. When Parliamentary
reform was promised by Palmerston's government in the opening of the 1857-
1858 Session, Cowen convened a meeting on 27 December of 'the friends of
political reform' in the Nun Street Chartist Institute.[49] Not only did Reed attend,
but he also moved a resolution, which was seconded by Cowen, calling for a
meeting of reformers early in 1858 'to consider the desirability of forming an
organisation for agitating the Northern Counties in favour of a radical measure
of Parliamentary reform'.[50] At the subsequent meeting the Northern Reform
Union was launched. Its purpose was to mobilise public opinion on behalf of

a campaign for manhood suffrage, the secret ballot and the abolition of the property qualification for MPs.[51] Although the real source of power in the Union was Cowen (who was the Treasurer) Reed gave up his trade to become its full time secretary, a position he held until the summer of 1861. It was a decision that changed his life. For Reed the Northern Reform Union became a crusade.[52] As Cowen's principal lieutenant he involved himself in a range of duties from public speaking, letter-writing, and distributing tracts, to managing the Union's publicity organ, the *Northern Reform Record*, and presenting quarterly reports to its thirty member Council. The Council was comprised of former Chartists, including influential middle-class figures, such as Thomas Doubleday and Charles Larkin,[53] skilled workers, trade unionists, members of friendly societies and mechanics' institutes, as well as newer recruits to the radical cause, such as the miners' leader, Richard Fynes, and Robert Warden of the Tyneside engineers.[54] The rank and file of the Northern Reform Union was drawn mainly from the pit villages and among the elite of the working classes; it also numbered, as was hoped, a sprinkling of lower middle-class shopkeepers as well as some professionals.[55] Finally, the Council attracted sympathetic publicity from influential Chartist leaders who could be paraded as ex officio members. Among them were Harney, who was in Jersey where he was editing the *Jersey Independent*, and G. J. Holyoake in London, who praised the Union in the *Daily News*.[56]

Reed's decision, on behalf of the Union, to support less than universal manhood suffrage, was a tactical shift designed to attract middle-class reformers. Clearly he was encouraged by success at local government level: in the late 1850s an advanced faction of the Ratepayers' Association, some of whose members were sympathetic to Chartist demands, had made significant progress in ending the Whig clique's long-standing domination of the Newcastle City Council.[57] Could the same formula be applied to parliamentary politics? The ultimate goal remained universal suffrage, but a new sense of realism encouraged Reed and Cowen to offer concessions that would make their campaign for parliamentary reform more appealing to middle class reformers.[58] The suffrage should be granted to all men, but based on a system of registration, and paupers, criminals and the insane were to be excluded.[59] Most importantly, Reed acknowledged that an elector should, 'by a fixed residence', give 'proof of his being an honest citizen'.[60] Even though they had compromised at the margins, Reed and Cowen had no difficulty in carrying their skilled supporters along with them on this revised platform of political rights, and it was sufficiently radical to count on strategic support from both Ernest Jones's nationally-circulating *People's Paper*,[61] and the largest Tyneside Chartist branch based in Newcastle.[62] They did, however, face charges of elitism from two quarters. Robert Mathison, reflecting the views of the Berwick Chartists, objected to the exclusion of paupers from the franchise,[63] and Jeanette Natham articulated the resentment felt by some of the wives and daughters of the Union's members at being left off the agenda. As she wrote to Reed:[64]

> At present I do not feel inclined to become a member of any society which as a society is purely selfish in its objects and does not recognise the principles of justice and rights for all ...

It was good point. For all that it was disappointing, Reed's reply went further than some former Chartists: the Union had settled for the formula of enfranchising men first and women later.[65]

Renewed expectations of reform from the Conservative government in 1859 prompted the Union to step up its activities. A campaign of meetings was set in motion across the North East at which petitions were to be signed advocating the Union's programme as the basis for the anticipated Reform Act. Just as the campaign reached its climax early in February 1859, Reed penned a revealing letter to Holyoake that allows us glimpse inside the operation of the Union, and to better appreciate the activity it conducted on an impressive scale. Since the beginning of the campaign, he reported, representatives of the Union had addressed no less than eighty meetings with an aggregate attendance of 'between 60,000 and 70,000 persons'. 'All our village organisations', Reed continued, 'are in good working order and the petitions are being extensively signed'. Moreover, the strategy of courting support from the middle classes seemed to be bearing fruit:[66]

> In Newcastle, 7,000 signatures have been obtained, and the professional class, such as clerks, accountants etc. have signed in a greater proportion than even working men. In Gateshead 3,000 signatures have been got, and altogether in the two counties about 30,000.

Although this fell short of the total number of signatures obtained in the halcyon days of early Chartism,[67] it was an impressive achievement. 'I am working like a "hack horse" and Mr Cowen is ditto', Reed confessed, but the results were a cause for optimism. Even a 'live lord', Lord Durham, 'has given us an unqualified adhesion', Reed boasted.[68]

The agitation culminated with a large public meeting in Newcastle Town Hall on 8 February at which the petition was collated. This meeting also recalled the days of the mass agitation for the Charter: over 4,000 were present with some groups of supporters marching into the Hall in an ordered manner headed by their village band and colourful banners.[69] An estimated six hundred yards of petition was finally presented to the House of Commons on 29 February by the veteran radical Perronet Thompson MP.[70] Reed's and Cowen's understandable pride at the success of the Union campaign only served to deepen their disappointment when the terms of Disraeli's Reform Bill were made known. A meeting of the Union was called in Newcastle on 2 March 1859 in order to begin a new phase of protest against it.[71] Radicalism was not a creed for those who were easily deflected.

There were two other aspects to the Northern Reform Union's work in which Reed played an active part: firstly, P. A. Taylor's campaign for Newcastle at the General Election of 1859; and, secondly, following revelations of malpractice at Berwick-upon-Tweed during the election, an attempt to expose corruption as a means of convincing middle-class voters of the gross inadequacies of the existing electoral system.[72] The initiative to bring Taylor to Newcastle under the auspices of the Union was Cowen's. Taylor had sound Chartist and republican credentials and with Cowen's backing he was unanimously adopted as a Radical candidate at the beginning of June 1858.[73] Unfortunately, Cowen's ultimate aim of presenting a broad Radical front to challenge the two Whig-Liberal incumbents foundered for a combination of reasons relating to personality, policy and social class.[74] Although he canvassed hard in 1859, Reed confessed to Holyoake that Taylor was not the right man.[75] For one thing, he felt that Taylor lacked warmth in man-to-man relations; for another he was devoid of both tact and discretion. Some of Taylor's public pronouncements on sensitive issues, such as religious toleration, undoubtedly upset the Dissenting elements within the radical Newcastle Ratepayers' Association. Moreover, the Association had fielded Peter Carstairs, a retired Bombay merchant, on a platform of strict temperance, Sabbatarianism and the promise of widening the franchise at the previous General Election of 1857, and were anxious to run him again. Ostensibly the impasse was resolved when the Association withdrew Carstairs as a candidate, but this did little to help Taylor.

Thirdly, the General Election result of 1859 made it abundantly clear that social class was still a key factor in determining voting behaviour. When they learned that Taylor had secured only 463 votes, compared with the 2,687 and 2,680 that were cast for the sitting Whig-Liberals, T. E. Headlam and G. Ridley, Reed and Cowen were horrified. As Muris comments, defeat meant that 'their efforts over the 15 months to woo the liberal electorate had failed'.[76] The hopes for a new political alignment proved fanciful. In a widely circulated letter written on behalf of the Union's Council in October 1859,[77] Reed and Cowen pinpointed class interests as the major cause of defeat. Specifically they blamed the 'shopocracy' for leaving them powerless. The previous campaign to gather the petition had convinced them that this particular constituency had been won over, but this was clearly not the case. For all their manoeuvring to secure a cross class cooperation, Reed and Cowen were never prepared to compromise the basic principle of manhood suffrage. The platform of the Northern Reform Union thus remained too radical for the middle-class electorate to embrace. The dynamics of class politics meant that only the most 'advanced' radical middle-class reformers – the occasional doctor, business man, and a few progressive shopkeepers – were ready to work with ex-Chartists like Reed in a movement based around working-class rights.[78]

The 1859 General Election also embroiled the Union in the prosecution of the so-called 'Berwick Bribers'. One of the achievements of the Union during its four-year life was the setting up of 'vigilance committees' in order to monitor the conduct of both local and parliamentary elections. At the request of the Chartist, Robert Mathison, who, despite his former criticism, was extremely active on the Union's behalf in Berwick-upon-Tweed, Reed visited the constituency to gather evidence of the malpractice that had allegedly taken place not only during the General Election, but also in an ensuing by-election. On behalf of a Berwick Election Committee consisting of himself, Cowen, and J. T. Gilmour, Reed prepared a full and frank report that was published in December 1859.[79] The main target was a Whig-liberal, D. C. Marjoribanks, who had been defeated at the General Election but had managed to get himself returned by the thinnest of margins – one vote – in a by-election held four months later. Between the two dates Marjoribanks, it was claimed, had come to an arrangement with one of the victorious Conservatives to vacate the seat, only to find that the local Conservatives had taken umbrage and proceeded to field their own candidate. Cowen and Reed were determined to take even stronger action: they consulted a Jedburgh attorney and brought a private prosecution in Reed's name under the Corrupt Practices Act of 1854. As both Muris and Milne have shown, the whole business was a disaster from start to finish.[80] Strategically, it cost the Union a great deal of middle class support; legally, they were badly advised; and financially Cowen's bank balance was drained of £2,500. Reed's bribery petition received short shrift in court. A Parliamentary Commission did eventually find that one person had been guilty of bribery, but it was a Pyrrhic victory. Much to Reed's disappointment, Marjoribanks was exonerated and, to the disgust of the Union's working-class supporters in the town, Berwick retained both its seats until the Redistribution Act of 1885. Despite the disastrous results, Reed enjoyed the legal work, telling Mathison during the proceedings that he would have liked a career as a lawyer, and he continued for a time to play an active part in the Vigilance Committee's work in overseeing Newcastle's municipal elections.[81]

In terms of its own agenda it is tempting to see the Northern Reform Union as a dismal failure.[82] They had made no discernible impact on the government's Reform proposals, the campaign to woo the shopocracy was rebuffed, and the attempt to prevent electoral manipulation back-fired. Viewed from a wider perspective, however, the Northern Reform Union played a vital role in convincing the public in the North East that political reform was necessary. As one commentator recalled, when the[83]

> Liberal Party took up the question of Parliamentary Reform there was no part
> of England better prepared, from knowledge of the question and interest in the

settlement, than the district which Mr Cowen and his coadjutors of the Northern Reform Union had so thoroughly and efficiently instructed in the rights and duties of the people.

The importance of Reed's contribution to placing Tyneside in the vanguard of change should not be overlooked. In the last quarter of the nineteenth century Tyneside was a beacon that prompted radicals in other towns and cities, including London and Birmingham, into bringing the question of democratic reforms back into the public domain.[84]

During his time as secretary of the Northern Reform Union Reed was involved in two other activities which, in different ways, brought more immediate benefits to working people, both at home and abroad. As soon as the Berwick case was over, Reed became actively involved in fundraising for the Italian nationalist, Giuseppe Garibaldi. The high point of British interest in Garibaldi and the Italian Question came in the years 1859-61. Working- and middle-class radicals across Britain were fascinated by the military progress of the General's 'Thousand Red-Shirts' through Sicily and on the Italian mainland in 1860.[85] In Newcastle, Cowen had already established such a strong reputation as a supporter of oppressed nationalities, and of working class internationalism, that he had come under the surveillance both by the security forces and by agents of foreign governments.[86] By 1859 Cowen had all but completed his acquisition of the Newcastle Daily Chronicle which was immediately opened up as a platform for actively propagandising on Garibaldi's behalf.[87] In 1860, a Garibaldi Fund Committee was openly established in Newcastle and the columns of the Daily Chronicle were then used to portray the General as 'the hero of liberty' and to advertise the fact that the newspaper's office acted as a depository for funds.[88] Reed's role was to ensure that both the money raised (over £340[89]) and the military assistance offered by those who wished to enlist in the General's army of liberation, got through. This task went beyond routine administration as it involved avoiding the detection of some activities that were prohibited by the Foreign Enlistment Act. Reed's letters to Holyoake provide an interesting if understandably brief glimpse of the sort of covert aid that British radicals provided to their European counterparts. It would appear that guns for Garibaldi were secretly manufactured not only in Newcastle, but also under contract in Sheffield.[90] Nothing has been unearthed to suggest how many rifles left the Tyne concealed in consignments of bricks from Cowen's Blaydon factory. It is clear that Reed's role was to act as a go-between, informing Holyoake, a veteran of gun-running to Orsini, when shipments were ready and when they might arrive in the capital. In London Holyoake's function was to liaise with Garibaldi's aide-de-camp, to ensure their successful passage to the Italian battlefields.[91] Reed must have been well satisfied with the outcome: the official declaration of the new and free Italy in March 1861. Some money continued to come in for Garibaldi at the *Chronicle's* office, and in 1864 the Fund Committee divided about £21 equally between Garibaldi's sons, Menotti and Riccotti.[92]

The Garibaldi agitation overlapped with a cause much closer to home. In May 1860 the House of Lords rejected Gladstone's attempt to repeal the duty on paper, the removal of which would have further enhanced the freedom of expression.[93] There was a public outcry not least on Tyneside and Reed, fresh from his experiences of editing the *Northern Reform Record*, was extremely active in organising protest meetings and the collection of a petition.[94] The chief opponent of repeal in the House of Lords was Lord Monteagle of Brandon in Kerry.[95] A commissioner for the state paper office, Monteagle had come out of retirement on this issue. Reed's strength of feeling about the defeat and the anti-aristocratic opinions it encouraged in him, were fully revealed in a letter to Holyoake on 22 May, the day after the Lords voted. 'So the Lords have done it as I expected', he told Holyoake,[96]

> I propose we abolish the 'House of Incurables'. London ought to be thoroughly agitated upon the question of privilege. Lords Derby and Monteagle ought to be mobbed at once. Tar and feathers will be cheaply enough bought at London.

Ever the optimist Reed consoled himself with a positive thought: 'Perhaps after all the rejection of the Paper Duty Repeal Bill by the Lords will effect the agitation for reform better than any other thing'.[97] The agitation for the franchise does not appear to have been helped in the North East by this adverse decision, but a year later the Paper Duty was successfully removed by the Liberals. It was a reform that must have been helpful to Reed in the next stage of his career as editor and then as the general business manager overseeing the commercial success of the *Newcastle Daily Chronicle*.

Five months after the *Northern Reform Record* closed in July 1859, Cowen purchased the *Newcastle Daily Chronicle* from its owner, M. W. Lambert, in order to obtain greater publicity for the Northern Reform Union. Although the reasons remain obscure, in January 1861 Cowen decided to dismiss the incumbent editor, John Baxter Langley, despite Langley's standing as a middle-class radical.[98] Cowen made no secret of his admiration for Reed's 'great intelligence, shrewdness and business capabilities' and, a month later, he appointed the former chainmaker as editor and then, shortly afterwards, as general manager of the newspaper.[99] As general manager Reed's control extended to every department of the *Chronicle*.[100] Reed's upward mobility was remarkable: from lowly iron worker in depressed Winlaton he had, within the space of four years, attained a professional position at the top of the world of provincial journalism, an office that carried with it considerable social weight and influence both in and beyond the North East. Following heavy investment by Cowen, by 1867 Reed managed at least 210 office, literary, commercial and printing staff.[101] Unfortunately, no evidence has been unearthed to indicate the kind of financial remuneration that Reed received. A guide, however, can be gained from the salary levels of two of his contemporaries in the North East: in Sunderland, the manager of the *Sunderland Daily Echo*, W. A. Brignal, who was its highest paid employee, received an annual salary of £208 in 1874;[102] and at the *Newcastle Weekly Chronicle*, James Annand was paid £250 per annum on the commencement of his editorial duties in 1871.[103] Given that by the mid 1860s the *Newcastle Daily Chronicle* had the highest circulation in the North East, it is likely that Reed was paid at least the same if not more than Annand. There are other indicators of his considerable wealth: from the size of his family – he and his wife, Jane, had sixteen children (seven sons and five daughters survived him) – which led to the acquisition of a 'substantial house' in Forest Hall on the outskirts of Newcastle,[104] to the fact that he left estate valued at £30,447 when he died in 1908.[105]

One of the first political campaigns that Reed was involved in on behalf of the *Chronicle* concerned the parliamentary representation of Newcastle. In mid March 1864 his name appeared in a published list of influential ratepayers and electors who not only wanted further political reform, but were also dissatisfied with the conduct of their two sitting Whig- Liberal MPs, T. E. Headlam and S. H. Beaumont.[106] At a public meeting held in March a loose alliance was formed between Radical middle-class reformers, Dissenters and ex-Chartists that led, in turn, to the adoption and successful return (at Beaumont's expense), of Joseph Cowen's father on a broadly radical platform at the General Election in mid July 1865.[107] Cowen senior was in favour of household rather than manhood suffrage,[108] but his support for the secret ballot and triennial parliaments did much to lay the groundwork for the renewed agitation for a further extension of the suffrage that occurred in 1866.[109]

The renewed agitation produced a national organisation consisting of a powerful extra parliamentary alliance of trade unionists, middle-class radicals and ex-Chartists. This was the Reform League. Joseph Cowen junior became a vice president of the Reform League in 1866, but by November (much to the delight of Harney as noted at the beginning of this chapter) he had decided to launch a separate Northern Reform League based in Newcastle. For all intents and purposes the Northern Reform League was a revival of the Northern Reform Union. As Todd has noted, 'the objects and rules of the League, including manhood suffrage, were those of the Union except for a few minor alterations made in Cowen's handwriting'.[110] The chief difference was that the Northern Reform League was more securely based within the working class: for example, at least a third of the one hundred members of the League's governing council were miners.[111]

As a former Chartist and now a senior member of the 'fourth estate', Reed had an important influence on the course of the Reform debate during 1866 and

1867. Reed became a member of the Council of the Northern Reform League at its inaugural meeting in November 1866, taking his place alongside old friends from the Northern Reform Union together with new members representing the Tyneside trades.[112] Thereafter he attended a number of Reform Demonstration Committee meetings and ensured that the agitation enjoyed a high profile in the columns of the *Chronicle*.[113] In May 1867, Reed took part in the delegation from the Reform League, which included Edmond Beales, George Potter, P. A. Taylor and James Stansfeld, that met with middle-class members of the National Reform Union at the Westminster Palace Hotel in London. According to the report in *The Times*, the object of the meeting was 'to consider the propriety of holding, as soon as possible, public meetings in London on the present position of the question of reform in Parliament'.[114] Agreement was reached on the need to keep up the pressure on Disraeli, whose Reform Bill was making little headway in Parliament, by organising jointly a series of reform meetings amongst 'those sections of the inhabitants of the metropolis which have not hitherto pronounced on this important question'.[115]

At this point, however, Reed became increasingly preoccupied with his managerial duties at the *Chronicle*, and, following the Reform Act of 1867, when the borough franchise was granted to the working class, he played only a secondary part in the Northern Reform League's later campaign to obtain the franchise for the local miners. Nevertheless, as noted earlier, Reed did receive credit for his role in the campaign that resulted in the triumphant election of Thomas Burt for Morpeth in 1874. There was plenty to occupy his attention at the *Chronicle*. Cowen's energy and financial backing made the *Newcastle Daily Chronicle* one of the most powerful newspapers in the land in the second half of the nineteenth century. In the counties of Northumberland and Durham its political influence was enormous.[116] On trade union matters, co-operatives, political reform, human rights and international affairs the *Chronicle* was the required reading of the politically conscious working class in the North East.[117] At the same time the paper broadened its appeal by covering sporting events, church news, local chit-chat, crime, literary and theatrical events, and book reviews.[118] Farming and agricultural news too was given its own column, a decision that would have appealed to the many thousands of former Chartists among the urban working classes who had subscribed to the Chartist Land Plan in the hope of achieving rural resettlement as independent land holders.[119] Not surprisingly, the circulation figures of the paper were spectacularly transformed: in 1860 when Cowen gained control the *Chronicle* had a daily circulation of only 2,500 copies; by 1893, it had become one of the largest provincial newspapers with 120,000 copies sold daily.[120]

It was Reed's enterprise that made this possible: as one historian has aptly put it, he found 'his true *métier* as manager of the *Chronicle*'.[121] According to Reed's perceptive colleague, W.E. Adams, he was nothing short of a 'newspaper genius'[122]

> Newspaper success depends even more upon skilful management than upon skilful writing. One of the most skilful managers of the time of which I am writing, and long after-wards, was Richard Bagnall Reed. No shrewder intellect than his, I think, was ever connected with the press. If he did not write much himself, he knew how to instruct and inspire others to write. And his energy was amazing. Nothing in any department of the paper escaped his watchful eye. Added to untiring zeal was a marvellous capacity for gauging the tastes and requirements of the reading public.

Reed's inventiveness, resourcefulness and technical genius in advancing the influence of the provincial press have been well documented.[123] No acknowledgement, however, has been made of the way in which his radicalism shaped his relationships with the many staff under his charge. First and foremost, Reed was 'a friend of the people' who worked in the large offices of the *Newcastle Daily Chronicle* on Westgate Street in the city centre.

Reed spelt out his workplace philosophy early in his professional career at the centenary celebrations of the *Chronicle* in March 1864. Before a gathering of distinguished guests, newspaper editors, journalists and printers, Reed typically began by praising the paper's manual labour force – the handworkers – as 'worthy samples of the mechanics of England':[124]

> The literary writers might expose a job or gibbet an infamous deed; but it was upon the steadiness and industry of the compositors that they could calculate to a moment the time to be occupied in setting that leader, or a report of a speech.

Equally important were those 'who had the management of the complicated machinery in what was best known in newspaper offices as "the downstairs department"'. All the efforts of 'what was termed the more intellectual portion of a newspaper staff', he confessed, would be to little avail without the 'attention, skill, steadiness, and industry of these men'.[125] Clearly, Reed had not forgotten his early years as a manual labourer in Winlaton.

Not surprisingly, Reed gained a reputation for rolling up his sleeves when necessary, and for his compassionate treatment of his employees.[126] As one of them recalled:[127]

> to any complaint or suggestion with a view to remedying any defect or grievance, he was always ready to listen, and when any dispute or feeling of dissatisfaction arose, he believed in and acted upon, the principle of both sides being fairly and fully heard. Towards all with whom he came in contact he exhibited a frank and straightforward disposition.

The evidence of length of service among Reed's immediate subordinates lends further weight to this positive assessment of his management style. As Lucy Brown has shown, nineteenth century journalism was seen as a specialised craft that called for particular qualities including disciplined writing skills, an ability to meet deadlines and working unsociable hours.[128] Consequently, a common feature of many journalistic careers was mobility: 'many men moved from job to job at bewilderingly frequent intervals'.[129] The last feature was not the pattern at the *Chronicle*. During Reed's long career – he did not retire until 1900 – several of his senior colleagues, including W. E. Adams (editor of the *Weekly*), William Duncan (a sub editor at the *Weekly*) and Richard Ruddock (editor of the *Daily*), all matched his impressive length of service. The only exception was the dismissal of James Annand, the editor before Ruddock, in 1878 after seven years in the post, but this was a direct result of differences with Cowen over the reporting of the Eastern Question.[130] Reed also enjoyed long and harmonious relations with the more junior staff. For example, Thomas Hutchinson, the chief sports writer, worked for forty-two years until his death at the age of fifty-four; and John Lumley, the chief printer, was employed for a record fifty-seven years.[131] As Aaron Watson noted enthusiastically in his memoirs about working on the *Chronicle*, Reed was 'a very remarkable manager'.[132]

The final aspect to Reed's radicalism was his involvement in self-improvement societies, particularly the fraternity of Freemasons. In his Introduction to the first volume of the *Dictionary of Labour Biography* in 1972, John Saville noted with some surprise the large number of working men who became Freemasons in the nineteenth century, but only recently has further research into this question got under way.[133] Freemasonry in Britain underwent a long process of gentrification that became particularly rapid in the second half of the nineteenth century. This was a time when Lodges were filled increasingly by professionals and businessmen.[134] Tyneside, however, appears to have retained a strong tradition of working-class Freemasonry which consciously overlapped with the craft-based tradition of radically inspired Friendly Societies. Both traditions actively fulfilled and were mutually reinforced by a strong commitment to welfare.[135] Like Cowen, Reed was attracted to Freemasonry by its long-standing tradition of working-class self-help, rather than because it offered an opportunity for social advancement. Although it would be naïve to argue that Reed did not benefit professionally from his contact with the newer middle-class recruits to the Order, what he seems to have valued most was the camaraderie, etiquette and the chain of command in which he became a master in his own right.[136] Reed's energy and drive helped his Lodge, The Lodge of Industry, to not only survive but to prosper, including a successful move to new premises in Gateshead in January 1882. Although Reed was a stalwart of The Lodge of Industry, Andrew Prescott has pointed out that it was not in regular craft Freemasonry that he made his most important contribution to the movement. As Prescott notes, there are various additional degrees and extra Orders that enthusiastic Freemasons can join. One of these, for example, was Mark Masonry which was a completely separate organisation that established its own Grand Lodge in England in the 1860s, though its origins may well have been Scottish. It was to Mark Masonry that Reed became particularly devoted, and it was as a Mark Mason (rather than in conventional craft Freemasonry) that he served for many years as Deputy Provincial Grand Master of the Freemasonry Lodges for the whole of Northumberland and Durham.[137] When failing health forced him to retire from active Freemasonry duties in 1896, Reed was presented with an address and a life-size painting in oils of his portrait in recognition of his 'wise counsel'. His wife, Jane, was given a diamond ring 'as a memento of the great esteem in which her husband was held by his brethren in Mark Masonry'.[138]

Richard Bagnall Reed died on Thursday 27 February 1908, aged 77. His funeral service – an elaborate and dignified Masonic ceremony[139] – took place at Long Benton on the following Sunday, and he was then buried in the family vault in the parish churchyard. The report in his beloved *Chronicle* was accompanied by a short piece from a 'correspondent', who evidently felt moved to write in affectionate remembrance on hearing of Reed's death. Recalling fifty years of struggle, the correspondent noted how 'Reed was one of the principal political reform educators of the present-day old radicals and reformers, who belonged to Tyneside and the North of England forty or fifty years ago'. 'And in the present day', the anonymous correspondent continued, 'we should not forget, that when it was not popular to be a reformer, Mr Cowen and Mr Reed kindled a desire for knowledge and liberty among the people of the North of England'.[140]

The anonymous correspondent worried unnecessarily: Reed's legacy would be evident in the lives of his children. By the time of Reed's death one of his seven surviving sons, Joseph Reed, had already succeeded him as managing director of the *Chronicle*. It was the sort of dynastic succession that was common in radical politics. Joseph later completed the rise begun by his father when he received a knighthood in 1922.[141] It is a testimony to the openness of the British aristocracy and to the extraordinary trajectory of a genealogy of Chartism.

Another of Reed's sons, John Hastings Reed, had also begun his working life at the *Chronicle* before an interest in chemistry took him to Germany to further his studies. After returning to England John Reed also followed a familiar path in a radical family: he emigrated. At first he went to America – the nation his father deeply admired – before going on to Australia.[142] During the second half of the nineteenth century the Australian colonies became the repository of a great deal of Chartist aspiration: here was a 'working man's paradise' where hard work and self-reliance – the values exemplified by Richard Bagnall Reed – held out the prospect of wealth and social independence. By 1883, a leading English socialist, H.M. Hyndman, lamented the fact that the 'clearest-sighted of our working class politicians' had 'abandoned the apparently hopeless struggle against class inequality and class greed at home to seek a wider field in new countries ...'[143]

Like McDouall, John Reed must have been tempted by the opportunity to help forge a better Britain in the antipodes. In Victoria Reed worked as a humble 'Jackaroo' – an Australian farm hand – before emulating his father's rapid rise in social standing by accepting a position as a chemist with what would become one of Australia's leading companies, Colonial Sugar Refining (CSR). By 1897 Reed had moved to north Queensland to manage CSR's mill and plantations at Hambledon outside of Cairns. Here he became a pillar of the community, applying his scientific skills to the eradication of the natural pests that threatened the livelihood of ordinary cane-growers. As a vociferous advocate of development through commercial expansion Reed went on to be a founding member of the Cairns Stock Exchange in 1906.[144] Few of those who travel along Reed Street in Cairns in far north Queensland today would know that it leads to the village forge in Winlaton on Tyneside where a humble chainmaker dreamed of becoming a friend of the people.

Notes

[1] W. E. Adams, *Memoirs of a Social Atom*, 1903, repr. New York, 1969, p. 493.

[2] *Newcastle Weekly Chronicle*, 29 December 1866.

[3] K. Harris, 'Joseph Cowen – The Northern Tribune', *Bulletin of the North East Group for the Study of Labour History*', no. 5, 1971, pp. 1-7. See also Adams, *Memoirs*, p. 495.

[4] C. Muris, 'The Northern Reform Union, 1858-1862', M.A., University of Newcastle, 1953, pp. 13-14.

[5] A. Watson, *A Newspaper Man's Memories*, London, 1925, pp. 46-47; A. J. Lee, *The Origins of the Popular Press in England, 1855-1914*, London, 1976, p. 174.

[6] *The Cowen Collection*, D449, 27 March 1894, Cowen to W. Longstaffe. See also M. Milne, 'Richard Bagnall Reed (1831-1908), Radical Reformer' in J. Saville & J. Bellamy (eds), *Dictionary of Labour Biography*, vol. iv, London, 1977, pp. 142-146, particularly p. 142.

[7] *Newcastle Weekly Chronicle*, 3 March 1900.

[8] K. Blind to G.J. Harney, 8 November 1879, in F. G. Black & R. N. Black (eds), *The Harney Papers*, Assen, 1969 p. 174.

[9] G. J. Holyoake, *Sixty Years of an Agitator's Life*, London, 1892, vol.1, p. 2. Holyoake noted that Reed, who had 'a journalist's instinct for incidents', was one of a group of radical friends who had urged him to write his memoirs.

[10] R. Fynes, *The Miners of Northumberland and Durham*, 1873, repr. Sunderland, 1923, p. 300.

[11] Muris, 'The Northern Reform Union'.

[12] Milne, 'Richard Bagnall Reed', p. 145.

[13] N. Todd, *The Militant Democracy: Joseph Cowen and Victorian Radicalism*, Tyne and Wear, 1991; J. Hugman, 'Joseph Cowen of Newcastle and Radical Liberalism', PhD, University of Northumbria at Newcastle, 1993; J. Hugman, 'Print and Preach: The Entrepreneurial Spirit of Nineteenth Century Newcastle', in R. Colls & B. Lancaster (eds), *Newcastle Upon Tyne. A Modern History*, Chichester, 2001, pp. 113-132. See also K. G. E. Harris, 'Joseph Cowen, Radical Reformer, Politician and Co-operator', in Saville & Bellamy, (eds), *Dictionary of Labour Biography*, vol. 1, pp. 81-86.

[14] These include the *People's Paper*, the *Jersey Independent*, the fairly extensive Reed-Holyoake correspondence, and the recently published political papers of the Reform League. See *The Holyoake Papers*, MM96636/Reel 3, Co-operative Union Library, Manchester, letters nos. 1137 to 1258; J. Breuilly, G. Niedhart & A. Taylor (eds), *The Era of the Reform League: English Labour and*

Radical Politics 1857-1872, Mannheim, 1995.

[15] R. Whitfield, *The History of the Lodge of Industry, No. 48, of Freemasonry, From 1725 to 1911,* Newcastle upon Tyne, 1911, pp. 1-3. Sir Ambrose Crowley was knighted in January 1706, served as Sheriff of London in 1707, and died in 1713 while he was MP for Andover.

[16] Hugman, 'Joseph Cowen', pp. 17-18.

[17] Whitfield, *The History of the Lodge of Industry,* p. 28.

[18] Ibid., pp. 49-51.

[19] T. J. Nossiter, *Influence, Opinion and Political Idioms in Reformed England. Case Studies from the North East 1832-74,* Brighton, 1975, pp. 13-14.

[20] *Northern Tribune,* vol. 1, no. 2, January-May 1854.

[21] Hugman, 'Joseph Cowen', p. 18.

[22] A. R. Schoyen, *The Chartist Challenge,* London, 1958, pp. 42-47.

[23] D. J. Rowe, 'Tyneside Chartism', in N. McCord (ed.), *Essays in Tyneside Labour History,* Newcastle, 1977, pp. 62-87, particularly p. 65; Nossiter, *Influence, Opinion and Political Idioms,* p. 153.

[24] *Newcastle Weekly Chronicle,* 15 January 1898.

[25] Ibid.

[26] *Northern Tribune,* vol.1, no. 2, January-May 1854.

[27] Ibid.

[28] *Newcastle Weekly Chronicle,* 29 February 1908. This source also appears as a cutting in R. W. Martin, *Northern Worthies,* 1932, vol. 1, pp. 389-391.

[29] Milne, 'Richard Bagnall Reed', p. 142.

[30] Ibid.

[31] Muris, 'The Northern Reform Union', pp. 150-151.

[32] T. Tholfsen, *Working Class Radicalism in Mid Victorian England,* London, 1976, p. 285.

[33] Muris, 'The Northern Reform Union', p. 150.

[34] R. Challinor & B. Ripley, *The Miners Association – A Trade Union in the Age of the Chartists,* London, 1968, p. 248.

[35] *Northern Tribune,* vol. 1, no. 2, January-May 1854.

[36] Todd, *The Militant Democracy,* p. 39.

[37] *Northern Tribune,* vol.1, no. 2, January-May 1854.

[38] Todd, *The Militant Democracy,* p. 38.

[39] *Northern Daily Express,* 2 January 1856.

[40] *Newcastle Weekly Chronicle,* 14 May 1881; *The Holyoake Papers,* MM 96636/ Reel 3, letter 1218, Reed to Holyoake, 20 May 1860; Muris, 'The Northern Reform Union' p. 150; *The Cowen Collection,* C1556, C1562.

[41] Hugman, 'Joseph Cowen', p. 57.

[42] P. Brock, 'Joseph Cowen and the Polish Exiles', *Slavonic and East European Review,* vol. xxxii, 1953, pp. 52-69; N. J. Gossman, 'British Aid to Polish, Italian, and Hungarian Exiles 1830-1870', *South Atlantic Quarterly,* vol.68, Spring 1969, pp. 231-245; Hugman, 'Joseph Cowen', pp. 57-66. In all their work the Newcastle Committee distanced itself from the hysterically anti-Russian views of the outspoken Tory, David Urquhart, who was dictating policy to members in branches elsewhere in the country. See R. Shannon, 'David Urquhart and the Foreign Affairs Committees', in P. Hollis (ed.), *Pressure from Without in early Victorian England,* London, 1974, pp. 239-261; Hugman, 'Joseph Cowen', p. 66.

[43] *Northern Tribune,* vol.1, no. 5, January-May 1854.

[44] Nossiter, *Influence, Opinion and Political Idioms,* p. 149. See also Schoyen, *The Chartist Challenge,* p. 42; Rowe, 'Tyneside Chartism', pp. 68-73; C. Godfrey, *Chartist Lives. The Anatomy of a Working Class Movement,* New York, 1987, p. 352.

[45] Tholfsen, *Working Class Radicalism,* pp. 149-150.

[46] For a detailed account of the campaign of persecution see O. R. Ashton, *W. E. Adams: Chartist, Radical and Journalist (1832-1906),* Tyne and Wear, 1991, pp. 73-79.

[47] *People's Paper,* 17, 24 April 1858.

[48] Ibid., 24 April 1858.

[49] Muris, 'The Northern Reform Union', p. 3.

[50] Ibid.

[51] Ibid., pp. 33-34.

[52] Ibid., p. 13.

[53] For the influence of Doubleday and Larkin in Newcastle Chartism, see B. Harrison & P. Hollis (eds), *Robert Lowery, Radical and Chartist,* London, 1979, pp. 64-65; Nossiter, *Influence, Opinion and Political Idioms,* p. 152.

[54] These men were members of the Council as individuals and not in their capacity as trade unionists or leaders of working-class self-help groups.

[55] Muris, 'The Northern Reform Union', pp. 22-24, 125.

[56] See, for example, *Jersey Independent and Daily Telegraph,* 10 March 1858, 18 April, 12 November 1860; Black & Black (eds), *The Harney Papers,* pp. 108-109, 143-144; *Holyoake Papers,* MM 96636/ Reel 3, letter1187, cutting from *The Daily News,*10 February 1860, 'The Nature of the Demand for Reform' by Disque (Holyoake).

[57] F. E. Gillespie, *Labour and Politics in England,* London, 1966, pp. 119-120, 136.

[58] See Muris, 'The Northern Reform Union', p. 39.

[59] Ibid., p. 41.

[60] Milne, 'Richard Bagnall Reed', p. 143.

[61] *People's Paper,* 14 August 1858.

[62] Muris, 'The Northern Reform Union', p. 125.

[63] Ibid., p. 35.

[64] Quoted by Todd, *The Militant Democracy,* p. 43.

[65] Some Chartists believed that the enfranchisement of women was unnecessary; the common assumption was that the interests of women would be protected by male suffrage in the family context. See conclusion below.

[66] *Holyoake Papers,* Part 1, General Correspondence 1840-1879, FN 96188/6, Miscellaneous Letters A-W, Reed to Holyoake, I February 1859.

[67] In 1842 the Chartist petition contained 92,000 signatures from Newcastle and district. See *Hansard,* 2 May 1842, col. 1375.

[68] *Holyoake Papers,* Reed to Holyoake, I February 1859.

[69] Ibid.

[70] Hugman, 'Joseph Cowen', p. 73.

[71] Muris, 'The Northern Reform', p. 20.

[72] Milne, 'Richard Bagnall Reed', p. 144.

[73] *People's Paper,* 5 June 1858.

[74] Muris, 'The Northern Reform Union', pp. 53-54.

[75] *Holyoake Papers,* letter 1232, Reed to Holyoake, 25 July 1860.

[76] Muris, 'The Northern Reform Union', p. 60.

[77] Ibid., pp. 140-144, where it is reproduced in full in Appendix B.

[78] Todd, *The Militant Democracy,* pp. 47-48. See also P. A. Pickering, *Chartism and the Chartists in Manchester and Salford,* Basingstoke, 1995, pp. 181-3; N. Kirk, *Change, continuity and class: Labour in British Society,* 1850-1920, Manchester, 1998, pp. 89-91.

[79] Muris, 'The Northern Reform', pp. 145-148.

[80] Ibid., pp. 88-111; Milne, 'Richard Bagnall Reed', pp. 144-145.

[81] Muris, 'The Northern Reform Union', pp. 108-109.

[82] Nossiter, *Influence, Opinion and Political Idioms,* p. 159.

[83] E. R. Jones, *Life and Speeches of Joseph Cowen MP,* London, 1885, p. 25.

[84] Muris, 'The Northern Reform Union', p. 133; Hugman, 'Joseph Cowen', p. 280.

[85] Gossman, 'British Aid', p. 236.

[86] Todd, *The Militant Democracy,* p. 15.

[87] Ibid., p. 17.

[88] *Holyoake Papers*, MM96636/Reel 3, letter 1224 Reed to Holyoake, c. May 1860.

[89] Gossman, 'British Aid', p. 239.

[90] *Holyoake Papers*, MM96636/Reel 3, letter 1232, Reed to Holyoake, 25 July 1860; letter 1235, Reed to Holyoake, 7 August 1860; letter 1239, Reed to Holyoake, 13 August 1860.

[91] G. J Holyoake, *Sixty Years of An Agitator's Life*, 1894 repr. New York, 1984, vol. 2, pp. 102-103.

[92] *Newcastle Weekly Chronicle*, 14 May 1864.

[93] The Advertising Duty on newspapers had been repealed in 1853 and the Excise Duty in 1855.

[94] Muris, 'The Northern Reform Union', p. 126.

[95] For Monteagle's career see *Dictionary of National Biography*, Oxford, 1921, vol. xviii, pp. 835-837.

[96] *Holyoake Papers*, MM 96636/ Reel 3, letter 1218, Reed to Holyoake, 20 May 1860. See also letter 1256, Reed to Holyoake, n.d. [c. late May 1860].

[97] Ibid.

[98] Breuilly, Niedhart & Taylor (eds), *The Era of the Reform League*, p. 333, for a brief profile of Langley's career as a radical.

[99] *Newcastle Weekly Chronicle*, 29 February 1908.

[100] Reed's position as secretary of the Northern Reform Union was taken by Charles Hadfield, who remained in the post until the organisation folded in 1862. See Muris, 'The Northern Reform Union', p. 12.

[101] *Newcastle Weekly Chronicle*, 28 December 1867.

[102] M. Milne, 'Survival of the Fittest? Sunderland Newspapers in the Nineteenth Century', in J. Shattock & M. Wolff (eds), *The Victorian Periodical Press: Samplings and Soundings*, Leicester, 1982, pp. 192-223, particularly 218-219.

[103] G. B. Hodgson, *From Smithy to Senate: The Life Story of James Annand. Journalist and Politician*, London, 1908, p. 53.

[104] Milne, 'Richard Bagnall Reed', p. 146.

[105] Ibid. Little is known of Reed's wife other than that she spent twelve of the adult years of her life pregnant with sixteen children. She died in 1900.

[106] *Newcastle Weekly Chronicle*, 26 March 1864.

[107] Ibid., 15 July 1865. The result was: J. Cowen senior, 2,941; T. E. Headlam, 2,477; S. E. Beaumont, 2,060.

[108] Ibid., 8 July 1865.

[109] Todd, *The Militant Democracy*, p. 80.

[110] Ibid., p. 81.

[111] Ibid.

[112] *Newcastle Weekly Chronicle*, 10 November 1866.

[113] Ibid., 29 December 1866; 9 February, 23 March 1867.

[114] *The Times* 11 May 1867 cited in Breuilly, Niedhart & Taylor (eds), *The Era of the Reform League*, pp. 234-237.

[115] Ibid., p. 237.

[116] Watson, *A Newspaper Man's Memories*, p. 29.

[117] T. Burt, *An Autobiography*, London, 1924, p. 184; M. Milne, *The Newspapers of Northumberland and Durham*, Newcastle upon Tyne, 1971, pp. 64-65, 73-81.

[118] Todd, *The Militant Democracy*, pp. 58-59.

[119] See *Newcastle Weekly Chronicle*, 18 March 1882; Ashton, *Adams*, p. 45.

[120] L. Brown, *Victorian News and Newspapers*, Oxford, 1985, p. 53.

[121] Milne, 'Richard Bagnall Reed', p. 145.

[122] Adams, *Memoirs of a Social Atom*, p. 493.

[123] Milne, *The Newspapers of Northumberland and Durham*, pp. 123, 155-156; Todd, *The Militant Democracy*, pp. 54-55, 60-61.

[124] *Newcastle Weekly Chronicle* 2 April 1864.

[125] Ibid.

[126] Watson, *A Newspaper Man's Memories*, p. 38.

[127] *Newcastle Weekly Chronicle*, 29 February 1908.

[128] Brown, *Victorian News and Newspapers*, pp. 80-81.

[129] Ibid., p. 81.

[130] Watson, *A Newspaper Man's Memories*, pp. 46-47.

[131] *Newcastle Weekly Chronicle*, 27 February 1869; 3 March 1900.

[132] Watson, A *Newspaper Man's Memories*, p. 27.

[133] J. Saville, 'Introduction', in Saville & Bellamy (eds), *Dictionary of Labour Biography*, vol. 1, p. ix-xiii. G. J. Holyoake, Charles Bradlaugh and Ben Brierley, for example, were Freemasons. The Centre for Research into Freemasonry was established at the University of Sheffield's Humanities Research Institute in 2001. We are grateful to Professor Andrew Prescott, its first Director, for providing us with information on both the Lodge of Industry and some of Reed's activities in Mark Masonry.

[134] S. Knight, *The Brotherhood: The Secret World of the Freemasons*, London, 1983, pp. 35-36.

[135] Hugman, 'Joseph Cowen', pp. 113-116.

[136] Whitfield, *The History of the Lodge of Industry*, pp. 49-51; *Newcastle Weekly Chronicle*, 29 February 1908.

[137] Letter to the authors from Professor A. Prescott, 14 Nov. 2001. See also *Newcastle Weekly Chronicle*, 2 July 1898

[138] Ibid.

[139] *Newcastle Weekly Chronicle*, 7 March 1908; *Newcastle Weekly Journal and Courant*, 7 March 1908.

[140] *Newcastle Weekly Chronicle*, 7 March 1908.

[141] See Milne, 'Richard Bagnall Reed', p. 146.

[142] See K. Earl, 'John Hastings Reed – First CSR Manager of Hambledon Mill', *Bulletin of the Historical Society of Cairns*, no. 414, May 1995.

[143] H.M. Hyndman, *The Historical Basis of Socialism in England*, London, 1883, p. 266. See also P.A. Pickering, 'A Wider Field in a New Country: Chartism in Colonial Australia', in M. Sawer (ed.), *Elections, Full, Free & Fair*, Sydney, 2001, pp. 28-44. This section has benefited from discussions with Nev Kirk who is completing a major study of the notion of Australia as a 'workers' paradise'.

[144] Earl, 'John Hastings Reed'; D. Jones, *Trinity Phoenix: A History of Cairns and District*, Cairns, 1976, pp. 371, 409. We are also grateful to Jeremy Hodes, Manager of the Information Unit at ATSIC, who provided us with information from his list of place and street names for far north Queensland.

CONCLUSION

FRIENDS OF THE PEOPLE

In a recent review of a major collection of Chartist documents Miles Taylor has characterised the leading Chartists as nothing more than 'clever speakers and racy journalists'.[1] Although Taylor undoubtedly had his tongue in his cheek when he penned this unfortunate quip, it is a timely reminder of the ingrained prejudice that smothered the history of the movement for much of the nineteenth century. The image of Feargus O'Connor in the House of Commons, isolated and 'baited on all sides', exclaiming 'the Charter and No Surrender' like Barnaby Rudges's raven croaking 'never say die', is a powerful one.[2] The life of a friend of the people was not easy: those studied here risked and, in some cases, sacrificed, reputation, social standing, income and even liberty. Criticism was often the least of their concerns, as James Scholefield remarked with a note of resigned indifference, a hostile press was 'ever ready to publish anything that is said or written against me'. But if a thick skin was the first characteristic that was shared by the six Chartist leaders studied in this book, what else can we learn by comparing and contrasting their sociological and ideological characteristics? Were they simply 'clever speakers and racy journalists'? Our 'friends' constitute a small and utterly random sample that precludes the sort of rigorous statistical analysis that often accompanies prosopography, but that is not the aim here. Rather, a consideration of their careers collectively is undertaken in the hope of finding some pointers to more common attitudes and experiences. Surely, the value of biography – individual and multiple – rests in the light that it can shed on what is nowadays called the 'big picture'.

Although our six Chartists were not of the same generation – their ages when the People's Charter was published ranged from 7 to 48 – some interesting observations can be made about their age. First, it is notable that three of them (Scholefield, Sankey and Parsons) had been born in the 'magical 1790s' and were an average of 44.6 years old in 1838. This is much older than the average age of others samples of Chartists. Although Christopher Godfrey is at pains to emphasise that Chartism was not a movement of 'teen-age hooligans', his samples of Chartist prisoners had median ages of 31, 29 and 24. Similarly, a study of thirty Chartist leaders in Manchester, undertaken by one of the present authors, showed that the average age in 1840 was 36.6 (median 33).[3] On the other hand, 44.6 is comparable to the average age of members of the Manchester

Anti-Corn Law Association (47 in 1840) and remarkably similar to the average age of 45 identified by Brian Harrison in his study of temperance leaders active in the mid-1830s.[4] An examination of the age at which they became politically active, however, reveals a more complex picture. Richard Reed gave his first political speech at age 20 (in 1851) and McDouall was not much older (age 24). Likewise, both Scholefield and Solly first became politically active at the relatively tender age of 27. Only Sankey and Parsons were latecomers to the public platform: Sankey at age 45 and Parsons at age 43 (although he did not join the ranks of the Chartists until 1847 when he reached 50). Nevertheless, in terms of Chartism, four of the six were older than the norm when they embraced the cause, and, although none was venerable by antiquity, it is likely that their higher social standing was enhanced by their age.

Reed might have given his first speech at twenty, but even by this time he was a political veteran. In a very familiar pattern in post-war radical culture, Reed imbibed his politics as an infant at his parents' table. As we have seen, as a young boy Reed was brought into close contact not only with local activists, but also with figures of national standing in the movement, most notably George Julian Harney, who became his life-long friend and ally. McDouall too could point a radical family member – a grandfather who fought alongside Washington – and James Scholefield's mentor, William Cowherd, was said to have freely encouraged radical opinions among his congregation. Of the group, William Sankey could boast the most enduring political genealogy that stretched back for five generations, although he was apparently the first radical of the clan. Whereas Reed's experience of kitchen politics was typical of nineteenth-century radicalism, Sankey's familial links to the political elite, including into Number 10 Downing Street, were exceptional, and perhaps even unique, among the Chartists. Sankey was also unlike the other five in that he was politically active for only five years (his career ended abruptly and inexplicably in 1842). For the others, the platform was a way of life, and, as a consequence, we can see in their careers some of the continuities of radicalism through the nineteenth and into the twentieth century. From Scholefield, who first became active before Peterloo and remained so until just before his death in the 1850s when he helped to found the Parliamentary and Financial Reform Association in Manchester, to Reed whose career spanned the last years of Chartism, the Reform League, and the early years of Edwardian Liberalism.

Sankey's claim to a radical pedigree was bolstered by his marriage to a Swiss, a nation highly regarded in radical circles for its democratic institutions. In fact all six of the Chartists studied here were married men, and each had a large family: the McDoualls had five children, as did the Sollys; Sankey and his wife had six children; the Parsons had seven; the Scholefields had eight; and the Reeds had sixteen! At an average of eight children per couple, this was nearly double the national average for the decade 1840-9.[5] Even if the Reeds are discounted, each of our couples had more children than was usual at the time. Given their size, these families might have been expected to put down deep roots, but this was only true in half the cases (Scholefield, Parsons, and Reed). The others were surprisingly mobile: the Sollys moved parish on several occasions, the Sankeys relocated on at least three occasions before settling in Camden; and McDouall's wife and offspring followed in the wake of their peripatetic husband and father even to Australia.

Marriage and family life were obviously very important to each of our subjects, but they had little in common when it came to their attitudes to the separate rights of women, and, indeed, to the extent to which their own wives were active alongside them. Charlotte Scholefield died in 1835 at the age of thirty, and there is no evidence about her activities up to that point other than childbirth (in 1822, 1824, 1825, 1827, 1829, 1832, 1833, and 1835). Scholefield's daughters, however, actively supported his pastoral work by running his day-school and they also shared his enthusiasm for dietary reform by becoming involved in the Vegetarian Society later in the 1840s.[6] As a Unitarian Rebecca Solly belonged to a denomination that was well known for encouraging the intellectual development of its women members, and she actively participated alongside her husband in many of his social and political activities, including campaigning on behalf of Henry Vincent at a local parliamentary by-election. It was somewhat different in the case of Mary-Ann McDouall. For most of her husband's career, she remained in the background, which is understandable given that she had sole care of five young children for long periods of time. But while her husband languished in prison, Mary-Ann stepped into the limelight, speaking and writing on his behalf and showing us glimpses of a sharp intellect and tenacious personality. Sankey's wife too was noted for her 'solidity of judgement, liveliness of imagination, and … extraordinary facility in expressing her thoughts and feelings', and reference has been made to the fact that her husband bathed in the reflected glory of her nationality. Given that Sophia was apparently little restrained by the conventions that weighed heavily on others of her class, it is all the more surprising that her husband upheld a very conservative view on the separate rights of women. 'Females in every instance – in every rank – and in every situation', he stated in 1838, 'should be considered as represented by their husbands – or fathers or brothers – or nearest male relative'.[7] Virtually nothing is known about Jane Reed apart from the fact that she was pregnant for a total twelve years in her adult life.[8] Her husband's attitude to women's rights went further than some Chartists (such as Sankey) in that he apparently settled for the formula of enfranchising men first and women later. Similarly, little is known about the life of Amelia Parsons, but in this case her husband's views on women were advanced, even among radicals. Convinced that the minds of girls were equal to those of boys, he offered the same educational opportunities to both sexes at his school and, in 1842 he outlined his views in a controversial tract *The*

Mental and Moral Dignity of Woman.

In terms of the educational background of our cases, Reed and Sankey stand out as almost polar opposites. On the one hand, Reed's experience closely follows the classic story of the radical autodidact. While completing his apprenticeship as a blacksmith, Reed used his spare time to educate himself at the village library and the Winlaton Literary and Mechanics' Institute. Venues for working class self-education from debating clubs to more or less formal societies like the Winlaton Institute proliferated in nineteenth century Britain. Although it was not always easy to do as Reed did and use them to research 'questions of a political character', they were a very common feature in Chartist lives.[9] In addition to Reed, Scholefield, Solly and McDouall participated in institutions of this sort, and later in life Parsons, Scholefield and Solly actively promoted and supported them as part of their circle of reforms. All of our cases (except Reed) had something more than a rudimentary formal education: Scholefield and Parsons attended different forms of religious seminary and McDouall completed a medical apprenticeship. In two cases formal education included university. As we have seen, Solly attended London University, and, at the other extreme to Reed, Sankey's university career was exceptional even among patricians. Two points can be made. Firstly, the level of formal education of our group was considerably better than for the typical Chartist. Godfrey's study of the Chartists interviewed by the prison authorities in 1840-41 (which included many local and national leaders) highlighted only a handful who had had anything like the level of formal education of our subjects.[10] Secondly, it is important to note that irrespective of the educational route taken, all of our 'friends' ended up as highly articulate, intelligent and prolific writers and speakers. Among this group it seems that Winlaton Mechanics' Institute was as efficacious as Cambridge University.

At least four of our 'friends' (McDouall, Solly, Sankey and Scholefield) used poetry as a means of expression. In this respect they took their place among legions of aspiring Chartist muses whose collective efforts repeatedly led the editor of the *Northern Star* to issue harsh rejection notices in a vain attempt to discourage them. Although our poetical 'friends' all published verse in various forums, none was anything more than a pedestrian poet. To the modern reader their poetry invariably lacks the emotional range and the deftness of touch that is indicative of extraordinary talent. Nonetheless, even mediocre Chartist poetry was more than a means of individual reflection and amusement; it took its place in collective rituals that combined inspiration and entertainment. The radical press was full of reports of 'stirring' verses enlivening Chartist dinners and festivals. Many Chartists would have agreed with a correspondent to the Scottish *Chartist Circular* that poetry was a 'lever of commanding influence' that 'penetrates to every nerve and fibre of society, stirring into irresistibility its innermost current, and spiriting into life and activity the obscurest dweller of the valley'.[11] Our 'friends' did their small part in the development of this important feature of nineteenth century radical culture.

The question of their social class is complex. Apart from Sankey (unequivocally a member of the upper class when measured against any objective sociological criterion) each of our 'friends' was 'middle class', but, as A.J. Kidd and David Nicholls have recently reminded us, the rapidly expanding middle class was 'stratified, with enormous differentials in power and influence, income and status, between the *haute bourgeoisie* at one extreme and the petit bourgeoisie at the other'.[12] It is difficult to offer conclusions on the basis of a handful of cases, but some general observations are possible. First, it is important to note the incidence of social mobility, both upwards and downwards. Contrast Reed's spectacular rise from penury in a village cottage in the 1840s to luxury at a suburban mansion (with three servants) by the 1880s,[13] with McDouall's sharp decline from a property-owning medical professional in the 1830s to itinerant hawker of pills, pamphlets and politics in 1840s. In the case of Reed, Solly and Parsons, their status as young men fluctuated greatly with their family fortune. Financial ruin engulfed Solly's father in 1837, Reed's father was left unemployed by the collapse of the local ironworks, and Parsons effectively dropped out of the 'middle class' to pursue a trade as a result of the financial collapse and subsequent death of his father.

These experiences point to a second observation: the life of a friend of the people was a precarious one. For Edward Gibbon Wakefield it was vulnerability – 'care, trouble, [and] perplexity' – that was the key to understanding why many in the 'middle class' – capitalists, manufacturers, commercial men, farmers and professionals – were 'uneasy'. 'By the uneasy class', Wakefield wrote, 'I mean those who, not being labourers, suffer from agricultural distress, manufacturing distress, commercial distress, distress of the shipping interest, and many more kinds of distress ...'[14] Overwhelmingly our case studies were members of this 'uneasy' middle class. As noted, McDouall lived from hand to mouth during the 1840s, clinging to the notion that he was a member of the middle classes long after the decline in his material circumstances made this impossible. Although less dramatic than McDouall, in the case of Scholefield and Solly, their outspoken political views also imperilled their financial security: for Scholefield it was threatened by a brush with the law in 1843, and in Solly's case by disgruntled members of his congregation after he took to the national political stage. It is important to note, however, in both cases their financial security was already fragile. Solly began his career as a Minister on a salary of £65 per annum, well below the £100 that was widely considered to be the minimum income of a petit bourgeois,[15] and thereafter his income was always subject to the whim of his congregation. Scholefield did not draw a stipend from his congregation, but he did profit from them, and the wider community, by charging a fee to christen, educate, marry, counsel, heal, and, eventually, bury them. Parsons was ostensibly more secure in his post due to his large and admiring congregation, but it was not so when he first went to Ebley and, presumably, anxiety about the future (and a repetition of the fate that befell his father) never completely left him.[16] For all Reed's spectacular rise, the memory of the 'hungry forties' must have remained with him also. Even Sankey, the archetypal leisured patrician, was profoundly 'uneasy': in his case, he perceived a threat to the future of his class from its refusal to come to terms with democracy. As Wakefield recognised, the 'uneasiness' of the middle class was a fertile breeding ground for radical opinions. According to an eminent sociologist and political scientist, C. Wright Mills, for the modern intellectual-cum-social activist alienation and idealism are different sides of the same coin.[17]

When examining the process of politicisation beyond that provided by family background, and by this pervasive sense of unease, three points of connection stand out: religiosity, experience, and observation. In terms of religion, each of our six cases rejected what McDouall called the 'rotten, slimy slough of Churchism', but the first point that needs to be stressed is that there is no evidence that this led on to either secularism or atheism, both of which formed an important strand in nineteenth century radicalism.[18] For Scholefield, Parsons, Sankey and Solly, opposition to the Established Church was evident in active campaigns against church rates, and in Parsons' case, in strident support for voluntarism in education as well as strict Sabbatarianism. It is important to remember, however, that nineteenth century Nonconformity was neither homogeneous nor free from jealousies, disputes and inter-denominational controversy. Congregationalists (Parsons) often clashed bitterly with Unitarians (Solly) over practical and theological matters, and many Dissenters would have seen a cloven foot lurking in Scholefield's heterodox rationalist eschatology. Nevertheless, for all their theological differences, Solly, Parsons, Scholefield, and Sankey were vociferous advocates of a similar form of radical Christianity that we have detailed extensively in the foregoing chapters. For each man God provided the ultimate sanction for radical opinions and, in each case (and for McDouall too) religion provided a strong impetus to public life: an unswerving belief that religion must involve deeds as well as words. Taken together these careers underscore the point made by Brian Harrison that many of the reform movements of this era were powerfully influenced by religious forms of radicalism, and especially by strong-minded members of small and often idiosyncratic sects.[19]

Experience and observation were also key elements in the process of politicisation. Solly's social conscience was stirred by the poverty he witnessed in London during the commercial depression of the late 1830s, and he was shocked by the degradation he saw on his first visit to Manchester in 1841. For McDouall and Sankey it was exposure to the 'White Slavery' of the factory system and to modern urban life more generally that produced a potent mixture of horror, outrage and determination. As we have seen, in the ancient capital of the Scots, Sankey was moved by a 'mixture of pain and indignation' to put pen to paper and, shortly afterwards, to get involved with the Chartists. After a couple of years of practising among the factory towns of Lancashire, McDouall's condemnation of urban industrialism was brimming with moral indignation:[20]

> I point to the empty cottage of the workman, to the half-clad body of his wife, and to the famished look of the child. Here you have one crippled in his limbs, there you have another stunted in his faculties. On the one side is the crowded pawn shop, on the other the frequented gin palace. Mark the wounded cripple bending to the hospital, see there is one just hurried to the jail. See the grey-haired slave tottering to the workhouse and watch, oh! watch pale-faced consumption pointing to the grave, to which a tide of miserable scourge driven mortals are hurrying. Then turn from the prison to admire once more the cotton palace; turn from the scaffold to praise the factory, from the grave to applaud the system ...

This was a perspective that Reed understood. Although it is too simplistic to reduce Chartism to a 'knife and fork' question, economic issues had been crucial for Reed's father and, presumably, left a lasting impression on his son. The right to vote was meant to be the way to put food on the table. For McDouall and Sankey too political reform was not only about abstract philosophical concepts, it was also about practical solutions. The spectre of trade unions and other combinations, Sankey told fellow members of his class, could easily be dispelled: 'there would be no necessity for combination at all, were it understood that no wage should be less than would be sufficient to feed a family on wholesome food; clothe and educate them; pay the rent of airy apartments, and leave still, something over to meet exigencies ...' McDouall agreed, as he stated in 1842: 'if the people in the manufacturing districts had had their social miseries remedied by the law in former times, they would never have sought for political remedies now'.[21]

For all that Sankey got angry, he was not personally affected by the harsh reality of modernity in the way that our other 'friends' were. At a time when the infant mortality rate was the scandal of the age, they shared a tragic experience: the death of at least one child. The circumstances are not always clear, but in some cases infant death was directly related to our subjects' social and political mission. McDouall, for example, blamed himself for the death of his eldest daughter while he languished in a prison cell. Similarly, Solly's eldest daughter contracted scarlet fever while accompanying his wife on one of her visits to the Cheltenham slums where she was actively engaged in helping the poor. The very location of Scholefield's chapel in the heartland of working-class Manchester put his family in harm's way. The death of his wife and three youngest children in the space of four months did not crush him, it spurred him on to greater effort, not only in pursuing practical piecemeal reforms such as cleaning up

Manchester's festering slums, but also in advocating self-improvement among his flock in Ancoats.[22] Although our 'friends' condemned the system, each of them was a conspicuous advocate of various forms of individual and collective self-help from vegetarianism to freemasonry. Scholefield, Solly and Parsons were active members of temperance organisations and, although it is unclear whether or not he drank alcohol himself, Sankey claimed that no one could 'deplore' the degradation arising from 'inveterate habits of intemperance' more than he. Despite a longstanding habit of calling into a well-known radical pub in Manchester for a 'social glass', McDouall also publicly advocated total abstinence.[23] The 'little doctor' was much clearer about the importance of dietary reform, as was Parsons, and Scholefield was a staunch vegetarian. All six Chartists were strong advocates of the other pillar of self-improvement, education. Ostensibly there were some disagreements. For example, Solly enthusiastically supported the plan for a National Association linking education and the suffrage promoted by William Lovett and other London Chartists, that McDouall and Sankey angrily rejected. For all his support for educational initiatives, Parsons, put the voluntary principle first. Nevertheless, the broad support for self-improvement through education is impressive. Sankey was a life-long supporter of the Lancasterian system of mutual education; Scholefield, Solly, and Parsons, all ran schools in connection with their church, and all three, together with Reed, were actively involved in local organisations devoted to adult education. In Solly's case, his contribution to adult education was perhaps his best known and enduring achievement.

In addition to those already noted, what other causes did they champion? A general conclusion is difficult to draw on the important question of trade union rights. Long after he had risen from the ranks of manual labourers Reed enjoyed strong and effective links with a range of trade unions on Tyneside, and, a generation earlier, McDouall had been one of the foremost among the Chartists to advocate their formal incorporation into Chartism. Scholefield, Solly and Parsons, on the other hand, had apparently little to say about trade union rights, and as noted above, Sankey set about convincing members of his own class that one of the benefits of democracy would be to obviate the need for 'combinations' altogether. All of our Chartists (with the exception of Reed who was too young), however, were opposed to the Corn Laws, not on the basis of doctrinaire economic liberalism, but as part of a broadly based radical crusade against privilege and monopoly. For them the bread tax was one of the most blatant examples of the system of 'Old Corruption' that buttressed the economic and political power of the landowners. By increasing the price of bread for the poor the Corn Laws placed the burden of a parasitic and heartless aristocracy on the backs of the people. Not surprisingly, four of our 'friends' were involved in the Anti-Corn Law League. Given that accounts of the relationship between the Chartists and the League have often emphasised a handful of violent confrontations, this is a point worthy of emphasis.[24]

Even more than Corn Law Repeal and the suffrage itself, opposition to the 1834 Poor Law Amendment Act was a litmus test for popular radicalism in the late 1830s and early 1840.[25] All of our 'friends' (again with the exception of Reed because of his age) passed this test with flying colours by vehemently opposing it, but it is illuminating to linger over the reasons for this opposition. First, it was rejected on a combination of moral, religious and humanitarian grounds: the 'Whig Starvation Law' introduced a harsh regime that was uncharitable, unnatural and punitive. Secondly, the alteration to the system of poor relief was seen as part of the almost inexorable encroachment of centralised government. The poor law commissioners would be followed, or so the argument ran, by a centralised police – a Frenchified *gendarmerie* – and a standing army, concepts that evoked deep loathing in popular ideology. Sankey, in particular, appears to have had an almost hysterical ability to see the malevolent hand of centralism lurking behind every Act, but the others were all against any perceived concentration of power in Westminster.

Thirdly, and closely related, our 'friends' opposed the New Poor Law on historical grounds. The new system was compared unfavourably with the previous system of poor relief that had first been implemented during the reign of Elizabeth I ('Good Queen Bess'). On the one hand, this is a reminder of how important notions of lost rights were for many Chartists, including our 'friends'. Sankey, for example, claimed that the People's Charter was based on the ancient Saxon Constitution and McDouall urged his fellow Chartists to study their history for this reason. At the same time, implicit in the unfavourable comparison between the Old and New poor law was an organic view of society based around the idea of a community of interests between all its members. As we have seen, Sankey urged members of his own class to embrace democracy because of their identity of interests with those seeking to regain lost rights. Parsons too upheld the concept of 'the whole people' with shared interests. 'Every human being is a *child of God*', he wrote in the first number of his celebrated *Tracts for Fustian Jackets and Frock Smocks*, 'and our Heavenly Father feels himself dishonoured when any member of his great family, whether prince or peasant, is treated with injustice or contempt'.[26] Likewise Solly's notion of a working-class 'gentleman', involved in club-work and promoting fellowship between the classes, was based upon a notion of an essential identity of interests across the social spectrum. Similarly, McDouall, the most uncompromising of our 'friends', was committed to a just balance between salary and wage earners, profit-takers and labourers, because they had 'identical' interests. When the 'little doctor' took his own advice and delved into history he rediscovered an ancient British institution that seemed encapsulate all the ideal characteristics of a Chartist society that reinforces this point. Membership of McDouall's 'Primitive Parliament', the 'Kyfr-y-then', was open to all 'warriors, wise men, and all who did service to their country'. 'Worth, service and duty were at the bottom of these congresses of the early Britons', he wrote.[27]

This highly functionalist (and optimistic) view of society had strong communitarian overtones which were also evident in Scholefield's involvement with the Christian Chartist Community at Chat Moss on the outskirts of Manchester, and in Sankey's vision of 'one great mutual co-operation society' that would obviate the need for government itself.[28] It is too easy to characterise this organic view of the social order as either utopian, backward looking or reactionary, although it undoubtedly drew on a romantic understanding of a past 'golden age' that was a common feature of a wider European romantic revolt against modernity. Our 'friends' were in good company. Modern sociology also offers useful insight on this point. '[H]istorically, those alienated from certain aspects of the normative order, but who have been committed to societal values in some idealistic form,' writes the author of an important study of middle-class radicalism in the 1960s, 'have often played a key role in the achievement of social reforms and the extension of individual liberties'.[29] The important point for the student of Chartism is that for 'friends of the people' (if our case studies are anything to go by), class conciliation was not merely a question of tactics, it was inherent in their conception of an ideal society. Nowhere among the thinking of these men is there any evidence of a belief in the inevitability of class struggle, an idea that would become axiomatic in some sections of the labour movement in years to come.

On Tyneside, however, Reed's efforts to fashion political alliances between middle- and working-class radicals were largely failures, except over questions of foreign affairs. Margot Finn has argued that continental struggles for freedom provided rallying points around which cross class alliances were concluded in the 1860s.[30] Reed's career certainly supports this claim, but for the rest of our 'friends', four of whom were dead by 1860, the important point to note is their longstanding commitment to internationalism. For Solly and Parsons (both stalwarts of the Peace movement) as well as Scholefield and Sankey, this stemmed from a religiously-inspired concept of the fellowship of man that was reflected in an abiding commitment to pacifism both at home and abroad. Despite their association with O'Connor, Solly, Parsons, and Scholefield were archetypal 'moral force' Chartists, both in their commitment to self-improvement and in their rejection of violence under any circumstances. As Parsons warned the 'Fustian Jackets and Frock Smocks' in characteristically florid language, 'Not a pike, a blunderbuss, a brickbat, or a match must be found in your hands'. Support for continental struggles for freedom and national independence, however, was not always compatible with pacifism. As we have seen, Reed was prepared to defend those who advocated tyrannicide and was involved in gun running for Garibaldi, and McDouall was involved in clandestine plots for an armed uprising much closer to home. Solly, Parsons, and Scholefield would have regarded these activities as anathema. On this point then it is impossible to suggest a representative characteristic, although we suspect that Sankey was probably typical of most Chartists, not just 'friends of the people'. As noted, the aristocrat of Chartism regarded himself as a consistent 'friend of peace' and 'carefully abstained from attempting to describe War and Combat in over charged and glowing language' in his poetry, but his sense of indignation and outrage led him to use what he called the 'bold language of Britons' which to the ears of his opponents (and to some historians) appeared to countenance violence.

To conclude our survey of the attitudes, activities and attributes of our 'friends', a couple of further points need to be made about the nature of their political careers. The first is the relative absence of electoral politics. Reference has been made to Scholefield's commitment to practical reform which, in part, he assiduously pursued during a lengthy career as an elected representative at the local government level. In this respect, however, he was atypical of our 'friends'. For all that these were men committed to electoral reform because, presumably, they felt that politics could make a difference, they did little to seek public office in their own right. Only McDouall and Sankey stood for election to the House of Commons (the latter only on one occasion) and Reed, Solly and Parsons apparently never sought elective office at all. The combination of principled social activism with limited interest in public office is consistent with what the author of a recent study of a middle-class protest movement has called 'expressive politics' (as distinct from 'instrumental politics'). 'Expressive politics', writes Frank Parkin, 'is that which is mainly concerned with the defence of principles, even if this means relinquishing power'.[31]

For all that this concept seems to illuminate important aspects of the careers of our 'friends of the people', by pointing to an apparent reluctance to take public office, it is not intended to demean or trivialise their commitment, far from it. As noted, being a Chartist was a risky business that invited abuse and threatened career, reputation, and liberty. At the very least all of our 'friends' were vilified as mavericks, adventurers, and trading politicians. Their involvement in different parts of the country and at various levels of responsibility bolstered the calibre of the national leadership and enhanced the vitality of branch life in the localities. Despite being vulnerable themselves, they were invariably better able than others to stand up to the authorities (local and national). We have seen that this sort of intervention took many forms. Whether it was McDouall exposing those employers engaged in the pernicious practice known as 'truck' before a parliamentary enquiry, Scholefield throwing open the doors of his Sunday school to children persecuted for wearing radical insignia, Solly insisting that he put the case for the Charter to an Anti-Corn Law League conference, Sankey using his aristocratic connections to obtain an interview with the Home Secretary on behalf of one of his 'constituents', or numerous other acts of representation and advocacy, this was a vital contribution to the movement.[32]

Second, for all that they were vilified by their opponents, the 'friends of the people' were undoubtedly charismatic figures in the movement they served. In the cases of McDouall, Parsons and Scholefield, there is ample evidence of charisma. Scholefield's popularity in Ancoats was second to none, and was based, in part, on a belief in his almost mystical powers of healing. Similarly, Parsons was renowned for the fierce loyalty he inspired from a large congregation; and McDouall thrilled and enchanted audiences up and down the country earning him an extensive following that was reflected in the large number of votes he received in elections for the executive of the National Charter Association. Parsons, Scholefield and McDouall were powerful orators: here were men who could smite opponents or evoke visions of a better future with equal enthusiasm. Although he was not generally regarded as a good speaker Sankey too was undoubtedly a charismatic figure whose charm and 'extremely prepossessing appearance' produced a 'most powerful effect' on O'Connor. 'The people know', stated O'Connor after meeting Sankey in London, 'when their superiors in rank mix with them from choice'.[33] For all that Solly deprecated charismatic leadership in his later memoir and novel – he called it demagoguery – he too was a persuasive and courageous orator who enjoyed the plaudits of the crowd. Little is known about Reed as a speaker, but there is ample evidence that he inspired considerable loyalty and affection among his extensive staff working on the *Newcastle Chronicle*. It would be a mistake, however, to confuse their interventions with paternalism and, thereby, dismiss them as anachronisms. First and foremost our 'friends' were democrats who treated the working people whose cause they championed as equals: the loyalty, respect and deference that they enjoyed was reciprocated. On this point Scholefield can be allowed to speak for them all: as he told a Chartist meeting in 1841, 'the character of a labouring man was the greatest honour he could possess'.

Finally, as noted in the introduction to this book, the fact that each of our 'friends' was associated for some or all of their career with the mainstream of the movement that revolved around the leadership of Feargus O'Connor, did not preclude them (with the exception of McDouall) from becoming directly involved with the more conciliatory initiatives within the movement, and with middle-class reform campaigns separate from it. In this respect it is important to note again that four were involved with the Anti-Corn Law League (Reed was too young to have done so), including all three clergymen attending the League's National Conference of Ministers of Religion in 1841. Similarly, two (Parsons and Solly) were active supporters of the Complete Suffrage Union in the first half of the 1840s, and four (Scholefield, Solly, Parsons and Reed) were involved in several organisations that sought to bring middle- and working-class reformers together in alliance in the 1850s. On the one hand, this suggests that middle-class reform politics in the age of the Chartists was more radical than is often acknowledged, but, at the same time, it also helps us to understand the ease with which the nascent Liberal party later captured the support of many former Chartists. Miles Taylor is undoubtedly correct when he argues that as 'part of the diagnosis of what had gone wrong in 1848 radicals and Chartists became more flexible over the issue of class', but it is equally important to note, as Margot Finn has done, the new found willingness of many middle-class reformers to tone down the *laissez-faire* rhetoric which had characterised Manchester School liberals. Furthermore, Neville Kirk has drawn attention to the efficacy of middle-class support for self-help initiatives and municipal improvements, as well as the promotion of civic pride, in preparing the ground for cooperation.[34] Critical also was the practical role played by 'friends of the people' in a range of organisations from Freehold Land Societies to the Reform League. The mid-Victorian consensus was built on the credibility, trust and inter-personal relationships that these men, and others like them, sustained during the difficult 1840s and into the 1850s and 1860s.

Nevertheless, popular liberalism was not all pervasive, universally attractive, and without problems, as we have seen in Reed's failed campaigns to forge cross-class political alliances on Tyneside; in Solly's desperate attempts to distance himself from the lingering memory of Feargus O'Connor; and in McDouall's decision to go in search of what one commentator called 'a wider field' in a new country (an option also taken by one of Reed's sons).[35] The persistence of a tradition of independent working-class radicalism meant that 'friends of the people' were unfashionable to those determined to follow leaders from their own order. In a symbolic gesture of enormous significance, Keir Hardie brought this tradition to its logical climax in 1893 when he stood in the House of Commons dressed in a work-a-day suit and wearing a cloth cap to move an amendment to the Queen's Speech calling for measures to tackle unemployment.[36] The parallel with a fustian-jacketed Feargus O'Connor standing at the gates of York Castle in 1841 is compelling. Nevertheless, 'friends of the people' continued to play a significant part in popular politics, and still do. There are unmistakable echoes of the Chartists studied here in the lives of many latter-day 'friends of the people' from Tom Maguire, William Morris and H.M. Hyndman, to Hugh Gaitskell, Tony Benn, (both Chartist scholars), and Tony Blair.[37] Blair, for example, was born in Edinburgh, the city that McDouall and Sankey knew so well, and he was educated at elite schools there and in Durham before reading law at Oxford and going into politics. In the House of Commons Blair represents a Durham seat where the sound of Reed's anvil still lingers in the air, but he is no more a worker than was Sankey, McDouall, Scholefield, Solly, Parsons, or Reed himself later in his life. At the beginning of the twenty-first century those within 'New Labour' who seek to link Blair to Hardie have missed the point, as have those who have characterised him simply as a Gladstonian Liberal.[38] The current occupant of Number 10 Downing Street is the heir to a nineteenth century tradition of popular politics – a Chartist one – he is a 'friend of the people'.

Notes

[1] M. Taylor, 'Knife and Fork Question', *London Review of Books*, 29 November 2001, p. 29.

[2] *Nation*, 9 March 1850. In this conclusion we have generally only referenced material not cited directly in previous chapters.

[3] C. Godfrey, *Chartist Lives: The Anatomy of a Working-Class Movement*, New York, 1987, pp. 59-60; P.A. Pickering, *Chartism and the Chartists in Manchester and Salford*, Basingstoke, 1995, p. 140.

[4] P.A. Pickering & A. Tyrrell, *The People's Bread: A History of the Anti-Corn Law League*, Leicester, 2000, p. 219; B.L. Harrison, *Drink and the Victorians*, Keele, 1994, p. 139.

[5] The national birth/marriage average for 1840-49 was 4.425. See E.A. Wrigley and R.S. Schofield, *The Population History of England 1541-1871*,Cambridge, Mass., 1981, pp. 189-91.

[6] Ms. *Register of Christ Church, Every Street, Manchester*, Manchester Public Library, n.p.; *Vegetarian Messenger*, July 1851.

[7] W.S.V. Sankey, *Popular Control of Hasty Legislation*, Edinburgh, 1838, p. 13n.

[8] Jane Reed died in Newcastle in 1900 aged 61 years.

[9] See *inter alia* T. Cooper, *The Life of Thomas Cooper*, 1872, repr. Leicester, 1971, pp. 103-7; W. Lovett, *The Life and Struggles of William Lovett*, 1876, repr. London, 1967, pp. 29-30; W.E. Adams, *Memoirs of a Social Atom*, 1903, repr. New York, 1968, pp. 116-17; B. Harrison & P. Hollis, *Robert Lowery: Radical and Chartist*, London, 1979, pp. 72-3.

[10] Godfrey, *Chartist Lives*, p. 61.

[11] *Chartist Circular*, 24 October 1840. For a study of a humble Chartist poet see P.A. Pickering, '"Glimpses of Eternal Truth": Chartism, Poetry and the Young H.R. Nicholls', *Labour History* [Australia], no. 70, May 1996, pp. 53-70. For a discussion of Chartist poetry see Y.V. Kovalev, 'The Literature of Chartism', *Victorian Studies*, vol. 2, no. 2, December 1958, pp. 117-138; M. Vicinus, *The Industrial Muse*, London, 1974, chapter 3; O.R. Ashton & S. Roberts, *The Victorian Working Class Writer*, London, 1999. Only Sankey is represented in Kovalev's collection. See *An Anthology of Chartist Literature*, Moscow, 1956.

[12] A.J. Kidd & D. Nicholls (eds), *The Making of the British Middle Class*, Stroud, 1998, p. xxv.

[13] We are grateful to Dr David Gatley for this information from the 1881 Census.

[14] E.G. Wakefield, *England & America: A Comparison of the Social and Political State of Both Nations*, 1834, repr. New York, 1967, p. 61.

[15] See J. Seed, 'From "Middling Sort" to Middle Class in late Eighteenth Century and Early Nineteenth Century England', in M.L. Bush (ed.), *Social Orders and Social Classes in Europe Since 1500: Studies in Social Stratification*, London, 1992, p. 121.

[16] Parsons also ran a school for financial gain. See *Dictionary of National Biography*, vol. XV, p., 397.

[17] C. Wright Mills, 'The Social Role of the Intellectual', in I.L Horowitz (ed.), *Power, Politics and People*, New York, 1963, pp.292-304.

[18] See E. Royle, *Radical Politics 1790-1900: Religion and Unbelief*, London, 1971. In a recent book Callum Brown has argued, in contrast to the orthodox view, that religious association remained strong during the nineteenth century. See C. C. Brown, *The Death of Christian Britain*, London, 2001.We are grateful to Alex Tyrrell for bringing this book to our attention.

[19] B. Harrison, *Drink and the Victorians*, pp. 36, 159, 363. See also A. Tyrrell, *Joseph Sturge and the Moral Radical Party in Early Victorian Britain*, London, 1987.

[20] *McDouall's Chartist and Republican Journal*, 3 April 1841.

[21] W.S.V. Sankey, *A Voice for the Operatives*, Edinburgh, 1837, p. 9; PP. *Select Committee of Payment of Wages*, 1842, (471), vol. IX, p. 107

[22] As Alex Tyrrell has shown, for Joseph Sturge the death of his wife and child was a catalyst for

renewed activity. See Tyrrell, *Joseph Sturge*, pp. 62-4.

[23] Sankey, *A Voice for the Operatives*, p. 6; F. O'Connor (ed.), *The Trial of Feargus O'Connor Esq. and Fifty-Eight Others at Lancaster on a Charge of Sedition, Conspiracy and Riot*, 1843, repr. New York, 1970, p. 117f; *Northern Star*, 22 August 1840. Later McDouall advocated moderation as opposed to total abstinence. See *People's Paper*, 6 November 1852.

[24] On this point see Pickering & Tyrrell, *The People's Bread*, chapter 7.

[25] See P. A. Pickering, 'And Your Petitioners &c: Chartist Petitioning in Popular Politics 1838-48', *English Historical Review*, vol. CXVI, no. 466, p. 375.

[26] B. Parsons, *Tracts for the Fustian Jackets and Frock Smocks*, n.d.,[1847], no. 1, pp. 2-3.

[27] *McDouall's Chartist and Republican Journal*, 8 May 1841.

[28] [W.S.V. Sankey], *Thoughts on the Currency as affecting production, suggested by the late Commercial Crisis &c in a letter addressed to the Honourable the Secretary of the American Treasury*, Edinburgh, 1837, p. 7.

[29] F. Parkin, *Middle Class Radicalism: the Social Bases of the British Campaign for Nuclear Disarmament*, Manchester, 1968, p. 31

[30] M. Finn, *After Chartism: Class and Nation in English Radical Politics 1848-1874*, Cambridge, 1993.

[31] Parkin, *Middle Class Radicalism*, p. 34. Parkin points out that most political activity combines elements of both.

[32] See D. Thompson, *The Chartists*, London, 1984, p. 172.

[33] *Northern Star*, 19 January 1839.

[34] See M. Taylor, *The Decline of British Radicalism 1847-1860*, Oxford, 1995, p. 109; Finn, *After Chartism*, pp. 234-9; N. Kirk, *Change, continuity and class: Labour in British society, 1850-1920*, Manchester, 1998, pp. 7, 84 & *passim*. See also C. Godfrey, *Chartist Lives*, pp. 331-337.

[35] The export of Chartism after 1850 has been largely ignored; it remains one of the most potentially fruitful areas for further research. Paul Pickering is currently undertaking a major study of Chartism in Australia and New Zealand for the Australian Research Council. For a preliminary assessment see P.A. Pickering, 'A Wider Field in a New Country: Chartism in Colonial Australia', in M. Sawer (ed.), *Elections, Full, Free & Fair*, Sydney, 2001, pp. 28-44.

[36] See F. Reid, *Keir Hardie: The Making of a Socialist*, London, 1978, pp. 158-9. Hardie was supported by only two radical-liberals in the subsequent division: Murray MacDonald and L.E. Atherley Jones, son of Ernest Jones, the last of the national leaders of Chartism.

[37] As Kenneth Morgan has noted Labour has always been a 'deferential party'. See K.O. Morgan, *Labour People: Hardie to Kinnock*, Oxford, 1992, p. 1.

[38] To coincide with the Labour Party's centenary, the cover of its magazine, *Inside Labour*, placed Blair and Hardie side by side implying a direct link between them. This was brought to our attention by Tony Taylor in a paper he gave at the 12th Australasian Modern British History Association Conference, LaTrobe University, Melbourne, February 2001. See also R. Spalding, 'Spinning History: Labour and Its Centenary', *New Politics*, vol. VIII, no. 2, 2001, pp. 1-2. Comparisons between Blair and Gladstone are far more common and have been encouraged by Blair himself.

BIBLIOGRAPHICAL NOTE

A full statement of the sources used in this book will be found in the notes at the end of each chapter. Detailed lists of the sources for the study of Chartism can be found in two book length bibliographies: J.F.C. Harrison and Dorothy Thompson (eds), *Bibliography of the Chartist Movement 1837-1976*, Sussex, 1978; O.R. Ashton, R. Fyson and S. Roberts (eds), *The Chartist Movement 1839-1994*, London, 1995. In cases where we have identified sources not listed in either of the above we have generally indicated as much in the relevant note. The end notes also indicate those sources that have been published since 1995.

INDEX

Adams, William E, 43, 44, 47, 127, 132, 140-2, 142
Aitken, William, 12, 17, 19, 26
Allsop, Thomas, 132
Ancoats, Manchester, 101, 102
Annand, James, 139, 140
Anti-Bread Tax Circular, 88
Anti-Corn Law League, 4, 38, 63, 74, 81, 87-9, 92, 94, 117, 150, 156-7, 160
Conference of Ministers (1841), 29, 35-6, 88, 90, 117, 159
aristocracy, 56, 61-2, 69-70, 74-5, 134
opposition to, 45, 88, 89, 131, 138, 156
Ashton, brothers, 9-10, 11
Ashton-under-Lyne, Lancashire, 11, 18, 19
Aspland, Rev. Robert, 31
Attwood, Charles, 131
Attwood, Thomas, 68
Australia, 143-4
Chartism in, 143, 163
emigration to, 21, 143

Bainbridge, John, 33, 34, 35, 36, 37, 39, 45, 48
Barker, Rev. Joseph, 42
Barmby, John Goodwyn, 17
Bartlett, George M, 34, 50
Beales, Edmond, 140
Beaumont, S.H., 139
Beggs, Thomas, 90
Berkeley family, 42
Bernard, Simon, 132
Berwick-upon-Tweed, Northumberland, electoral corruption, 136
Bible Christians of Manchester and Salford, 102, 103-7, 109
Building Society, 109, 118
education and, 105-6
temperance and, 108-9, 121
vegetarianism and, 108-9, 122
Black, Adam and Charles, 74
Blair, Tony, 161-2, 163
Blind, Karl, 128
Borthwick, Peter, 86, 97-8

Bowly, Samuel, 46, 90, 94, 99-100
Bridport, Dorset, 36, 38
Brignal, W.A., 139
British Association, 9, 61
British Constitution, references to, 12, 63, 70-1, 85, 157
Brooks, John, 115
Brotherton, Joseph, 104
Brown, James, 131
Brown, Rev. Morton, 44, 46
Bull-Ring Riots, Birmingham (1839), 11
Burder, Rev. John, 83, 86, 87, 90, 96
Burnley, Lancashire, 8, 21
Burt, Thomas, 128, 140

Cabet, Etienne, 17, 26
Cairns, Queensland, 144
Carlile, Richard, 107, 123
Carstairs, Peter, 135
centralism, opposition to, 66-7, 94, 115, 157
Chainmakers' Journal, 130
Channing, Rev. William Ellery, 31
charisma, evidence of, 15, 84-5, 102-3, 115, 160
Charter, 55, 62
Chartism, plans for organisation of, 15, 72
Chartist Land Company, 18, 21, 40, 109, 140
Chartist, characteristics of typical, 1, 149-63 passim
Cheltenham Free Press, 43-4
Cheltenham Spa, Gloucestershire, 30, 42, 86
Cheltenham Working Men's Institute, 44-6
Cheshunt College, Hertfordshire, 84
children, death of, 7, 19, 46, 101, 155
Christian Chartist Community, Chat Moss, 109, 158
Christian Socialism, 47, 53
Church of England,
attitude to, 8, 37, 69, 92-3, 111, 117, 129, 154
Church Rates, campaigns against, 69, 81, 86, 89, 113-14, 154
class, 153-4, 157-8

fustian as symbol of, 1, 91-2, 103, 161
hostility, 37, 43, 117, 135
identity of interests between classes, 20, 43, 69-70, 87, 141-2, 157-8
reconciliation of, 39, 40, 43, 44, 47, 87, 89, 90, 118
social mobility, 153
'uneasy', 3, 7, 42, 43, 49, 153-4
Close, Rev. Francis, 43-4, 45, 46, 86
Cobbett, William, 94, 103, 116
Cobden, Richard, 46, 64, 77, 94
Coffin, Dr A.I., 13
Colne Bridge, Yorkshire, 103
Colonial Sugar Refining company, 144
Complete Suffrage Union, Conferences, 4, 29, 37-9, 40-1, 89, 90, 92, 95, 160
Cooper, Thomas, 44, 46, 47, 64
Corn Laws, repeal of, 15, 36, 56, 73, 87, 88, 90, 94, 117, 156
Cowen junior, Joseph, 2, 127, 128, 130, 131, 132, 133, 134, 135, 136, 137, 138, 139, 142, 143
Cowen senior, Joseph, 139
Cowherd, Rev. William, 103-7, 109, 111
Crawford, William Sharman, 66
Cromwell, Oliver, 57
Crowley, Ambrose, 128-9, 144

Dawson, George, 44
debating clubs, 11, 13, 84, 152
Democratic Improvement Society, Yeovil, 39, 40-1
Democratic Teetotal Society, Stroud, 89-90
Detrosier, Rowland, 107
dietary reform, belief in, 14, 89, 151
Dobell, Sydney, 46
Doubleday, Thomas, 133
Duncan, William, 142
Duncombe, Thomas Slingsby, 3, 13, 26
Dunning, Thomas, 12

Ebley, Gloucestershire, 84, 95
Eclectic Review, 81, 82, 93, 96
Edinburgh, 21, 55, 59, 60, 61, 62, 74, 155
Edmunds, John, 33
education, attitude to, 34-5, 37, 41, 43, 85-6, 107-8, 152, 156
educational institutions, 30, 44-6, 47, 82, 84, 96, 102, 105-6, 152
Elections, Chartist policy, 72, 159
Berwick-upon-Tweed, 135, 136
Carlisle, 27,

Marylebone, 72-3
Manchester, 115
Newcastle, 135-6, 139
Northampton, 15-16
Nottingham, 16
Tavistock, 41
Engels, Frederick, 9, 102
English Chartist Circular, 38, 41
European struggles for freedom, 46, 71, 130-2, 137, 158
expressive politics, concept of, 159

factory system, opposition to, 9-11, 21-2
Fethard, County Tipperary, 57, 75
Fife, John, 131
Fletcher, Matthew, 11
Foreign Affairs Committee, Newcastle, 131-2
Fox, William Johnson, 31
France, 7, 17, 21, 132
French Revolutions, attitude to, 44, 71, 85
Freehold Land Societies, 109, 161
Freemasonry, 127, 128, 142-3
The Lodge of Industry, 128, 142
Mark Masonry, 142-3
friendly societies, 89, 128, 133
Fustian Jackets and Frock Smocks, tracts for, 81, 91-4, 100
Fynes, Richard, 128, 133

Gammage, Robert, 11, 12, 15, 17, 28, 29, 33, 89
Garden City movement, 29, 47
Garibaldi, Giuseppe, 131, 139
Garrison, William Lloyd, 41
General Convention of the Industrious Classes, 1839, 1, 11, 55-6, 62-3, 67-8, 129
gentleman, working class, 33, 45, 157
Gilmour, J.T., 131, 136
Glenister, J.P., 43, 44, 46
Goding, John, 43, 44, 97
Grant, brothers, 8-9, 10
Gregson, Thomas, 131

Hardie, Keir, 161
Harney, George Julian, 4, 26, 63, 118, 127, 129, 130, 131, 133, 139, 150
Harper, Samuel Charles, 43-4, 97
Headlam, T.E., 135, 139
Hewlett, William, 33, 35
Heywood, Abel, 18, 117
Hill, William, 17, 18, 23
history, Chartist interest in, 22, 57-8, 60, 157-8

Hollis, William, 43, 44, 97
Holyoake, G.J., 47, 128, 133, 134, 137, 138,
    144, 148
Hooper, Emanuel, 33
Hulme Philosophical Society, 105
Hume, Joseph, 'Little Charter', 94
Hunt, Henry, 2, 32, 101-2, 112, 113
    monument to, 101, 114, 115
Hunter, William, 131
Huntingdon's Connexion, Countess of, 83-4
Hutchison, Thomas, 142
Hyde, Lancashire, 9-10,
Hyett, William, 86
Hyndman, H.M., 143, 161

Icarie, 17
insurrection, need for, 11, 18, 23
    'physical force', 15, 16, 63, 65, 158-9
Ireland, 55, 57-8, 64-6, 74
    Chartist attitude to, 64, 117
    repeal of Legislative Union, 66, 114
    federal solutions and, 66

Jessop, C. Hale, 44
Jomard, E-F, 59-60
Jones, Ernest, 133
Jude, Martin, 130, 131

Kane, John, 130, 131
Kyfr-y-them, 'primitive parliament', 22-3,
    157-8

Lancashire Public Schools Association, 105
Lancasterian, system of mutual instruction,
    59-60, 72, 156
Langley, John Baxter, 138
Larkin, Charles, 133
Leach, James, 18
Leno, J.B., 18
Linton, William, 22, 46
Livesey, Joseph,
London, 3, 31, 154
    radical culture in, 72
Lovett, Mary, 3
Lovett, William, 1, 30, 33, 34-5, 36, 39, 40, 45,
    48, 64, 72, 156
Lowery, Robert, 64
Lumley, John, 142

machinery, opposition to, 10, 115
Manchester Political Union, 114
Manchester, 16, 21, 32

social conditions in, 36, 38, 109-110, 154
    Chartism in, 109, 114-15, 118, 149
    local government in, 115-17
Marjoribanks, D.C., 136
Mathison, Robert, 133, 136
Maurice, F.D., 47, 53
Mazzini, Giuseppe, 46, 130
McDouall, Andrew, 8
McDouall, Mary-Ann, 12, 19, 21, 151
McDouall, Peter Murray, 3, 4, 7-28 passim, 61,
    69, 72, 89, 143, 149-63 passim
McDouall's Florida Medicine, 13-14
McDouall's Chartist and Republican Journal,
    13
McDouall's Manchester Journal, 13, 19-21
Mechanics' Institutes, 41, 127, 133, 152
medicine, 20-1, 89, 102, 105
    alternatives to orthodox, 13-14, 109-110
    education in, 8
Miall, Edward, 37
middle-class reform, 4, 34, 130, 131, 133, 135-
    6, 139, 140, 160-1
mid-Victorian Liberal consensus, 4, 92, 96,
    118, 128, 161
Monarchism, 22, 66, 157
    attitudes to monarchy, 36-7, 39, 70, 112-13,
    130
Monteagle, Lord, 138
moral force, advocacy of, 30, 33, 93, 158
Murray, George, 115

Napoleon III, 131, 132
Natham, Jeanette, 133-4
National Association, 33, 39, 72, 156
National Charter Association, 1-2, 3, 7, 15, 18,
    33, 34, 39, 40, 43, 91
    Executive of, 1, 7, 15, 16, 17, 18, 21, 35, 160
National Chartist Conference (1842), 16-17,
    101-2, 117, 119
National Parliamentary and Financial Reform
    Association, 4, 94, 117-18, 150
National Petition,
    (1839), 63, 68
    (1848), 91, 92
National Republican Brotherhood, 130-1
New Poor Law Amendment Act (1834),
    opposition to, 15, 73, 89, 110, 115, 117, 157
Newcastle Daily Chronicle, 137, 138-42, 160
Newcastle Weekly Chronicle,127, 139, 140
Newcastle Ratepayers' Association, 133, 135
Newport riots, 1839, Frost, Williams and
    Jones, 33, 108

Newton Stewart, Wigtownshire, 8, 13
Nibley, Gloucestershire, 82
Nonconformist, 93
North East (England), 3, 129, 134, 140
  Chartism and radicalism in, 129, 130, 131-2,
  133, 134, 137, 139-40, 143
Northern Reform League, 139
Northern Reform Record, 133, 138
Northern Reform Union, 128, 131-2, 132-7,
  138, 139, 147
Northern Star, 38, 90, 92, 93-4
Northern Tribune, 130

O'Brien, James Bronterre, 63
O'Connell, Daniel, 64, 65, 66, 74
O'Connor, Feargus, 1, 3, 4, 17, 18, 30, 34, 35,
  37, 39, 40, 41, 48, 58, 63, 64, 65, 66, 67, 68,
  72, 74, 90, 92, 96, 101, 102, 103, 114, 117,
  118, 149, 158, 160, 161
'Old Corruption' analysis, 88, 95, 112, 116,
  156
O'Neill, Arthur, 34, 40
Operative, 55, 62
Orsini affair, 132

parks, provision of, 94, 109, 117
Parsons, Amelia, 84, 151
Parsons, Rev. Benjamin, 1, 3, 44-5, 81-100
  passim, 102, 103, 117, 149-63 passim
Parthenon, Manchester, 105
Paulton, A.W., 87
peace, Peace movement, 41, 46, 64, 81, 93, 94,
  158
Peddie, Jane and Robert, 68
People's International League, 46
People's Paper, 132, 133
Peterloo, massacre of, 9, 102, 111-12, 113
Philosophical Enquiring Christians, 105
Philp, R.K., 90
Plug Plot strikes, 1842, 16-17, 39, 41, 81, 101-2
poetry, 8, 10, 12, 22, 60-1, 68-9, 70, 71, 122,
  152-3
poor relief, provision of, 102, 110-1
poverty, experience of, 32, 82, 95, 129
practical reform, commitment to, 103, 109,
  115, 155
prison, 12, 18-19, 33, 68
  Kirkdale gaol, 18-19

Queen Caroline affair, 112-13

Radical Electors' Assocation, Manchester, 118

Ramsbottom, Lancashire, 8-9, 14, 61
Rechabite Society, Stroud, 90
Reed, Jane, 139, 143, 151
Reed, John Hastings, 143-4
Reed, John, 129
Reed, Joseph, 143
Reed, Richard Bagnall, 3, 127-48 passim, 149-
  63 passim
Reform League, 127, 139, 150
religion, 8, 30, 45-6, 47, 59, 69, 82, 83-4, 158
  radical, 69, 90-1, 92-3, 95, 103, 111-12, 113,
  118, 154, 157
  dissent, 8, 42, 85-6, 135
  motivation, 38, 93, 108, 119
representation,
  Chartist concept of, 67-8, 73, 116
  Burkean notion of, 67-8
Republicanism, 22, 130-1, 135
retrenchment, support for, 93, 116, 118
Reynolds, G.M.W., 71
Ridley, Ruffey, 34, 39
Roberts, William Prowting, 18
Rochdale, Lancashire, 84
Ruddock, Richard, 142
Russell, Lord John, 63, 86, 87, 88, 97
Russia, attitudes to, 66, 145

Sabbatarianism, 81, 85, 94, 135
Salford Grammar and Academy of Sciences,
  105-6
Sankey, Hieronymous (Jerome), 57-8
Sankey, Richard, 57
Sankey, Sophia, 59, 151
Sankey, William Senior, 58, 74
Sankey, William Stephen Villiers, 3, 39, 55-79
  passim, 92, 116, 149-63 passim
Scholefield, Charlotte, 101, 107, 151, 155
Scholefield, Rev. James, 3, 16, 36, 67, 86, 101-
  25 passim, 149-63 passim
Scholefield, William, 107
Scholefield's Bottle, 110
Scotland, 3, 8, 12, 14-15, 18, 68
Scrope, G.P., 87, 88, 100
secularism, 107, 111, 154
self-help, 20-1, 43, 94, 128, 142-3, 156
Shepton Mallet, Somerset, 30, 41-2
slavery, campaign against, 29, 47, 58, 81, 86-7
Smiles, Samuel, 8, 9, 10
Solly, Rev. Henry, 3, 29-53 passim, 117, 149-
  63 passim
Solly, Rebecca, 35, 41, 46, 151, 155
Spencer, Rev. Thomas, 38

Stanton, W.H., 88, 94-5, 100
Steele, Thomas, 74
Stephens, Rev. Joseph Rayner, 11, 12, 25, 114-15
Stevens, John, 33, 37, 48
Stockbridge, Hampshire, 60
Stowell, Rev. Hugh, 108
Stroud, Gloucestershire, 83, 86, 87, 90
Stroudwater, Chartism in, 88-90, 91, 98
Sturge, Joseph, 16, 29, 37, 40, 41, 64, 89-90, 95
Swansea, Wales, 84
Swedenborg, Emanuel, 103, 104, 105, 106, 108, 111
Swedenborgianism, 103-7, 111, 123
Switzerland, 59
Symonds, Jelinger C., 87, 90, 94-5, 98

Tavistock, Devon, 30, 40
taxation, opposition to, 116, 117
Taylor, P.A., 46, 135, 140
Taylor, Robert, 'Devil's Chaplain', 107
Tchorzewski, Stanislaus, 132
teetotalism, temperance, 30, 37, 41, 43, 44, 46, 81, 89-90, 108, 150, 156
    Chartism and, 43, 87, 91, 95, 109
    Temperance Society, of Manchester and Salford, 108-9
Ten Hour Working Day, campaign for, 109
Thompson, Colonel Perronet, 98, 115, 134
Thompson, George, 36
trade of agitation, 13, 14-15, 23
trade unions, 127, 130, 133, 139, 140, 155, 156
    Chartism and, 15, 16, 20, 127, 146
Truelove, Edward, 132
Tweedie, William, 44

Unitarianism, 29, 30-1, 32, 33, 42, 43, 49, 154
    education and, 30, 35
    women and, 35, 151
United States of America, 13-14, 17, 37, 131, 143
University,
    Cambridge, 59
    Edinburgh, 59
    London, 31
    Paris, 59
    Trinity College, Dublin, 59

vegetarianism, Vegetarian Society, 108, 151
view of society, 19-20, 70, 157-8
Villiers, Charles Pelham, 56, 74, 77
Vincent, Henry, 34, 40, 41, 47, 72, 87, 89-90, 151
Voluntarism, 85-6, 94, 105, 156

Wakefield, Edward Gibbon, 3, 153-4
Walmsley, Joshua, 94
Warden, Robert, 133
Watson, Aaron, 142
Watts, Rev. J, 90
West Country (England), 4, 30, 39, 89
West, John, 18-19
Wheadon, George,
White, George, 19, 26
Wilberforce, William, 58
Wilkes, Edwin, 43, 44
Winlaton, Durham, 128-9
    Literary and Mechanics' Institute, 129-30, 152
women, 3, 85
    attitude to rights of, 81, 85, 133-4, 146, 151-2
Working Men's Club movement, 29, 30, 45, 46-7
Wroe, James, 112, 116

Yeovil, Somerset, 30, 31-3, 36

Other Titles in the Chartist Studies Series from The Merlin Press

Images of Chartism
Stephen Roberts and Dorothy Thompson

Seventy contemporary images of the Chartist Movement

1998 ISBN: 0850364752 paperback £15.95

The Chartist Legacy
Edited by Owen Ashton, Robert Fyson & Stephen Roberts

Eleven essays by leading scholars

1999 ISBN: 0850364968 hardback £25.00
085036484 paperback £14.95

Forthcoming – Spring 2003

The People's Charter
Democratic Agitation in Early Victorian Britain
Edited by Stephen Roberts

A collection of essays – previously published in scholarly
journals and therefore of limited availability – on aspects of
Chartism

Chartist Studies Series, Volume 4
ISBN: 0850365147 paperback £14.95 approx.